CHAPTER 1: WELCOME TO CANVA

Canva stands as a transformative platform within the realm of digital design, uniquely crafted to accommodate a diverse array of users, from novices embarking on their creative journeys to seasoned professionals seeking efficient tools for sophisticated projects. The platform's foundational appeal lies in its intuitive user interface, which demystifies the design process by making it accessible to individuals with varying levels of experience and expertise. The simplicity with which one can navigate the dashboard is not merely an aesthetic choice; it is an essential aspect of its functionality, encouraging users to engage with design elements without the intimidation often associated with traditional graphic design software.

Upon entering the Canva workspace, the user is greeted by a clean and organized layout that prioritizes ease of use. The design dashboard serves as a central hub from which all creative endeavors can be initiated. At the top, one finds the menu bar, featuring options that allow for the creation of new designs, the access of existing projects, and a search function to locate specific templates or elements. This design philosophy underscores Canva's commitment to efficiency; users can swiftly transition between tasks, fostering a fluid workflow that enhances productivity.

The main section of the dashboard showcases a diverse array of templates categorized by their intended purpose, such as social media posts, presentations, flyers, and more. Each template is designed with flexibility in mind, allowing users to modify elements to suit their unique vision. This modular approach to design encourages experimentation, as users can select a template that resonates with their goals and customize it to reflect their personal style or branding requirements. The breadth of available templates also alleviates the pressure of starting from scratch, providing a robust starting point for users who may be uncertain about design principles or aesthetic choices.

One of the standout features of Canva is its extensive library of design elements, which includes graphics, images, fonts, and icons. These elements are not merely decorative; they are integral to crafting effective visual communications. The library is organized and searchable, enabling users to find specific items with ease. This wealth of resources empowers users to think creatively, combining various elements to produce original compositions. Additionally, Canva's partnerships with stock image providers ensure that users have access to high-quality visuals, further enhancing the platform's utility for creating professional-grade designs.

Understanding how to customize one's workspace within Canva is vital for maximizing efficiency and personalizing the design experience. Users have the ability to rearrange toolbars, adjust the size of panels, and even save frequently used elements for quick access. This adaptability fosters a tailored environment that aligns with individual workflows. For example, a user focused on social media marketing may prioritize quick access to specific image sizes and templates relevant to that medium, while a graphic designer may prefer a layout that facilitates extensive editing capabilities. This level of customization not only enhances user satisfaction but also reinforces the notion that design is not a one-size-fits-all endeavor; rather, it is a highly personalized process that varies from one creator to another.

Navigating through the various design tools available in Canva is a journey in itself. The toolbar on the left side of the screen houses essential functionalities, including the options for adding text, images, and elements to the design canvas. Each tool is equipped with contextual menus that offer specific settings and adjustments. For instance, when a user selects a text box, options for font style, size, color, and alignment appear, enabling comprehensive customization that is both straightforward and effective. This direct approach to adjustments eliminates the steep learning curves often associated with graphic design software, allowing users to focus on their creativity rather than grappling with complex technicalities.

One cannot overlook the collaborative features embedded within Canva. The platform recognizes the importance of teamwork in the design process, particularly in settings such as marketing teams or educational environments. Users can invite others to view or edit designs, facilitating real-time collaboration that fosters creative dialogue and collective input. This capacity for collaboration is particularly advantageous for those working in fast-paced environments where feedback and revisions are necessary. By streamlining communication and ensuring that all stakeholders can engage with the project, Canva positions itself as a vital tool in the modern design toolkit.

Moreover, Canva's ability to integrate with other applications enhances its functionality even further. Users can connect their designs with platforms like Google Drive, Dropbox, and social media channels, enabling seamless sharing and publishing of their work. This interoperability ensures that once a design is completed, the transition to distribution is effortless. The capacity to export designs in various formats—such as JPEG, PNG, and PDF—means that users can tailor their output to fit specific needs, whether for digital use or print media.

As we embark on this exploration of Canva, it is essential to recognize the platform's commitment to continual improvement and user support. Canva offers a wealth of educational resources, including tutorials and design courses, which serve to enhance the user experience. This emphasis on learning reflects an understanding that design is a skill that evolves over time, and Canva is dedicated to nurturing that growth by providing users with the tools and knowledge they need to succeed.

In conclusion, the journey into the world of Canva begins with an understanding of its user-friendly interface, the wealth of customizable features, and the myriad of design elements at one's fingertips. This chapter lays the groundwork for harnessing the power of this tool, equipping users with the knowledge necessary to navigate the platform effectively and creatively. As we move forward, the exploration of more advanced functionalities will build upon this foundation, enhancing your ability to create compelling designs that communicate effectively and resonate with your audience.

As I continue to explore the depths of Canva, it becomes evident that one of the platform's most remarkable features is its extensive range of design templates. These templates are not merely a collection of static images; they are meticulously crafted frameworks designed to inspire creativity and streamline the design process. Each template embodies a professional aesthetic, catering to a wide variety of contexts —from social media graphics and business presentations to educational infographics and marketing materials. This versatility allows users to initiate their projects with a solid foundation, effectively reducing the time and effort required to create visually appealing designs from scratch.

When selecting a template, I am often struck by the sheer

diversity available within Canva's library. Each template is categorized by its intended use, making it effortless to locate options that align with specific goals. For instance, if I am creating an Instagram post, I can browse through templates specifically tailored for social media, ensuring that the dimensions, layouts, and styles are optimized for the platform. This not only saves time but also ensures that the design meets the necessary specifications for its intended audience, enhancing its overall effectiveness.

The process of customizing these templates is equally engaging. Once a template is selected, I am immediately taken to the design canvas, where I can manipulate every element to suit my vision. The drag-and-drop functionality of Canva is particularly noteworthy; it allows me to reposition text boxes, images, and graphics with ease, providing a tactile sense of control that is essential in the creative process. Moreover, I can change colors, fonts, and sizes to reflect my branding or personal style. This ability to personalize designs fosters a sense of ownership over the creative output, making it feel less like a replication and more like a unique expression.

An integral component of Canva's design philosophy is its emphasis on user empowerment through customization. As I delve deeper into the editing tools, I discover the vast array of options available for fine-tuning each design element. For instance, the text tool offers not only font choices but also options for letter spacing, line height, and text effects. I can create striking headlines or subtle captions, allowing the text to complement the visuals rather than overpower them. This attention to detail is crucial, as typography plays a pivotal role in establishing tone and conveying messages effectively.

Beyond typography, Canva's image editing capabilities are another highlight. The platform allows me to upload my own images or choose from its extensive library of stock photos, illustrations, and icons. Once an image is integrated into my design, I can enhance it using a variety of editing tools. Cropping, filtering, and adjusting brightness and contrast can elevate a good image to a great one, ensuring that it resonates with the intended audience. The ability to apply effects and overlays adds an additional layer of creativity, enabling me to craft visuals that are not only eye-catching but also narratively cohesive.

Collaboration emerges as a key feature in Canva that aligns with contemporary work practices. The platform's design interface includes functionalities that facilitate teamwork, allowing multiple users to contribute to a single project simultaneously. This real-time collaboration feature fosters a sense of community and encourages the exchange of ideas, ultimately leading to a more robust design outcome. As I invite colleagues or peers to edit or comment on my designs, I can witness the synergy that emerges from collective input, reinforcing the notion that creativity thrives in collaborative environments.

Furthermore, Canva's integration with various social media and marketing platforms amplifies its utility as a design tool. Once a design is finalized, the options for sharing and publishing are both comprehensive and intuitive. Users can publish directly to their social media accounts, schedule posts, or export designs in multiple formats tailored to specific needs. This seamless transition from design to distribution is a crucial aspect for professionals seeking to enhance their online presence or market their products effectively. The ability to export designs in high-resolution formats ensures that the quality remains uncompromised, which is vital for print materials and promotional content.

Engaging with Canva also opens the door to an expansive community of creators, educators, and professionals who share insights and inspiration. The platform not only offers design tools but also serves as a hub for learning and growth. Through tutorials, design courses, and user forums, I can access a wealth of knowledge that enhances my skills and understanding of design principles. This commitment to education reflects Canva's broader vision of empowering users to become more proficient and confident in their creative endeavors.

As I reflect on the features and functionalities that Canva offers, it becomes clear that the platform is designed not only to facilitate the act of creating but also to inspire creativity itself. The inherent flexibility within the interface allows for experimentation, encouraging users to push boundaries and explore new design possibilities. By providing a space where both novice and experienced designers can flourish, Canva cultivates an environment where creativity is not just encouraged but celebrated.

Ultimately, the journey into the world of Canva is about more than just mastering a design tool; it is about embracing the creative process itself. The platform's design features, collaborative capabilities, and educational resources all converge to create a rich ecosystem that supports and nurtures creativity. As I navigate this landscape, I am continually reminded of the transformative power of design in communication and expression. With a solid understanding of Canva's foundational elements, I feel equipped to harness its potential fully, embarking on my creative journey with confidence and enthusiasm. This initial exploration paves the way for deeper dives into more advanced functionalities, which will further enhance my design capabilities and broaden my creative horizons.

As I immerse myself further into the functionalities of Canva, it becomes increasingly apparent that the platform is built upon principles that prioritize user empowerment and creative expression. This focus is reflected not only in its interface but also in the wealth of design resources that are readily accessible. A particularly noteworthy aspect of Canva is its vast library of educational content, which serves as an invaluable resource for users at all skill levels. Through tutorials, webinars, and instructional articles, Canva fosters an environment where users can continually expand their knowledge and refine their skills, making the journey of learning about design both enjoyable and impactful.

The design community that surrounds Canva is vibrant and dynamic, comprising individuals from diverse backgrounds who contribute to a rich tapestry of creativity. By engaging with this community, I find inspiration and support that enhances my own creative endeavors. The shared experiences and insights from other users create a collaborative atmosphere where ideas can flourish. This communal spirit is essential, as it reinforces the notion that design is not just a solitary pursuit; rather, it thrives on the collective contributions of many voices and perspectives. Whether through design challenges, collaborative projects, or sharing finished works, the community encourages exploration and innovation, pushing the boundaries of what can be achieved with the tools at hand.

One of the most compelling features of Canva is its adaptability across various mediums and applications. As I explore the platform, I recognize that Canva is not merely limited to digital designs. The ability to create printed materials, such as brochures, business cards, and posters, broadens its appeal and utility. This versatility is critical for professionals who must navigate both digital and print environments, allowing for a cohesive visual identity that translates seamlessly across all platforms. The export options available in high resolution ensure that designs maintain their integrity, whether displayed on a screen or printed on a physical medium. This capability is especially valuable in today's multi-faceted marketing landscape, where a unified brand presence is paramount.

The analytical tools that Canva provides further enrich the user experience. Understanding the performance of designs, particularly in the context of social media, is vital for refining strategies and optimizing outreach. Through integrated analytics, I can track engagement metrics, viewership statistics, and audience interactions. This data not only informs future design decisions but also allows for a more strategic approach to content creation. By analyzing which designs resonate most with audiences, I can tailor my efforts to meet their preferences and expectations more effectively. This iterative process of creation and analysis embodies the essence of modern design practice, where data-driven insights inform artistic choices.

In addition to its analytical features, Canva promotes the idea of sustainability in design. The platform recognizes the importance of eco-conscious practices in today's world. By providing options for digital sharing rather than solely print, Canva encourages users to think critically about their design choices and their impact on the environment. This consideration extends to the types of materials used for printed designs, where the platform offers guidance on selecting sustainable printing options. Such initiatives reflect a broader awareness within the design community about the need for responsible creativity, an aspect that I find both commendable and essential in fostering a more sustainable future.

As I navigate through various design projects on Canva, the integration of brand kits becomes increasingly valuable. This feature allows me to maintain brand consistency across all my designs by storing specific colors, logos, and fonts in a centralized location. When I create a new project, I can easily access these elements, ensuring that every piece of content aligns with my overall branding strategy. This capability is crucial for professionals and businesses that require a cohesive visual identity. The ease with which I can implement these brand elements into my designs fosters a sense of professionalism and reliability that is essential in building trust with audiences.

Exploring the concept of accessibility within Canva is another key aspect that enriches the user experience. The platform is designed with inclusivity in mind, ensuring that users with varying abilities can engage with the tools available. Features such as keyboard shortcuts, screen reader compatibility, and alternative text options for images demonstrate Canva's commitment to making design accessible to everyone. This focus on inclusivity not only reflects ethical considerations but also expands the creative community, allowing individuals from diverse backgrounds to share their perspectives and contribute to the richness of the design landscape.

Moreover, the continual evolution of Canva's features signifies its responsiveness to user needs and industry trends. As I delve deeper into the platform, I observe that new tools and functionalities are regularly introduced, reflecting a commitment to innovation. This adaptability ensures that Canva remains relevant and useful, accommodating the ever-changing demands of the design world. Whether it's the introduction of new animation options, enhanced collaboration tools, or advanced editing features, each update reaffirms Canva's position as a leader in the design software space.

As I conclude this exploration of Canva, I am left with a profound appreciation for the platform's comprehensive approach to design. It has equipped me with the tools and knowledge to create compelling visual content while fostering a sense of community and collaboration. The seamless integration of educational resources, analytical tools, and brand management features enriches my creative process, allowing me to navigate the complexities of design with confidence. With a firm understanding of Canva's capabilities, I am not only prepared to embark on my design projects but also excited to continue exploring the endless possibilities that lie ahead. This journey is one of continuous learning and creative exploration, underscoring the transformative power of design in communication and expression. The foundational skills I have acquired in this initial phase will serve as the bedrock for deeper explorations into more advanced functionalities, enabling me to harness the full potential of this dynamic platform as I advance in my design journey.

CHAPTER 2: SETTING UP YOUR FIRST PROJECT

Initiating a design project in Canva marks an important step in my creative journey, as it lays the foundation for all subsequent design work. The process begins with a thoughtful consideration of the project type I wish to undertake, as each type comes with its own unique requirements and specifications. For instance, the approach to designing an Instagram post differs significantly from that of creating a business presentation or a printed brochure. Each medium not only dictates the visual elements but also influences the messaging and audience engagement strategies. By understanding these distinctions, I can tailor my design choices effectively to suit my objectives.

Upon entering Canva, the initial interface presents an array of options categorized by design type. This curated selection allows me to quickly identify the project I want to embark on. As I navigate this selection, I find it useful to reflect on the ultimate purpose of the design. If I aim to create social media content, I must consider the platform's specific guidelines regarding dimensions and aesthetic trends. For instance, an Instagram story requires vertical dimensions, while a Facebook post typically favors square or rectangular formats. Recognizing these distinctions allows me to select a design type that aligns seamlessly with my goals, ensuring that my design is not only visually appealing but also functional in its intended context.

Choosing the right dimensions is a crucial aspect of setting up my project. Canva simplifies this process by providing predefined templates that conform to the most common sizes for various platforms and print materials. However, there are occasions when I may need to customize dimensions to fit specific needs, particularly if I am creating unique content tailored to a niche audience. In such cases, I can easily input my desired width and height, granting me the flexibility to experiment with non-standard sizes. This adaptability empowers me to push creative boundaries while ensuring that the final design remains practical and aligned with my objectives.

Once I have determined the appropriate dimensions for my project, the next step involves selecting a template that resonates with my vision. The wealth of templates available in Canva is one of its most compelling features, offering a broad spectrum of styles and formats that cater to diverse design needs. As I browse through the selection, I pay careful attention to the layout, color scheme, and typography of each template. It is important to choose one that aligns with the tone and message I want to convey. For instance, a vibrant and playful template might suit a promotional event, while a more subdued and professional design may be better suited for a corporate presentation.

After selecting a template, I am presented with the design canvas, where the real creative work begins. The first thing I notice is the user-friendly interface, which allows for easy navigation of elements within the canvas. At this stage, I can begin to modify the template to better reflect my unique style and branding. Customization is a critical part of the design process, and Canva offers a plethora of options to achieve this. I can change colors, adjust fonts, and rearrange elements to create a layout that feels cohesive and aligned with my vision. The ability to experiment with different design choices in real time adds a layer of dynamism to the creative process, allowing me to visualize changes immediately.

Another important aspect of setting up my project involves the integration of branding elements. If I am designing for a business or personal brand, incorporating specific colors, logos, and fonts is essential for maintaining consistency across all visual content. Canva allows me to upload brand assets, which I can easily access and incorporate into my designs. This integration ensures that my project not only stands out but also reflects a unified identity that resonates with my audience. Maintaining this consistency across various platforms and materials helps establish trust and recognition, which are critical in effective branding.

In addition to branding, I find that understanding the principles of design is vital as I navigate the setup of my project. Concepts such as balance, contrast, and alignment play a significant role in creating visually appealing designs. For instance, I pay attention to the spacing between elements, ensuring that my layout is neither too cluttered nor too sparse. The arrangement of text and images can dramatically influence how the audience perceives the information being presented. Therefore, as I modify the template, I am continuously evaluating how each change impacts the overall aesthetic and effectiveness of the design.

The importance of utilizing high-quality images cannot be overstated when setting up a project in Canva. Whether I choose to use images from Canva's extensive library or upload my own, I must ensure that the visuals enhance the narrative of my design. Images should complement the text and support the message I am trying to convey. Additionally, I find it beneficial to consider the emotional impact of the images I select. Colors, subjects, and styles all contribute to the overall mood of the design, influencing how the audience engages with the content.

Throughout this process, I remain aware of the importance of iteration. Setting up a project is not a linear journey; rather, it involves continuous reflection and adjustment. As I work on my design, I often take breaks to step back and assess my progress. This distance allows me to view the design with fresh eyes, leading to valuable insights about areas that may need further refinement or rethinking. The iterative nature of design encourages a mindset of experimentation, where I feel free to explore various creative avenues without the fear of making mistakes.

As I finalize the setup of my project, I ensure that I have thoroughly reviewed all elements for coherence and effectiveness. The project should reflect a harmonious blend of visual appeal and functional communication. By meticulously considering each aspect of the design—from dimensions and templates to branding and image selection—I am not only preparing to create a visually stunning piece but also crafting a design that serves its intended purpose with clarity and impact. This foundational understanding of setting up a project in Canva empowers me to approach future design endeavors with confidence, equipped with the knowledge necessary to create meaningful and engaging visual content.

As I delve deeper into the intricacies of setting up my first project in Canva, I recognize that understanding the design environment is essential for optimizing my creative output. The design canvas serves as my playground, a space where ideas can be brought to life. In this stage, I pay close attention to the various tools and features available to me. The toolbars, often positioned to the left and top of the canvas, contain an array of options for adding text, images, elements, and backgrounds. Each feature is designed to be intuitive, facilitating a seamless transition from concept to execution.

The text tool, for instance, is a pivotal component of my design process. Text can convey messages in a manner that visuals alone often cannot. As I add text boxes to my design, I become acutely aware of the significance of typography in effective communication. Typography is more than just choosing a font; it involves considerations such as size, spacing, color, and hierarchy. Each decision impacts how the audience perceives the message. For instance, bold fonts can draw attention and convey strength, while softer, rounded fonts may evoke a sense of warmth and friendliness. I take care to select fonts that align with the overall tone of the project, ensuring consistency and clarity throughout.

Moreover, the ability to manipulate text directly on the canvas allows for real-time adjustments, which is invaluable. I can reposition text, adjust alignment, and change colors in a matter of clicks, enabling me to create a cohesive layout that guides the viewer's eye through the design. I find that experimenting with different arrangements often leads to unexpected yet compelling results. By layering text over images or incorporating transparent backgrounds, I can create depth and visual interest, transforming a straightforward message into a dynamic experience.

In conjunction with text, the integration of imagery plays a crucial role in enhancing the narrative of my design. Canva provides an extensive library of stock photos, illustrations, and icons, which I can easily search and incorporate into my projects. When selecting images, I remain mindful of the emotions and stories they convey. A well-chosen image can enhance the text, adding context or illustrating a concept. I often find myself pondering how each visual element interacts with the overall message, ensuring that every image I use serves a purpose rather than merely filling space.

As I explore the various options for images, I also take

advantage of Canva's editing capabilities. These tools allow me to adjust brightness, contrast, and saturation, ensuring that the images harmonize with the rest of the design. Furthermore, I can apply filters and effects that not only enhance the aesthetic appeal but also create a unified look across the project. For instance, if I desire a vintage feel, I can apply a specific filter to all images, ensuring they all maintain a consistent style. This attention to detail is crucial in crafting a professional and polished final product.

In the midst of designing, I often remind myself of the importance of balance. A successful design must guide the viewer's eye without overwhelming them. This principle of balance influences my decision-making process as I arrange elements on the canvas. I consider both symmetrical and asymmetrical compositions, weighing the visual weight of each element against others. For instance, if I have a large image on one side of the canvas, I may counterbalance it with smaller text or icons on the opposite side. This dynamic interplay creates visual tension and interest, encouraging the viewer to explore the design rather than passively consume it.

As I continue to develop my project, I find that color plays an instrumental role in establishing mood and tone. Canva's color palette feature allows me to explore various combinations and apply them effortlessly to my design elements. I often refer to color theory principles to inform my choices, such as complementary colors that create contrast or analogous colors that evoke harmony. By utilizing a cohesive color scheme, I can reinforce the message and enhance the emotional resonance of the design. The interplay of colors, paired with thoughtful typography and imagery, creates a holistic visual experience that captivates the audience.

Collaboration emerges as another vital component of my design process within Canva. The platform's real-time collaboration feature allows me to invite colleagues or clients to view and contribute to my project. This capability transforms the design process into a communal effort, where feedback and suggestions can be integrated seamlessly. I appreciate the ability to leave comments and track changes, as this fosters a dynamic dialogue around the design. Collaborative efforts often yield unexpected insights, enhancing the project in ways I might not have anticipated. This collaborative spirit aligns with the broader trends in creative industries, where teamwork and cross-disciplinary input are becoming increasingly vital.

Furthermore, as I approach the final stages of my project setup, I recognize the significance of reviewing and refining my design. Stepping away from the canvas momentarily allows me to return with fresh eyes, helping to identify areas that may require adjustment. During this review, I assess the alignment of elements, the clarity of the message, and the overall aesthetic appeal. I often find that even minor tweaks, such as adjusting the spacing between text lines or refining the color saturation of an image, can lead to significant improvements in the design's effectiveness.

Finally, I turn my attention to the aspect of accessibility. In today's diverse audience landscape, it is crucial to ensure that my designs are inclusive and can be enjoyed by all. Canva provides options for adding alt text to images, which enhances accessibility for individuals using screen readers. This consideration reflects a broader commitment to inclusive design practices, reminding me that the goal of effective communication is to reach as wide an audience as possible.

With the project setup nearing completion, I feel a sense of accomplishment. The meticulous attention to detail in selecting dimensions, templates, typography, imagery, and collaborative input has culminated in a design that not only meets my project goals but also reflects my unique creative voice. As I prepare to move forward with the next phases of the project, I carry with me the insights and strategies I have gathered during this foundational process, ready to tackle the challenges and opportunities that lie ahead.

As I finalize the setup of my design project in Canva, I begin to explore the functionality of layers and groupings, essential concepts that significantly enhance my creative process. Layers allow me to stack design elements in a way that can be manipulated independently, providing a deeper level of control over how components interact visually. This functionality becomes especially relevant when I am working with overlapping images or text, as it enables me to arrange elements in a manner that maximizes clarity and impact. For instance, by placing text over a colorful background image, I must ensure the text remains legible. Adjusting the layering ensures that important information is not lost or overshadowed, allowing for a harmonious balance between visual appeal and message clarity.

Grouping elements is another technique I find invaluable as I work on my designs. By selecting multiple components —whether they are text boxes, images, or shapes—I can group them together, allowing for simultaneous movement and adjustment. This becomes particularly useful when I am creating a complex layout that requires several elements to maintain relative positioning. Grouping elements simplifies the editing process, making it easier to reposition entire sections of my design without losing the intended arrangement. It fosters a fluid workflow, enabling me to iterate on designs efficiently as I experiment with different layouts and configurations.

The integration of grids and guidelines also plays a pivotal role in my design process. Canva provides the option to display gridlines, which assists me in aligning elements precisely. By snapping to these grids, I can create a structured layout that is visually balanced and appealing. The importance of alignment cannot be overstated; it contributes to the professionalism of the final product. When elements are well-aligned, the design appears cohesive and intentional, reinforcing the credibility of the message being communicated. I often toggle the visibility of these guides on and off as I make adjustments, allowing me to focus on both the finer details and the overall composition.

As I delve deeper into the technical aspects of Canva, I become increasingly aware of the importance of file formats, particularly when it comes to exporting my final design. Depending on its intended use—whether for social media, print, or web—I must select the appropriate format to ensure that the quality remains intact. Canva offers a range of export options, including PNG, JPEG, PDF, and more. For example, if I am preparing a design for print, I typically opt for PDF, as it preserves the high resolution and ensures that colors appear as intended when printed. Conversely, for digital platforms, a PNG format may be preferable, particularly if I require a transparent background.

In addition to file formats, I consider color profiles when preparing my design for export. Understanding the difference between RGB and CMYK color models is essential for achieving optimal results. RGB (Red, Green, Blue) is ideal for digital screens, as it captures the vibrant colors that display well on monitors. However, when preparing a design for print, I shift my focus to CMYK (Cyan, Magenta, Yellow, Black), as this model is tailored for printing processes. By ensuring that I am using the correct color profile, I mitigate the risk of color discrepancies that may arise during printing, ultimately delivering a product that meets my expectations.

Throughout this project setup process, I find that collaboration and feedback play a significant role in refining my designs. After finalizing the initial draft, I often share my work with trusted colleagues or friends to gather their insights. This feedback loop is invaluable; external perspectives can highlight aspects I may have overlooked or suggest enhancements that elevate the design further. In a collaborative environment, I appreciate Canva's functionality that allows others to comment directly on specific elements of the design. This feature facilitates constructive dialogue, making it easy to track suggestions and implement changes efficiently.

Moreover, I realize the significance of version control as I engage in collaborative design projects. As revisions are made, I find it beneficial to maintain a history of changes, allowing me to revert to earlier versions if necessary. Canva's automatic saving feature provides a sense of security, ensuring that my work is preserved as I navigate through different iterations. This capability alleviates the anxiety associated with making bold changes, as I know I can always return to a previous state if an idea does not resonate as I initially envisioned.

As I prepare to present my final design, I also contemplate the various formats in which I may want to showcase it. Depending on my audience and the context of the presentation, I might create a slideshow using Canva's presentation templates or prepare a series of social media graphics to share across platforms. This versatility in presentation formats allows me to adapt the same core design to fit different contexts, maximizing the reach and impact of my message. By repurposing design elements, I can maintain a consistent brand identity while tailoring my content to suit various audiences.

The final step in my design setup process involves a thorough review, not only of the design elements but also of the intended audience. Understanding who will engage with my design informs every decision I make, from color choices to imagery. I find it essential to consider the demographics and preferences of my target audience, ensuring that the design resonates with them on a personal level. This empathetic approach to design enhances the likelihood that my message will be received positively, fostering engagement and connection.

In conclusion, as I navigate the intricacies of setting up my first project in Canva, I am continuously reminded of the importance of both technical proficiency and creative intuition. The ability to manipulate layers, group elements, align components, and choose appropriate export formats all contribute to my success as a designer. However, it is the underlying principles of collaboration, feedback, and audience awareness that ultimately elevate my designs from mere visuals to impactful communications. Armed with this understanding, I feel prepared to embark on a creative journey that embraces both the art and science of design, leveraging Canva's powerful tools to bring my visions to life.

CHAPTER 3: EXPLORING CANVA'S TEMPLATES

As I delve into the extensive library of templates that Canva offers, I am immediately struck by their transformative potential. Templates serve as a foundational element in the design process, providing a framework that can significantly streamline my efforts while simultaneously enhancing my creative expression. The sheer variety of templates available covers a multitude of formats—ranging from social media graphics and marketing materials to presentations and print media. Each template is meticulously designed to cater to specific contexts, which not only saves time but also inspires innovative approaches to my projects.

When selecting a template, I first consider the purpose and audience of my design. Each template is crafted with a particular function in mind, and understanding the context in which I plan to use the design is crucial. For instance, if I am creating an Instagram post, I look for templates that are visually engaging and optimized for mobile viewing. These templates often employ bold imagery and concise text, designed to capture attention quickly as users scroll through their feeds. Conversely, for a business presentation, I prioritize templates that project professionalism and clarity, often opting for more subdued color schemes and structured layouts that facilitate information delivery.

Once I identify a template that aligns with my project goals, the customization process begins. Canva's user-friendly interface allows me to modify virtually every aspect of the template, ensuring that it reflects my unique style and branding. The first step in this customization journey often involves adjusting text elements. I find that the original text provided in the template serves as a useful starting point, guiding me in terms of layout and font size. However, I quickly realize the importance of adapting the text to fit my specific messaging. I pay attention to the tone and voice I want to convey; for example, a light-hearted promotional graphic might benefit from playful language, while a formal report requires more straightforward terminology.

In addition to textual adjustments, the ability to modify fonts is crucial in achieving the desired aesthetic. Canva's library includes a vast array of font choices, ranging from classic serif and sans-serif styles to more decorative options. I often experiment with different combinations, as the right typography can dramatically influence the perception of my design. For instance, pairing a bold header font with a more understated body font can create a visually appealing hierarchy, guiding the viewer's attention through the content. I am also mindful of readability; while decorative fonts may add flair, they must remain legible to effectively communicate the intended message.

Images are another significant component of the customization process. Canva provides access to an extensive stock photo library, which I frequently utilize to find visuals that enhance my designs. I can also upload my own images, ensuring that my projects maintain a personal touch. Once I incorporate images into the template, I delve into editing options that allow me to adjust aspects such as brightness, contrast, and cropping. This level of control is essential, as the integration of images must not only complement the text but also align with the overall tone of the design. A vibrant photo can energize a promotional graphic, while a muted image may be more suitable for a formal report.

The process of color adjustment is equally significant in customizing templates. Each template comes with a predefined color scheme, which often provides a strong starting point. However, I am keen to ensure that the colors reflect my brand identity or the specific emotions I want to evoke. Canva's color palette tool allows me to experiment with various combinations, and I often refer to color theory principles to guide my choices. For example, warm colors like reds and yellows can convey excitement, while cool colors like blues and greens often evoke calmness. By thoughtfully selecting colors, I can create a design that resonates emotionally with my audience, reinforcing the intended message.

As I immerse myself in the customization of templates, I begin to appreciate how these tools can enhance my creativity. The initial framework provided by the template alleviates the pressure of starting from a blank canvas, allowing me to focus on refining and personalizing the design. I find that this process fosters experimentation; as I make adjustments to text, images, and colors, new ideas often emerge that I hadn't initially considered. The template serves not only as a guide but also as a catalyst for creative exploration, encouraging me to push boundaries and explore different design possibilities.

Another vital aspect of using templates in Canva is the consideration of layout and composition. The pre-established arrangement of elements in a template can provide valuable insights into effective design principles. As I study the structure of the template, I learn about the importance of balance, alignment, and spacing. For example, a well-designed template may feature a grid layout that enhances organization and readability. By analyzing these successful layouts, I can apply similar principles to my own custom designs, ultimately improving my overall design skills.

The collaborative aspect of working with templates is also noteworthy. If I am designing for a team or organization, I can share the template with colleagues to gather their input. Canva's collaborative features allow multiple users to access and edit the same project simultaneously, fostering a sense of teamwork that enhances the creative process. This collaborative approach not only enriches the design but also ensures that the final product aligns with the collective vision of the team. Receiving feedback on the template customization can spark new ideas and lead to improvements I might not have considered independently.

As I navigate through the extensive library of templates, I am reminded of the importance of saving my customized designs. Canva allows me to organize my projects into folders, making it easy to locate and revisit previous work. This feature is particularly useful as I undertake multiple design projects simultaneously, enabling me to maintain a coherent workflow. By categorizing my templates based on themes or project types, I can streamline my creative process and easily access resources that align with my current focus.

In summary, exploring Canva's templates reveals their immense value in the design process. The initial framework provided by templates not only saves time but also inspires creativity and experimentation. Through the thoughtful customization of text, images, and colors, I can transform templates into unique expressions of my ideas and branding. By understanding the underlying principles of layout and composition, I can enhance my design skills while benefiting from the collaborative features that Canva offers. The process of working with templates ultimately enriches my creative journey, providing both structure and freedom as I navigate the world of design.

As I continue to explore the vast array of templates available in Canva, I become increasingly aware of the strategic advantages they offer in various design scenarios. Each template is not merely a decorative option; it is a carefully constructed tool designed to meet specific needs and enhance the effectiveness of the final product. One of the most significant benefits of utilizing templates lies in their inherent ability to save time. When embarking on a design project, the daunting task of starting from scratch can stifle creativity and lead to unnecessary delays. However, with a template as a foundational element, I am provided with a structured starting point that allows me to bypass many preliminary decisions, enabling me to focus on the creative aspects of my design.

Furthermore, the diversity within Canva's template library ensures that I can find options tailored to nearly any occasion or audience. Whether I am designing a promotional flyer for a community event or a sleek presentation for a corporate meeting, the templates are designed to resonate with the intended audience. This understanding of audience engagement is vital; each design should not only communicate information effectively but also connect with viewers on an emotional level. As I sift through the templates, I pay attention to the color schemes, imagery, and overall aesthetic, ensuring that the chosen design aligns with the expectations and preferences of my target demographic.

Once I select a template that fits my project's goals, the customization process becomes a rich canvas for expression. The first area I typically address is the visual hierarchy of the design. Effective visual hierarchy directs the viewer's attention to the most important elements of the design first, guiding them through the information in a logical and engaging manner. I often begin by adjusting the size and weight of the text elements within the template. For instance, I might increase the size of the headline while reducing the size of supporting text. This adjustment not only emphasizes key points but also creates a dynamic interplay between various text elements, enhancing the overall readability of the design.

In conjunction with text adjustments, I take great care in selecting images that complement the message I wish to convey. Canva's library is abundant with high-quality visuals, ranging from photographs to illustrations. When integrating these images, I consider their placement and impact on the overall composition. A well-placed image can serve as a focal point, drawing the viewer's attention and evoking the desired emotional response. As I explore different images, I often experiment with their sizing and positioning within the template, assessing how these changes affect the overall balance of the design.

The color palette is another critical aspect of customization. Templates typically come with predefined color schemes, but I find that adapting these colors to better align with my branding or project theme can greatly enhance the effectiveness of the design. Canva allows me to modify colors easily, enabling me to explore various combinations until I find one that resonates. As I delve into color theory, I understand that colors evoke specific emotions and reactions. For instance, bright and vibrant colors may communicate energy and excitement, while softer hues might convey calmness and sophistication. By carefully selecting a color palette that aligns with my intended message, I can create a cohesive and compelling visual narrative.

Another feature that amplifies the creative possibilities within templates is the ability to add design elements such as shapes, lines, and icons. These elements serve as visual enhancers that can guide the viewer's eye or create emphasis around specific areas of the design. For instance, incorporating geometric shapes can add structure and organization, while using icons can break up text and make information more digestible. As I layer these elements into my design, I pay close attention to their size and positioning, ensuring they enhance rather than clutter the visual experience.

Throughout the customization process, I find that the iterative nature of design is particularly rewarding. With Canva's user-friendly interface, I can make changes quickly and see the results in real-time. This immediacy allows me to experiment without hesitation, encouraging a playful exploration of different design directions. Often, I will create multiple versions of a design, each with slight variations, to determine which one best resonates with my intended message. This trial-and-error approach is not only effective in refining the design but also cultivates a deeper understanding of the principles of effective design.

Collaboration features within Canva also enhance the template experience. If I am working as part of a team, sharing a template allows for a collaborative approach to customization. Colleagues can leave comments directly on the design, offering feedback and suggestions that may improve the final product. This collaborative dynamic is particularly useful for larger projects where input from various stakeholders is necessary. The ability to track changes and revert to previous versions of the design adds an additional layer of flexibility, enabling the team to navigate the design process smoothly.

Moreover, I find that utilizing templates in Canva fosters a sense of community among users. Many designers share their customized templates online, providing inspiration and guidance to others. This exchange of ideas not only enriches my creative toolkit but also motivates me to experiment further with my designs. Engaging with this community cultivates a collaborative spirit, reminding me that design is a shared journey that thrives on the input and inspiration of diverse perspectives.

As I refine my designs using templates, I also remain mindful of the importance of consistency across various projects. When creating multiple pieces for a single campaign, maintaining a cohesive look and feel is crucial for establishing brand identity. Templates enable me to achieve this consistency with ease. By using the same template style across different formats—whether for social media, print, or presentations—I can ensure that each piece reinforces the overall branding strategy. This strategic alignment is essential for building recognition and trust with my audience.

Finally, I appreciate the educational resources that accompany Canva's template library. The platform provides tips and best practices for using templates effectively, which I often refer to as I refine my design skills. Understanding the nuances of effective design—from typography to color usage—empowers me to make informed choices as I customize templates. This ongoing learning process ensures that I continually evolve as a designer, equipped with the knowledge necessary to create visually impactful and meaningful content.

In conclusion, the exploration of Canva's templates unveils a powerful tool that not only enhances the design process but also inspires creativity. Through the thoughtful customization of templates, I can create compelling visual narratives tailored to my specific needs. The strategic use of text, images, colors, and design elements allows me to engage with my audience effectively while fostering collaboration and consistency across projects. As I immerse myself in the world of templates, I am excited by the possibilities they offer, paving the way for new creative adventures as I harness the full potential of Canva's robust design capabilities.

As I continue to immerse myself in the capabilities of Canva's templates, I realize that an essential aspect of effective design lies in the nuances of visual storytelling. Each template serves as a canvas not only for aesthetic choices but also for conveying a narrative. When I select a template, I am not merely choosing a layout; I am deciding how to communicate my message visually and emotionally. Understanding this narrative component influences every decision I make throughout the design process.

When customizing a template, I begin by considering the story I want to tell. For instance, if I am designing a flyer for a community event, I think about the atmosphere I want to create. Is it energetic and vibrant, or is it calm and inviting? This thought process informs my choice of colors, fonts, and imagery. A lively event might call for bright colors and dynamic typography, while a workshop might benefit from more subdued tones and clear, professional fonts. By aligning the visual elements with the intended message, I ensure that my design resonates with the audience on a deeper level.

As I modify the template, I pay close attention to the flow of information. Effective designs guide the viewer's eye through the content in a deliberate manner, emphasizing key points while maintaining coherence. I often employ techniques such as the rule of thirds, which helps me place elements in a way that creates visual interest. By strategically positioning images or text along these lines, I can create a balanced composition that naturally draws the viewer's attention to the most important aspects of the design. This principle becomes especially relevant when working with multiple elements, as it helps me avoid clutter and ensures that each component serves a purpose within the narrative.

In addition to visual balance, I consider the emotional resonance of my design. Colors evoke feelings, and understanding the psychology behind them allows me to choose palettes that support the narrative. For example, blues can evoke trust and calmness, making them suitable for corporate presentations or wellness content. On the other hand, warm colors like reds and yellows can instill a sense of excitement or urgency, which might be more appropriate for promotional materials or events. By thoughtfully selecting colors that align with the emotional tone of my message, I can create a stronger connection with my audience.

As I dive deeper into customization, the incorporation of imagery becomes increasingly vital. I explore Canva's extensive library, searching for visuals that not only enhance the design but also align with the narrative I want to convey. When selecting images, I consider their composition, subject matter, and relevance to the content. A well-chosen image can act as a powerful focal point, capturing attention and reinforcing the message. For example, if I am designing a poster for an environmental initiative, I might select images of nature that evoke a sense of beauty and urgency regarding conservation efforts. These images not only enhance the design visually but also enrich the narrative, drawing the audience into the story I am telling.

The editing tools available in Canva further empower me to manipulate these images, allowing for adjustments in size, cropping, and filters. I often experiment with various filters to achieve a consistent look across multiple images, ensuring that they align cohesively with the overall design aesthetic. The ability to apply overlays or transparency effects can also create depth, helping certain elements stand out while allowing others to recede, contributing to a layered storytelling approach. This flexibility allows me to craft a visual narrative that feels both dynamic and harmonious.

As I work through the template, I continually assess how each design decision supports the overall message. The iterative nature of this process is crucial; I find that taking breaks and returning to the design with fresh eyes can reveal inconsistencies or areas that need refinement. This reflective practice encourages me to ask critical questions about the effectiveness of my design. Does the layout facilitate a natural flow of information? Are the visual elements enhancing the message, or are they detracting from it? Engaging in this self-reflection not only improves the design but also hones my skills as a designer, deepening my understanding of how to communicate effectively through visuals.

Collaboration remains an essential element of the design process, particularly when working on projects that involve multiple stakeholders. Sharing the customized template with colleagues allows for a rich exchange of ideas, where each person's insights contribute to a more refined final product. The comments and feedback features in Canva facilitate this collaborative effort, enabling team members to leave suggestions directly on the design. This level of engagement fosters an environment where creativity thrives, as diverse perspectives often lead to innovative solutions and enhancements that I might not have considered independently.

As I finalize my design, I also consider the various formats in which it will be presented. The versatility of Canva's templates allows me to adapt a single design for different platforms, whether that be a social media graphic, a printed flyer, or a digital presentation. Each format presents its own unique challenges and opportunities; for instance, a design for social media must capture attention quickly, while a printed piece might require more detailed information and a different layout approach. By leveraging the existing template as a foundation, I can tailor my designs to meet the specific requirements of each format while maintaining a consistent brand identity.

I also appreciate the educational resources that accompany the use of templates in Canva. Tutorials and design tips within the platform enhance my understanding of effective design principles, enabling me to make more informed decisions as I customize templates. This commitment to ongoing learning fosters a growth mindset, encouraging me to continually refine my skills and expand my creative repertoire.

In conclusion, the exploration of Canva's templates reveals a multifaceted tool that transcends mere aesthetics. These templates serve as powerful instruments for storytelling, allowing me to weave narratives through thoughtful customization. By considering the emotional resonance of colors, the strategic flow of information, and the impact of imagery, I can create designs that not only captivate but also communicate effectively. The collaborative features and educational resources further enrich the design process, fostering a spirit of creativity and continuous improvement. As I continue to harness the power of Canva's templates, I feel empowered to bring my ideas to life, crafting compelling visual narratives that resonate with my audience and fulfill my project goals.

CHAPTER 4: MASTERING TEXT AND TYPOGRAPHY

As I delve into the intricacies of text and typography within Canva, I am reminded of the pivotal role that these elements play in effective design. Typography is not merely a means of presenting words; it is an art form that can profoundly influence how a message is perceived and understood. The ability to manipulate text effectively allows me to enhance the overall visual appeal of my designs while ensuring that the content is not only attractive but also easily readable. In this exploration, I will uncover the tools and techniques that Canva provides to master text and typography, transforming the way I communicate through design.

The journey begins with adding text to my design. Canva's interface makes this process straightforward, providing a text box feature that allows me to position text anywhere on the canvas. This flexibility is crucial, as the placement of text can significantly affect the composition and flow of the overall design. I often begin by selecting the type of text I want to include, such as headings, subheadings, or body text. Each category serves a distinct purpose within my design, and understanding the hierarchy is essential. For example, the heading grabs the viewer's attention, while the subheading provides additional context, and the body text conveys the primary message. By categorizing my text in this way, I establish a clear typographic hierarchy that guides the viewer through the content.

Once I have added my text, I turn my attention to formatting it. Canva offers a rich array of font options, each with its unique character and style. The selection of fonts is a critical decision, as it can significantly affect the tone of the design. For instance, a bold, modern sans-serif font might convey a sense of innovation and energy, while a classic serif font might evoke tradition and reliability. When selecting fonts, I consider the message I wish to convey and the audience I am addressing. This thoughtful approach ensures that the typography aligns with the overall narrative of the design. I often experiment with various fonts, pairing them thoughtfully to create contrast and visual interest. For example, I might use a bold font for the heading and a lighter, more understated font for the body text. This contrast not only enhances readability but also adds depth to the design.

In addition to font selection, the formatting tools within Canva allow me to adjust size, weight, and style. I find that these adjustments play a crucial role in establishing a visual hierarchy. For example, by increasing the size of the heading while decreasing the size of the subheading, I can effectively direct the viewer's attention to the most important elements of the design. Text weight also plays a critical role; using bold or italic styles can emphasize key points, drawing attention where it is most needed. I carefully consider how these formatting choices interact to ensure that the overall composition remains balanced and harmonious.

Alignment is another vital aspect of typography that I prioritize as I refine my designs. Canva provides several alignment options—left, center, right, and justified—each of which can significantly influence the visual flow of the text. I often opt for left alignment for body text, as it tends to be the most readable option for longer passages. However, center alignment can create a sense of formality and can be effective for headings or short pieces of text that need to stand out. The alignment of text must work in tandem with the overall layout of the design, ensuring that each element complements the others without creating visual clutter.

Once the basic formatting is complete, I turn my attention to spacing, which is an often-overlooked but crucial element of typography. Canva allows me to adjust both line spacing and letter spacing, giving me the power to enhance readability and aesthetics. I find that increasing line spacing can make text feel more airy and less cramped, which is particularly beneficial for body text. Conversely, reducing line spacing in a heading can create a sense of urgency or emphasis. Letter spacing, or kerning, can also be manipulated to achieve the desired effect; tighter letter spacing can lend a modern, sleek feel, while wider letter spacing may evoke a more classic aesthetic. By thoughtfully adjusting these spaces, I create a more polished and professional appearance.

The use of typographic hierarchy is essential for ensuring that my content is not only visually appealing but also easy to navigate. Canva provides tools to create this hierarchy effectively, allowing me to establish a clear order of information. I begin by clearly defining my primary, secondary, and tertiary text elements. Using size, weight, and color variations helps to delineate these different levels of information. For example, I might use a large, bold font for the main heading, a slightly smaller italicized font for the subheading, and a standard font for the body text. This structured approach not only guides the viewer's eye but also enhances the overall flow of information within the design.

As I continue to refine my designs, I am constantly aware of the importance of conveying my message effectively through typography. The interplay between text and visuals is crucial; they should work in harmony to reinforce the overall narrative. I consider how my text complements the imagery and other design elements, ensuring that the typography enhances rather than distracts from the intended message. This cohesive approach helps to create a unified visual experience that resonates with the audience.

Furthermore, I take advantage of Canva's features that allow for the inclusion of text effects. Options such as drop shadows, outlines, and highlights can add depth and emphasis to my text, enhancing its visual impact. For instance, applying a subtle shadow to a heading can make it pop against a background, drawing the viewer's attention instantly. These effects, when used judiciously, can elevate my design from the ordinary to the extraordinary, creating a polished finish that captures attention.

In conclusion, mastering text and typography within Canva is a multifaceted endeavor that requires careful consideration of font selection, formatting, alignment, spacing, and hierarchy. The ability to manipulate these elements empowers me to create designs that are not only visually appealing but also effectively communicate my intended message. As I continue to explore and refine my typographic skills, I am confident that the tools provided by Canva will enhance my ability to engage my audience and convey narratives through compelling visual design.

As I delve further into the mastery of text and typography within Canva, I begin to appreciate the nuances that differentiate effective communication from mere decoration. Typography is a language in itself, capable of conveying tone, emotion, and intention through the careful selection of typefaces and styles. My exploration continues with an emphasis on advanced text manipulation techniques, allowing me to elevate my designs and create a more engaging viewer experience.

One of the first aspects I examine is the significance of font pairings. While a single font can communicate a message, the combination of multiple fonts can create contrast and depth, enhancing the overall visual narrative. When selecting complementary fonts, I often adhere to certain principles. For instance, pairing a serif font with a sans-serif font can yield an appealing dynamic, as the contrasting styles can create a sense of balance and interest. The serif font often provides a classic, trustworthy feel, while the sans-serif can introduce modernity and clarity. I find that using a decorative font for headings combined with a simpler font for body text helps to maintain readability while still capturing attention.

In addition to selecting the right font pairings, I pay close attention to the overall visual weight of the text. Each typeface carries its own inherent weight, which influences the hierarchy within my design. For example, a bold typeface can act as a focal point, drawing the viewer's eye and emphasizing critical information. I utilize this principle by strategically placing bold text for headlines or key messages while employing lighter weights for supporting text. This contrast helps to establish a clear path for the viewer's gaze, guiding them through the design while making it easy to digest the information presented.

Alignment is another crucial element in the effective presentation of text. I recognize that the way text is aligned can significantly impact its readability and overall aesthetic. While left alignment is commonly used for body text due to its ease of reading, centered text can create a sense of formality or focus when used appropriately. In my designs, I consider the context and the message I wish to convey when choosing alignment. For instance, I might center-align a quote or an impactful statement to give it prominence, while maintaining left alignment for paragraphs of text to facilitate smoother reading. This thoughtful approach to alignment not only enhances clarity but also contributes to the overall harmony of the design.

As I further refine my designs, I explore the use of text spacing—both line spacing and letter spacing—known as leading and kerning, respectively. The manipulation of these spaces can dramatically enhance the overall legibility and aesthetics of the text. In particular, adjusting line spacing allows me to create a sense of rhythm within the text block. Tight line spacing may be effective for short, impactful messages, while increased spacing can promote readability in longer paragraphs. By carefully assessing the text layout, I ensure that the spacing creates an inviting reading experience, drawing the viewer in rather than overwhelming them with densely packed lines.

Kerning, or the adjustment of space between individual letters, is another critical consideration in typography. While many typefaces come with preset kerning, I often find that slight adjustments can enhance the text's appearance and readability. For instance, when working with a title, I might tighten the spacing between letters to create a more cohesive and impactful visual. Conversely, I may choose to increase the spacing in body text to enhance legibility, particularly for designs that will be viewed from a distance. By being attuned to these details, I cultivate a more polished and professional presentation in my designs.

Exploring Canva's text effects also contributes to my understanding of how to make text visually compelling. Options such as drop shadows, outlines, and glows provide additional layers of depth and emphasis. For example, applying a subtle drop shadow to a headline can create a three-dimensional effect, making it stand out against the background. However, I remain cautious not to overuse these effects, as they can detract from the overall message if applied indiscriminately. A well-placed effect enhances the text without overshadowing it, serving to clarify rather than complicate.

As I progress, I find that incorporating text boxes strategically can enhance the layout of my designs. Text boxes allow me to isolate specific content, such as quotes or call-to-action statements, from the rest of the text. This separation can draw attention to key messages, encouraging engagement from the viewer. Additionally, the ability to customize the shape and color of text boxes can create visual interest and help establish a consistent branding theme. By utilizing these features, I can create designs that are not only informative but also visually appealing and cohesive.

While designing, I remain cognizant of the importance of consistency in typography across multiple designs, particularly when establishing a brand identity. The thoughtful selection of fonts, sizes, colors, and spacing should align with my brand's values and messaging. Consistency fosters recognition, allowing audiences to associate specific visual styles with my work. I often create a style guide for my projects, detailing the fonts and typographic treatments I intend to use across different materials. This practice not only streamlines my workflow but also reinforces a cohesive brand image.

Another valuable feature within Canva is the option to create and save text styles. By establishing predefined text styles for headings, subheadings, and body text, I can ensure consistency and save time during the design process. This feature allows me to apply the same formatting across various designs effortlessly, creating a seamless transition from one piece to another. Additionally, the ability to adjust these styles globally means that if I decide to modify a font or size, the changes will automatically reflect across all instances, further enhancing efficiency.

In conclusion, mastering text and typography within Canva

encompasses a multifaceted approach that combines font selection, formatting, alignment, spacing, and creative effects. Through a nuanced understanding of these elements, I am empowered to craft designs that effectively communicate my message while captivating the viewer's attention. By leveraging the tools and features available within Canva, I can elevate my designs, ensuring that text is not merely an afterthought but a central component of a compelling visual narrative. As I continue to hone my skills in typography, I embrace the creative possibilities that await, ready to explore new dimensions of communication through the art of text.

As I delve deeper into the mastery of text and typography in Canva, I realize that the subtleties of font selection and manipulation are crucial to crafting a compelling design. The selection of a typeface is not merely a technical decision; it is an artistic choice that carries the weight of branding, emotion, and narrative. Each font possesses its own personality and tone, and understanding how to match these characteristics with the intended message of my design is essential. I find myself constantly exploring new fonts, evaluating their potential to convey different feelings—whether it be elegance, playfulness, seriousness, or creativity.

When I embark on a design project, I begin with a clear vision of the message I want to communicate. This vision guides my font selection process. For instance, if I am creating a flyer for a charity event, I may choose a serif font to convey a sense of tradition and reliability, reflecting the cause's importance. In contrast, a promotional piece for a youth-oriented product might benefit from a modern, sans-serif font that conveys a sense of fun and accessibility. This strategic approach to font selection enhances not only the aesthetic quality of my design but also its effectiveness in reaching the intended audience.

Once I have settled on the appropriate font, I focus on how to format it effectively. In Canva, I have the flexibility to adjust various attributes such as size, weight, and style. The size of the text can greatly impact its readability and visual hierarchy within the design. I often experiment with different sizes to ensure that the most important information stands out while maintaining an overall sense of balance. For example, I might use a larger size for the main headline to attract immediate attention, while using smaller sizes for supporting text to create a cohesive look.

Text weight also plays a significant role in creating emphasis. By varying the weight—bold, regular, or light—I can guide the viewer's focus to specific elements. A bold headline not only commands attention but also sets the tone for the rest of the content. Conversely, lighter weights for body text can enhance readability, making it easier for the audience to absorb information. This deliberate manipulation of text weight helps establish a clear visual hierarchy, ensuring that the design communicates its message effectively.

In addition to size and weight, the alignment of text elements is another area that warrants careful consideration. In Canva, I have access to multiple alignment options: left, center, right, and justified. Each alignment choice can evoke a different visual and emotional response. I often prefer left alignment for body text, as it is the most common and easiest for readers to follow, creating a natural reading flow. However, center alignment can create a striking effect for headlines or quotes, drawing attention and instilling a sense of importance. I continuously evaluate how each alignment choice impacts the overall composition, making adjustments as needed to ensure that the design remains visually appealing and functional.

Spacing is yet another critical factor in typography that I meticulously consider. The spacing between lines of text, known as leading, can significantly influence the legibility of the content. I find that slightly increasing line spacing in body text enhances readability, especially in designs where longer paragraphs are present. This adjustment allows the text to breathe, making it less daunting for the reader. In contrast, tighter line spacing might be suitable for headings or short phrases, where a more compact appearance can create a sense of urgency or impact. Similarly, letter spacing—or kerning—can be adjusted to refine the overall look. A tighter kerning can create a sleek, modern feel, while a wider kerning can convey elegance and sophistication.

As I work through the text formatting process, I also explore the potential of incorporating text effects available in Canva. Effects such as drop shadows, outlines, and highlights can add depth and emphasis to my typography, helping to distinguish important information within the design. For example, applying a subtle drop shadow to a key message can enhance its visibility against a complex background, ensuring that it remains legible and impactful. However, I am mindful to use these effects judiciously; overusing them can lead to visual clutter and detract from the overall message. Striking a balance between enhancement and simplicity is crucial in effective design.

Furthermore, I recognize that typography is not just about the aesthetics of individual letters; it's about creating a cohesive visual experience. The way text interacts with other design elements, such as images, shapes, and colors, plays a vital role in the overall composition. I strive to ensure that my text harmonizes with the visual components of the design, contributing to a unified look that enhances the message. For instance, if I am working with a vibrant color palette, I may choose text colors that provide sufficient contrast while still being visually appealing. This careful consideration of color contrast ensures that the text remains legible and striking against the background.

I also find it beneficial to create text styles within Canva, especially when working on projects with multiple components. By establishing predefined text styles for headings, subheadings, and body text, I streamline my design process and maintain consistency across different pieces. This organization is invaluable, particularly for branding purposes, as it helps reinforce a cohesive identity throughout various materials. The ability to apply these styles across multiple designs not only saves time but also ensures that the typography remains aligned with the overall brand aesthetic.

In exploring the impact of typography on overall design effectiveness, I come to appreciate the importance of feedback and iteration. After completing a design, I often seek input from colleagues or peers to gauge their perceptions of the typography choices I made. This external perspective can illuminate aspects I may have overlooked, such as readability issues or misalignment with the intended message. Engaging in this feedback loop allows me to refine my designs further, ensuring that the final product resonates well with the audience.

In conclusion, mastering text and typography in Canva involves a thoughtful and strategic approach to font selection, formatting, alignment, spacing, and effects. By understanding the nuances of these elements, I can create designs that effectively communicate my intended messages while remaining visually appealing. This exploration not only enhances my technical skills but also deepens my appreciation for the artistry of typography as a means of expression. With each design I undertake, I embrace the challenge of weaving together words and visuals, crafting compelling narratives that engage and resonate with my audience. As I continue to develop my expertise in typography, I look forward to pushing the boundaries of creativity and innovation within my designs.

CHAPTER 5: WORKING WITH IMAGES AND GRAPHICS

As I embark on the exploration of images and graphics within Canva, I recognize that these elements are crucial in crafting designs that not only capture attention but also convey messages effectively. Images have the unique ability to evoke emotions, illustrate concepts, and provide context, making them indispensable tools in the designer's arsenal. The journey begins with the fundamental task of integrating images into my projects, which involves understanding both the technical and creative aspects of image selection and placement.

The first step in working with images is to consider the purpose they will serve within the design. Whether I am creating a marketing flyer, a social media post, or a presentation, the images I choose must align with the overall message and tone I wish to communicate. When browsing through Canva's extensive library of stock images, I find it helpful to keep my target audience in mind. For example, if I am designing for a corporate audience, I might opt for polished, professional imagery that reflects the brand's values. Conversely, for a youth-oriented campaign, I might choose vibrant, dynamic images that convey energy and excitement. This thoughtful approach ensures that my images resonate with viewers and enhance the overall effectiveness of the design.

Once I have selected an image, I can upload my own or choose from Canva's library. Uploading my own images is a straightforward process that allows me to incorporate personal or brand-specific visuals into my designs. After uploading, I am often eager to explore the editing options available in Canva's built-in photo editor. This tool provides a variety of features that enable me to enhance and manipulate images to better suit my design goals. I begin by adjusting basic attributes such as brightness, contrast, and saturation, which can dramatically alter the mood of the image. For instance, increasing the brightness can create a more vibrant and inviting feel, while adjusting the contrast can add depth and drama.

Filters and effects are another valuable aspect of Canva's photo editor that I frequently utilize. By applying filters, I can instantly change the aesthetic of an image, giving it a cohesive look that aligns with the overall design. I often experiment with different filters to see how they affect the emotional tone of the image. For example, a vintage filter might evoke nostalgia, while a modern filter could impart a sleek and contemporary feel. This capability to manipulate images not only enhances their visual appeal but also allows me to maintain a consistent theme throughout my designs.

In addition to basic editing, I take advantage of Canva's cropping and resizing tools to ensure that images fit seamlessly within the layout. Cropping can help eliminate distractions and focus attention on the most relevant parts of the image. When I encounter an image with extraneous elements, I often crop it to highlight the subject, ensuring that it serves the intended purpose in the design. Resizing images is equally important, as I need to ensure they maintain their aspect ratio and quality when adjusted. This attention to detail is essential in preventing images from appearing stretched or pixelated, which can detract from the overall professionalism of the design.

Once I have edited and placed my images, I turn my focus to the overall composition of the design. The placement of images in relation to text and other elements is critical for achieving balance and harmony. I often consider principles such as the rule of thirds, which involves dividing the canvas into a grid and placing key elements along these lines. This technique can create a more dynamic and visually interesting layout. Additionally, I am mindful of the white space surrounding images, as it can enhance focus and prevent the design from feeling cluttered. By ensuring that images and text work together cohesively, I create a more engaging visual experience for the viewer.

Beyond photographs, I also explore Canva's extensive library of graphic elements, including icons, illustrations, and shapes. These elements provide additional layers of creativity that can elevate my designs. For instance, using icons can simplify complex ideas, making them more accessible to the audience. When selecting icons, I focus on their style and how they complement the overall design. A modern, minimalist icon set might work well in a contemporary design, while more ornate icons could enhance a traditional or formal aesthetic. This strategic selection of graphic elements contributes to a unified visual narrative.

Illustrations are another powerful tool within Canva that allow for more creative expression. Unlike photographs, illustrations can be tailored to fit the specific tone and message of my design. I often choose illustrations that convey a sense of whimsy or playfulness for projects aimed at children or creative industries. The flexibility of illustrations enables me to align visuals with the message more closely, providing a level of customization that photographs may not always achieve. Furthermore, combining illustrations with photographs can create interesting contrasts and visual intrigue, enriching the overall composition.

Integrating these graphic elements into my designs requires careful consideration of placement and size. I find that layering images and graphics can create depth and complexity, leading to a more engaging design. For instance, placing an icon over an image can enhance the message, while also adding a modern touch. This layering technique often involves adjusting the transparency of certain elements, allowing them to interact visually without competing for attention. By experimenting with layering, I can achieve a sense of cohesion and flow throughout the design.

As I navigate the creative process, I remain aware of the importance of consistent branding. When working on projects for a specific brand or organization, I ensure that the images and graphics I use align with the established brand guidelines. This includes maintaining a consistent color palette, style, and tone across all visual elements. Consistency fosters recognition and builds trust with the audience, making it essential for effective design. I often create mood boards to visualize how different images and graphic elements can come together to support the brand's identity.

Finally, I appreciate the value of feedback when working with images and graphics. Sharing my designs with colleagues or peers allows me to gather insights and perspectives that can enhance the final product. Others may spot issues I might have overlooked or suggest alternative images that could strengthen the design. Engaging in this collaborative process not only improves the quality of my work but also fosters a sense of community and creativity within the design process.

In conclusion, mastering the integration of images and graphics in Canva is a multifaceted endeavor that involves careful consideration of selection, editing, and placement. By leveraging the tools available within the platform, I can enhance my designs with compelling visuals that resonate with the audience and effectively convey the intended message. The combination of images, graphic elements, and thoughtful composition enables me to create rich and engaging designs that captivate viewers and leave a lasting impression. As I continue to refine my skills in this area, I embrace the creative possibilities that images and graphics offer, ready to explore new dimensions of expression in my designs.

As I continue to navigate the realm of images and graphics in Canva, I recognize the importance of employing best practices not only in the selection and editing of images but also in their integration into the overall design. This integration requires a strategic approach that considers how each visual element interacts with the others to create a harmonious and effective composition. One of the foundational aspects of this integration is understanding the context in which my images will be used, as different projects demand different visual strategies.

In corporate presentations, for example, images must convey professionalism and credibility. I often choose images that reflect the brand's ethos, featuring real people in relatable situations or high-quality graphics that enhance the content. These choices help to create an environment of trust, reinforcing the message I wish to communicate. In contrast, when designing for social media campaigns aimed at younger audiences, I may opt for more vibrant and playful images that elicit excitement and engagement. The context dictates not only the type of images I choose but also how I present them, ensuring that each visual supports the overall message and aesthetic of the design.

Once I have selected the images appropriate for the project,

I focus on how to position them within the layout. The placement of images can significantly affect the visual flow and impact of the design. I often employ the concept of visual hierarchy to guide my decisions. By placing a striking image prominently, I can capture the viewer's attention immediately. This technique works particularly well for headlines or key messages, where the visual component serves to enhance the text. Conversely, smaller images or icons can be placed strategically to support the main content without overwhelming it.

The use of grid systems within Canva helps me maintain a structured layout that enhances readability. Grids provide a framework for aligning images and text, ensuring that each element is well-positioned within the design. I often take advantage of Canva's alignment tools, which allow me to snap elements to the grid, creating a cohesive look. This level of organization not only improves aesthetics but also contributes to the clarity of the information being presented, guiding the viewer's eye naturally through the content.

As I integrate images into my designs, I also pay close attention to the backgrounds of these images. A well-chosen background can enhance the visual appeal of the design, while a poorly selected one can detract from it. I often experiment with different background options, considering whether to use solid colors, gradients, or even subtle textures that add depth without distracting from the main content. The background should complement the images and text, creating a unified visual experience that draws the viewer in. I find that using slightly muted or blurred backgrounds can help focus attention on the primary elements of the design, creating a more polished look.

In addition to background considerations, I am also mindful of the color palette I employ throughout the design. The colors in the images should harmonize with the overall color scheme, creating a sense of cohesion and professionalism. Canva's color picker tool allows me to sample colors directly from the images, ensuring that my design remains consistent. By matching text colors to the hues within the images, I create a more integrated look that enhances the overall impact of the design. This attention to detail reinforces the branding and messaging, ensuring that each element works together harmoniously.

Exploring Canva's extensive library of icons and graphic elements further enriches my designs. Icons serve as visual shorthand for concepts, making complex information more digestible. For instance, using a light bulb icon next to an idea can immediately signal creativity or innovation. When selecting icons, I pay careful attention to their style and color, ensuring they align with the overall design. A cohesive look across all graphic elements strengthens the visual narrative and contributes to a unified brand identity.

Illustrations offer a versatile alternative to photographs, allowing for more creative expression. Unlike static images, illustrations can be tailored to reflect the specific tone and style of the project. When I'm working on a playful or whimsical design, illustrations can evoke emotions that resonate with the target audience. This flexibility is particularly beneficial for designs aimed at children or creative industries, where a more light-hearted approach is often appropriate. I often combine illustrations with photographs to create interesting contrasts, merging different visual styles to enrich the overall composition.

As I integrate these graphic elements, I am conscious of the overall balance within the design. The placement of icons and illustrations must complement the images and text, contributing to the overall harmony. I frequently experiment with layering these elements, positioning them in a way that creates depth without causing visual clutter. This layered approach not only adds complexity to the design but also enhances engagement, encouraging viewers to explore the various elements more deeply.

Another important consideration is the use of image overlays, which can help blend images into the design seamlessly. By applying a semi-transparent overlay, I can soften the impact of a background image, allowing text to stand out more clearly. This technique is particularly useful when dealing with busy backgrounds that might otherwise compete with the text. I find that these overlays not only improve readability but also create a more cohesive look by tying different elements of the design together.

As I finalize my designs, I prioritize the review process to ensure that every image and graphic element serves its purpose. This reflective practice allows me to step back and evaluate the overall composition critically. I consider whether the images enhance the message or detract from it, and whether the placement of each element contributes to the visual flow. Gathering feedback from colleagues is also invaluable during this stage; fresh perspectives can often reveal areas for improvement that I might have overlooked. This collaborative approach not only enriches the design process but also fosters a sense of community and shared creativity.

In conclusion, mastering the integration of images and graphics in Canva is an intricate process that requires careful consideration of selection, editing, and placement. By leveraging the extensive tools available within the platform, I can enhance my designs with compelling visuals that effectively communicate my intended messages. The thoughtful combination of high-quality images, graphic elements, and strategic composition enables me to create rich and engaging designs that captivate viewers. As I continue to develop my skills in this area, I embrace the creative possibilities that images and graphics offer, eager to explore new dimensions of expression in my design journey.

As I delve deeper into working with images and graphics in Canva, I find that the strategic use of overlays, textures, and gradients can significantly enhance the visual impact of my designs. Overlays serve as a versatile tool that can help unify disparate elements, add depth, or even create a mood that aligns with the design's purpose. For instance, applying a subtle color overlay to an image can shift its emotional tone—transforming a bright photograph into something more muted and sophisticated. This technique is particularly effective when I need to ensure that text remains legible against a complex background. By adjusting the opacity of the overlay, I can find the perfect balance that allows the image to provide context without overshadowing the written content.

In addition to overlays, textures can bring an added dimension to my designs. Canva offers various textures that can create tactile qualities in visual presentations. These textures can evoke feelings of warmth or authenticity, making designs feel more approachable. When integrating textures, I often consider the overall theme of the project. For example, if I am designing for a rustic brand, incorporating wood or linen textures can enhance the organic feel of the design, making it resonate more deeply with the intended audience. Textures are not just decorative; they serve as a means of connecting with the viewer on a sensory level.

Gradients, too, play a pivotal role in enriching the design landscape. By transitioning between two or more colors, gradients can add depth and sophistication, creating a sense of movement or fluidity. I often use gradients as backgrounds to give a design a more modern touch, and they can also enhance the dimensionality of shapes and text. When applying gradients, I consider the direction of the transition—whether it flows from left to right, top to bottom, or radiates from a center point. Each direction conveys different emotions and visual rhythms, influencing how the design is perceived. I find that the combination of gradients with well-placed images can create striking focal points that capture the viewer's attention.

Another essential aspect of working with images and graphics is ensuring that they adhere to the principles of accessibility. This consideration is paramount in creating designs that are inclusive and can be appreciated by a diverse audience. I pay close attention to color contrasts, ensuring that text over images is easily readable. Canva provides contrast check tools that allow me to evaluate whether the color combinations I'm using are accessible to all viewers, including those with visual impairments. This attention to detail not only demonstrates professionalism but also reflects a commitment to creating designs that can be appreciated by everyone.

As I incorporate various graphic elements, such as icons and illustrations, I make a conscious effort to maintain consistency in style and color throughout the design. This consistency reinforces branding and creates a cohesive visual narrative. When selecting icons from Canva's library, I often look for those that share a similar line weight or design aesthetic. This approach helps unify the overall look, making the design feel intentional rather than pieced together. I also consider how icons interact with images and text. For example, placing an icon alongside a heading can enhance its meaning, offering visual reinforcement to the message being conveyed.

Illustrations serve as another powerful tool in my design toolkit. Unlike photographs, illustrations can be customized and stylized to align perfectly with the overall theme of a project. When I am working on a campaign that aims to evoke creativity or playfulness, illustrations allow me to embody those qualities in ways that photographs may not achieve. I often experiment with different illustration styles, such as flat design or hand-drawn aesthetics, to find the best fit for the message and target audience. The flexibility of illustrations allows me to communicate complex ideas simply and engagingly.

As I further refine my designs, I explore the option of creating custom graphics within Canva. The platform allows for the combination of shapes, text, and images to craft unique visual elements tailored specifically to my project. This capability empowers me to step beyond the limitations of stock imagery and graphic elements, giving me the freedom to express my ideas more fully. I find that creating custom graphics can also serve as a branding opportunity, reinforcing visual identity through unique and recognizable designs.

Throughout the design process, I am reminded of the importance of maintaining a clear visual hierarchy. The careful placement of images and graphics must guide the viewer's attention through the design in a logical and engaging manner. As I analyze my designs, I assess whether the images enhance or distract from the message. Each image, icon, and illustration should serve a purpose, whether it's to support text, evoke an emotion, or create visual interest. If an image doesn't contribute meaningfully, I am not afraid to replace or remove it, recognizing that simplicity often yields the most powerful results.

Moreover, the iterative process of design is invaluable as I continue to refine my use of images and graphics. I often step back from my work to gain a fresh perspective, which allows me to identify areas for improvement or new creative avenues to explore. Seeking feedback from peers is also integral to this process; their insights can reveal strengths and weaknesses I might not have noticed. Collaboration fosters a rich environment for creativity, enabling me to develop designs that resonate with audiences on multiple levels.

Finally, as I prepare to present my designs, I consider the various formats in which my work will be shared. Each platform may have specific requirements regarding image resolution and file type, which necessitates careful planning and adjustment. Canva simplifies this process by providing options for exporting designs in various formats, including PNG, JPEG, and PDF. Understanding the strengths of each format allows me to deliver high-quality images that maintain their integrity, whether for digital use or print.

In conclusion, working with images and graphics in Canva is a multifaceted journey that encompasses careful selection, thoughtful editing, and strategic integration. By mastering these elements, I create compelling designs that effectively communicate messages and engage audiences. As I refine my skills in using images and graphics, I remain excited about the creative possibilities they present, continually seeking to push the boundaries of expression and innovation in my design work. Embracing this dynamic interplay of visuals allows me to craft narratives that resonate and leave a lasting impression.

CHAPTER 6: UTILIZING CANVA'S DESIGN ELEMENTS

As I immerse myself in the rich array of design elements offered by Canva, I begin to understand how these components can significantly enhance my projects and create a more engaging visual experience. The power of shapes, lines, grids, and frames lies in their ability to organize content, create emphasis, and establish a cohesive design language. By thoughtfully integrating these elements into my work, I can elevate the overall aesthetic while ensuring that my designs effectively communicate their intended messages.

The exploration begins with shapes, which are fundamental building blocks in design. Canva provides an extensive library of shapes, allowing me to incorporate various geometric forms into my projects. Shapes can serve multiple purposes; they can be used as backgrounds, containers for text, or decorative elements that add visual interest. When I consider using shapes as backgrounds, I often choose to create overlays that provide contrast against the text. For instance, a semi-transparent rectangle behind a heading can enhance readability while adding depth to the design. This layering technique allows me to create a polished, professional look that guides the viewer's eye to the most important information.

Additionally, shapes can be utilized to segment content within my design. By employing shapes as containers for text or images, I create clear divisions that help organize information logically. For example, in an infographic, I might use circles to highlight key statistics while employing rectangles for descriptive text. This organization not only enhances readability but also helps the viewer process information more efficiently. The deliberate use of shapes can create a visual rhythm that draws the eye from one element to the next, facilitating a smooth flow through the content.

In addition to shapes, lines are powerful tools for adding structure and visual interest to my designs. Canva offers various line styles, including solid, dashed, and dotted, each of which can evoke different feelings and convey unique messages. For instance, a bold solid line may suggest strength and stability, while a dotted line might impart a sense of playfulness or informality. I often employ lines to create borders around images or text boxes, which can enhance focus and delineate space effectively. A well-placed line can serve as a visual cue, leading the viewer's eye and enhancing the overall composition.

When using lines, I consider their placement and direction carefully. Horizontal lines can create a sense of calm and stability, while vertical lines may evoke energy and movement. Diagonal lines, on the other hand, can introduce dynamism and tension. By experimenting with these different orientations, I can create visual narratives that resonate with the intended message of my design. For instance, if I am designing a promotional piece for an event, I might incorporate diagonal lines to convey excitement and action, reflecting the event's energetic atmosphere.

As I work with these elements, the concept of balance becomes increasingly significant. Achieving visual balance involves distributing elements in a way that feels harmonious and intentional. I often evaluate my designs for visual weight, considering how each shape and line contributes to the overall composition. For example, if I have a large graphic on one side of the design, I might balance it with several smaller shapes or lines on the opposite side to create equilibrium. This attention to balance not only enhances the aesthetic quality but also ensures that the viewer's eye moves fluidly through the design.

Moving beyond shapes and lines, I explore the use of grids and frames, which offer additional structure and organization. Grids are invaluable for ensuring that my content aligns neatly and cohesively. Canva allows me to set up a grid that helps maintain consistent spacing and alignment, which is particularly useful when working with multiple images or text elements. This grid system facilitates a cleaner layout, ensuring that everything feels intentional rather than haphazard. I often rely on grids to establish a clear visual hierarchy, allowing me to prioritize information in a way that guides the viewer's focus.

Frames serve a dual purpose: they can contain images while also adding an aesthetic element to the design. Canva's frames allow me to crop images into various shapes, adding creativity and flair to my projects. For instance, I might use circular frames for profile pictures or hexagonal frames for a modern twist on traditional layouts. This versatility enhances the visual appeal of the design while reinforcing brand identity through unique shapes. Additionally, frames can help create consistent styling across multiple elements, ensuring that my designs maintain a cohesive look.

While integrating these design elements, I also remain mindful of color selection. The colors I choose for shapes and lines can dramatically influence the overall mood and message of the design. I often draw inspiration from the brand's color palette to ensure that my designs are not only visually appealing but also consistent with established branding. Canva's color picker tool allows me to select and customize colors, ensuring that they harmonize with the overall composition. I find that creating a limited color palette often results in a more sophisticated look, as too many colors can lead to visual clutter and confusion.

In the iterative process of design, I frequently revisit and refine my use of shapes, lines, grids, and frames. After completing a draft, I take a step back to evaluate the overall composition. I ask myself whether the design elements work together to enhance the message or whether any adjustments are needed. Gathering feedback from peers is invaluable during this stage, as fresh eyes can identify areas for improvement that I might have missed. Engaging in this collaborative process not only strengthens my designs but also fosters a sense of community among fellow creators.

As I work on my projects, I also explore Canva's library of templates that already incorporate various design elements. These templates provide inspiration and can serve as a foundation upon which I can build. By analyzing how shapes, lines, and frames are utilized within these templates, I can glean insights into effective design practices. This exploration often sparks new ideas and encourages me to experiment with my own creations.

In summary, utilizing design elements such as shapes, lines, grids, and frames within Canva is a dynamic and rewarding endeavor. By understanding how to effectively integrate these components, I enhance my ability to create visually compelling designs that communicate messages clearly and engagingly. The thoughtful combination of these elements allows me to craft narratives that resonate with viewers and foster deeper connections. As I continue to refine my skills in this area, I am excited to explore the creative possibilities that await, eager to push the boundaries of expression and innovation in my design work.

As I delve deeper into the various design elements available in

Canva, I become increasingly aware of how effectively utilizing shapes, lines, grids, and frames can elevate my projects. Each element serves a distinct purpose, enabling me to not only enhance visual appeal but also improve the clarity and organization of information presented. Understanding the versatility of these components empowers me to craft designs that are not only aesthetically pleasing but also functional in communicating their intended messages.

Beginning with shapes, I recognize their multifaceted role in design. Beyond serving as backgrounds, shapes can act as containers for text and images, thereby creating visually distinct areas that help organize content. When I incorporate shapes as backgrounds, I often opt for semi-transparent overlays that allow the underlying image or text to show through while still providing contrast. For instance, placing a light-colored rectangle behind a dark-colored text block can enhance readability and create a focal point. This technique ensures that the text stands out clearly against the background, facilitating easier comprehension for the viewer.

I also take advantage of the different types of shapes available in Canva, such as circles, squares, and more complex polygons. Each shape can evoke different feelings and associations, which I leverage strategically in my designs. For example, rounded shapes often impart a sense of friendliness and approachability, making them ideal for designs aimed at children or casual settings. In contrast, sharp-edged shapes might convey professionalism and precision, which would be more appropriate for corporate or technical designs. This strategic selection of shapes helps me communicate subtle messages that enhance the overall impact of the design.

Moving on to lines, I find that they serve as powerful visual tools for creating structure and flow. Lines can guide the viewer's eye through the composition, establishing a pathway that directs attention to key information. When I incorporate horizontal lines, for instance, they can effectively separate different sections of a design, providing visual pauses that enhance readability. Vertical lines, on the other hand, can create a sense of strength and stability, while diagonal lines introduce movement and energy. I often experiment with varying line thicknesses and styles, such as dashed or dotted lines, to see how these choices affect the overall feel of the design. By strategically placing lines throughout my work, I create visual rhythms that keep the viewer engaged.

The integration of grids and frames adds another layer of sophistication to my designs. Grids offer a structured approach to layout, ensuring that elements align neatly and cohesively. In projects where multiple images or text blocks need to coexist, the grid system allows me to create a balanced composition that is easy for the viewer to navigate. I frequently use grids to establish a clear visual hierarchy, guiding the viewer's attention to the most important elements. For instance, in a presentation slide, I might employ a grid to arrange bullet points alongside images, ensuring that both elements complement each other without overwhelming the viewer.

Frames are particularly useful for cropping images into various shapes, allowing me to infuse creativity into my designs. I find that using frames not only enhances the visual appeal of an image but also allows for creative compositions that can set my work apart. For example, I might choose a circular frame for a profile picture, which lends a modern touch to a traditional layout. This versatility enables me to experiment with different visual styles, ultimately leading to a more dynamic design. Moreover, frames can serve to create consistent styling across multiple elements, reinforcing branding and thematic coherence.

While integrating these elements, I am continually mindful of the principles of balance and contrast. Each design element contributes to the overall composition, and ensuring that they work together harmoniously is crucial. I often evaluate whether the shapes, lines, and frames create a visual hierarchy that effectively communicates the message. If I notice any elements that feel out of place or overly dominant, I am quick to make adjustments, either by resizing, repositioning, or altering the opacity. This iterative process is essential; design is rarely perfect on the first attempt, and embracing the need for refinement leads to stronger outcomes.

Additionally, I recognize the power of color in relation to these design elements. The colors I choose for shapes and lines not only influence the mood of the design but also enhance readability and visual interest. When selecting colors, I often refer to the brand's established palette or consider the emotional impact of different hues. Canva's color picker tool allows me to experiment with various combinations, ensuring that the colors I choose work harmoniously with the overall design. For example, using a bright accent color for lines can draw attention to specific areas of the design, while softer colors in shapes can create a calming effect.

As I refine my designs, I also prioritize the inclusion of negative space—areas devoid of visual elements—that can enhance clarity and focus. Incorporating negative space allows the viewer's eye to rest and can improve the overall organization of the design. By strategically leaving certain areas blank, I can direct attention toward important content, ensuring that the viewer is not overwhelmed by visual noise. This balance of positive and negative space is vital in creating a visually appealing and functional design.

Furthermore, the iterative nature of design means that I often revisit my work after taking a break. This distance provides me with a fresh perspective, allowing me to identify elements that may need adjustment. During this review process, I critically assess whether the integration of images, shapes, lines, and frames effectively supports the design's goals. Gathering feedback from peers during this stage is equally valuable; their insights can highlight strengths and reveal areas for improvement that I may have overlooked.

Finally, as I prepare my designs for final presentation, I consider the various formats in which they will be shared. Whether for digital platforms, print, or social media, understanding the requirements for each format is essential. Canva simplifies this process by offering export options in various formats, ensuring that my designs maintain their quality and integrity across different media. By adjusting the resolution and file type according to the intended use, I can confidently deliver professional and polished designs that meet the audience's needs.

In conclusion, effectively utilizing design elements such as shapes, lines, grids, and frames within Canva is a multifaceted endeavor that enhances both the aesthetic quality and functionality of my projects. By strategically integrating these components, I can create compelling designs that resonate with viewers and communicate messages clearly. This exploration not only enriches my understanding of design principles but also empowers me to express creativity in innovative ways. As I continue to refine my skills in this area, I eagerly anticipate the opportunities for creative expression that await, ready to push the boundaries of design with each new project I undertake.

As I delve deeper into the capabilities of Canva's design elements, I begin to appreciate the subtleties of combining various components to create cohesive and visually compelling designs. One of the most powerful aspects of using shapes lies in their ability to act as visual anchors within a layout. Shapes can define areas of content, guide the viewer's eye, and establish a visual hierarchy that enhances the overall clarity of the message. I often utilize geometric shapes such as rectangles and circles as foundational elements that help organize my designs. For example, using a rectangle as a background for text not only provides a contrasting surface that improves legibility but also frames the text, making it stand out as a key focal point.

In my experience, the color of these shapes plays a crucial role in setting the mood and tone of the design. When selecting colors, I draw from a pre-defined palette that aligns with the brand identity or project theme. The strategic use of color can evoke emotions and influence perceptions, which is particularly important in designs aimed at specific audiences. For instance, warm colors like oranges and reds can convey energy and enthusiasm, making them suitable for promotional materials, while cooler tones such as blues and greens evoke calmness and professionalism, which may be more appropriate for corporate presentations.

Beyond simple backgrounds, shapes can also serve as containers for images, creating opportunities for innovative compositions. By combining images with various shapes, I am able to create unique layouts that capture attention. For example, placing an image within a circular shape can soften the visual impact and introduce a more playful element. This method of framing images not only enhances the visual appeal but also allows for greater creativity in presenting content. I often experiment with different shapes and their arrangements, seeking to find combinations that resonate with the theme of my design while maintaining a sense of balance and cohesion.

Lines, too, contribute significantly to the visual language of my designs. They can act as dividers, guides, or decorative elements that enhance the overall structure. For example, using a thin line to separate sections of text can improve readability by providing clear boundaries that help organize information. I find that varying the thickness and style of lines can also create a sense of hierarchy; thicker lines may denote importance or signify a strong division, while thinner lines can offer subtle guidance without overpowering other elements. Moreover, the orientation of lines—whether horizontal, vertical, or diagonal—can convey different emotions and dynamics. Diagonal lines, for example, often create a sense of movement and energy, while horizontal lines suggest stability and calmness.

Incorporating grids into my designs is another critical element that enhances organization and alignment. Grids help maintain consistency throughout the layout, ensuring that all elements are positioned harmoniously. I frequently set up grids to guide the placement of images, text, and other design components, allowing me to create a clean and orderly presentation. By aligning elements to the grid, I can ensure that my designs are visually balanced, which not only pleases the eye but also improves the user experience. This systematic approach is particularly beneficial in complex designs where multiple elements must coexist without overwhelming the viewer.

The flexibility of frames within Canva adds another layer of creativity to my designs. Frames allow me to crop images into unique shapes, enabling me to create interesting visual patterns that enhance the overall composition. For example, I might use a hexagonal frame to present a photo within a marketing campaign, which can inject a modern and trendy feel into the design. This ability to customize the shape of images encourages experimentation, and I often find that thinking outside the conventional rectangular frame leads to more engaging and innovative designs.

As I work with these design elements, I also recognize the importance of contrast. Ensuring that there is a clear distinction between different elements helps to draw attention to key components of the design. I pay close attention to the interplay of colors, shapes, and lines to achieve effective contrast. For example, placing a light-colored shape against a dark background enhances visibility and makes the text within it pop. This contrast not only improves legibility but also helps guide the viewer's focus toward the most important aspects of the design.

While integrating these design elements, I remain aware of the need for consistency. Maintaining a uniform style throughout the project is crucial in creating a cohesive visual narrative. I often establish a style guide that outlines specific colors, fonts, and design elements to be used throughout the project. This guide serves as a reference point, ensuring that all components work together harmoniously. By adhering to this consistency, I can reinforce brand identity and create a design that feels polished and professional.

In addition to consistency, I also emphasize the role of white space in my designs. White space, or negative space, is essential in providing breathing room for the viewer's eye and preventing the design from feeling cluttered. I often assess my layouts to ensure that there is enough space around key elements to allow them to stand out. This thoughtful use of white space not only improves readability but also enhances the overall elegance of the design. In fact, sometimes the absence of elements can be just as impactful as their presence, allowing the viewer to focus on what truly matters.

As I finalize my designs, I take the time to review and refine each element, ensuring that the integration of shapes, lines, grids, and frames enhances the overall message. This reflective practice allows me to step back and evaluate the design critically. I often ask myself whether each element contributes meaningfully to the composition or if any adjustments are necessary. Gathering feedback from colleagues or peers during this stage is invaluable; their perspectives can provide insights that I might have missed, allowing me to refine my work further.

In conclusion, utilizing Canva's design elements—shapes, lines, grids, and frames—offers a rich tapestry of possibilities that enhance the visual appeal and effectiveness of my designs. By thoughtfully integrating these components, I can create balanced and engaging compositions that effectively communicate messages to my audience. This exploration of design elements not only enriches my understanding of effective layout and organization but also empowers me to express my creativity in innovative ways. As I continue to develop my skills in this area, I look forward to the creative potential that these elements present, eager to explore new avenues of expression in my design journey.

CHAPTER 7: UNDERSTANDING COLOR THEORY

As I embark on my exploration of color theory, I find myself captivated by the profound impact that color can have on design. Color is not just a decorative element; it plays a critical role in shaping the emotional response of the viewer, influencing perceptions, and enhancing the overall effectiveness of a design. Understanding the principles of color theory is essential for creating compositions that are not only visually appealing but also capable of conveying the intended message clearly and effectively.

The journey begins with the fundamental concepts of color theory, including the color wheel, which serves as a foundational tool for understanding color relationships. The color wheel organizes colors into primary, secondary, and tertiary categories, allowing me to visualize how different hues interact. Primary colors—red, blue, and yellow—cannot be created by mixing other colors, while secondary colors—green, orange, and purple—are formed by mixing equal parts of two primary colors. Tertiary colors, which include hues like red-orange and blue-green, are created by mixing primary and secondary colors. This understanding of color relationships enables me to make informed decisions about which colors to use and how to combine them effectively in my designs.

One of the key principles of color theory that I frequently

apply is the concept of complementary colors. These are pairs of colors that are located opposite each other on the color wheel, such as blue and orange or red and green. When used together, complementary colors create a striking contrast that can enhance visual interest and draw attention to specific elements within a design. I often utilize this technique when I want to emphasize a particular piece of information or create a sense of dynamism. For example, in a marketing flyer, placing a bold headline in a complementary color to the background can create an eye-catching effect that immediately captures the viewer's attention.

In addition to complementary colors, I explore analogous colors, which are located next to each other on the color wheel. These colors typically share a common hue and create a more harmonious and cohesive look when used together. For instance, using shades of blue, green, and teal can evoke a calming and serene atmosphere, making this combination ideal for wellness-related designs. I often experiment with analogous color schemes when I aim to create a soothing or inviting ambiance, allowing the colors to flow seamlessly from one element to another without jarring contrasts.

Another vital concept within color theory is the use of warm and cool colors. Warm colors, such as reds, oranges, and yellows, tend to evoke feelings of warmth, energy, and excitement. These colors can stimulate emotions and create a sense of urgency, making them effective in promotional materials where I want to encourage action. Conversely, cool colors like blues, greens, and purples tend to impart feelings of calmness, tranquility, and professionalism. I often consider the emotional response I want to elicit from my audience when choosing between warm and cool color palettes. For example, a healthcare campaign may benefit from cool colors to convey trust and safety, while a sports event flyer may utilize warm colors to convey enthusiasm and energy.

As I dive deeper into the practical application of color theory in Canva, I become increasingly adept at utilizing the platform's color tools to create cohesive and visually engaging designs. Canva provides a range of options for selecting and customizing colors, including pre-made palettes, color pickers, and gradient generators. These tools enable me to experiment with different combinations, making it easy to explore various color schemes that align with my design goals.

Creating color schemes is a fundamental aspect of my design process. I often start by selecting a primary color that reflects the essence of the project. From there, I explore options for secondary and accent colors that complement the primary hue. Canva's color palette generator is particularly useful in this regard, as it allows me to input a single color and generates harmonious combinations based on color theory principles. This feature streamlines the process, ensuring that the colors I choose work well together and contribute to a unified visual narrative.

Understanding the psychology of color also informs my choices. Different colors elicit distinct emotional responses, and I strive to select colors that resonate with the message I wish to convey. For example, blue is often associated with trust and reliability, making it an excellent choice for corporate branding. In contrast, vibrant red can evoke passion and excitement, ideal for promoting an event or sale. By aligning my color choices with the emotional undertones of the project, I can create a more impactful design that connects with the audience on a deeper level.

As I work through the color selection process, I remain vigilant about maintaining balance and harmony within my designs. Too many colors can lead to visual chaos, distracting from the main message. I often adhere to the 60-30-10 rule, where I allocate approximately 60% of the design to a dominant color,

30% to a secondary color, and 10% to an accent color. This guideline helps create a sense of proportion and ensures that one color does not overpower the others, allowing for a more cohesive and visually appealing composition.

When applying color to text, I take care to ensure that there is sufficient contrast between the text and the background. This consideration is crucial for readability; for instance, light text on a light background can easily become illegible. Canva's contrast checker tool is invaluable in this regard, helping me evaluate whether the chosen color combinations provide adequate visibility. By ensuring that my text is easily readable, I enhance the overall effectiveness of the design and ensure that the intended message is communicated clearly.

In addition to standard colors, I also experiment with gradients, which can add depth and visual interest to my designs. Gradients transition smoothly between two or more colors, creating a dynamic effect that can be eye-catching and modern. I often use gradients as backgrounds or to highlight specific areas within a design. By manipulating the angle and intensity of the gradient, I can create a sense of movement or dimension that enhances the overall aesthetic.

As I finalize my designs, I engage in a thorough review of my color choices to ensure that they align with the project's goals and audience expectations. Gathering feedback from peers during this stage is invaluable, as their perspectives can reveal insights that I may have overlooked. This collaborative approach fosters a richer design process, encouraging creative discussions that often lead to innovative solutions.

In conclusion, understanding and applying color theory is a vital component of effective design. By exploring the relationships between colors, employing strategic color schemes, and utilizing Canva's color tools, I can create visually compelling designs that resonate with audiences.

This exploration of color not only enriches my understanding of design principles but also empowers me to express my creativity in impactful ways. As I continue to refine my skills in this area, I am excited to discover the endless possibilities that color offers, ready to transform my designs through the art of color.

As I deepen my understanding of color theory, I am increasingly aware of how the subtleties of color can transform a design, influencing not only its aesthetic appeal but also its effectiveness in communicating a message. The psychology of color is a critical component in this exploration, as each hue can evoke specific emotions and associations. For instance, warm colors like red, orange, and yellow can create feelings of excitement, energy, and warmth, making them ideal for promotional materials or events where I want to inspire action. In contrast, cool colors like blue and green often evoke calmness and trust, making them suitable for designs that require a sense of professionalism and reliability, such as corporate branding or health-related content.

In applying these principles, I find that the context of the design plays a significant role in determining which colors to use. When designing a product advertisement, for example, I might opt for vibrant, high-energy colors to capture attention and generate enthusiasm. Conversely, when creating a visual for a nonprofit organization, I may choose a more subdued palette that reflects the seriousness of the cause while still conveying hope and compassion. This thoughtful approach to color selection helps me tailor my designs to resonate with the intended audience and context.

Creating effective color schemes is another vital aspect of applying color theory in my work. I often begin this process by choosing a dominant color that embodies the essence of the design. From there, I explore secondary and accent colors that complement the primary hue. Canva's color palette generator is an invaluable tool during this stage, allowing me to input a color and receive suggestions for harmonious combinations. This feature not only streamlines my workflow but also inspires me to experiment with combinations that I might not have considered otherwise.

In addition to exploring traditional complementary and analogous color schemes, I delve into triadic color schemes, which involve selecting three colors that are evenly spaced around the color wheel. This method can create a vibrant and dynamic palette, adding a sense of playfulness to the design. When employing a triadic scheme, I pay close attention to the balance between the colors, ensuring that one color does not dominate the others. This balance is essential in maintaining visual harmony and allowing each color to contribute meaningfully to the overall composition.

As I integrate color into my designs, I find that understanding the principles of contrast is crucial for enhancing readability and visual impact. Contrast refers to the difference between colors, tones, or shapes and plays a significant role in guiding the viewer's eye through the design. High contrast between text and background is essential for ensuring legibility; for instance, dark text on a light background or light text on a dark background creates clear visibility. I often use Canva's contrast checker to evaluate whether my color combinations provide sufficient contrast, ensuring that all text remains readable regardless of the device or medium.

When working with color in typography, I am particularly mindful of the emotional implications of different colors. The choice of color for headings and body text can influence the perceived tone of the message. For example, using a vibrant color for a call-to-action button can create urgency, while a softer color may suggest calmness and reassurance. I strive to select colors that not only align with the overall palette but also reinforce the message being conveyed. This thoughtful consideration of color within typography enhances the effectiveness of the design as a whole.

I also find that the use of gradients can introduce depth and dimension to my designs. Gradients allow me to transition smoothly between colors, creating visually captivating backgrounds or effects that can draw attention. When applying gradients, I consider the direction and intensity of the color transition. A subtle gradient from a soft blue to a pale green can evoke tranquility, while a bold transition from red to orange may convey excitement and energy. This ability to manipulate gradients enhances my creative expression, allowing me to craft more dynamic compositions that resonate with viewers.

As I finalize my designs, I reflect on the emotional journey I want to take my audience on. The arrangement and interaction of colors should lead viewers through the content in a way that feels intuitive and engaging. I often evaluate whether the color choices align with the narrative I aim to tell. For instance, in a design intended to promote an environmental initiative, I might incorporate earth tones and greens to evoke a sense of harmony with nature. This thoughtful alignment of color choices with thematic elements ensures that my designs communicate effectively on both visual and emotional levels.

Gathering feedback from peers becomes an essential part of this process as I seek to refine my color choices and overall design. Their insights can shed light on aspects I might not have considered, such as cultural perceptions of color or the emotional resonance of my palette. Engaging in discussions about color allows me to expand my understanding and refine my designs further, ultimately leading to a more polished final product. This collaborative approach fosters a richer design process, encouraging me to explore new avenues and perspectives.

I also recognize the importance of consistency in my color application across different projects. Establishing a cohesive color palette for a brand not only enhances recognition but also reinforces the brand's identity. I often create a style guide that outlines specific colors to be used consistently across various materials. This guide serves as a reference point, helping to ensure that all visual elements work together harmoniously. By adhering to these guidelines, I create designs that are not only visually appealing but also aligned with the brand's overall messaging and identity.

As I wrap up my exploration of color theory in Canva, I appreciate how the understanding of color can elevate my designs to new heights. Each color choice I make carries weight and significance, influencing the way viewers perceive and engage with my work. By mastering the principles of color theory, I can craft designs that not only capture attention but also evoke emotions and communicate messages effectively. This journey through color has deepened my appreciation for its role in design, and I eagerly anticipate the creative possibilities that lie ahead as I continue to refine my skills and express my vision through the art of color.

As I further immerse myself in the intricacies of color theory, I am drawn to the profound implications of cultural perceptions of color, which can vary significantly across different societies. This awareness is crucial, especially when designing for diverse audiences. Colors can carry different meanings; for example, while white is often associated with purity and innocence in many Western cultures, it can symbolize mourning and loss in some Eastern cultures. This knowledge informs my color choices, allowing me to create designs that resonate positively with the intended audience and avoid unintentional misinterpretations. I often conduct research or consult cultural guides when developing designs aimed at specific demographic groups, ensuring that my color palette aligns with their cultural context and emotional associations.

In my design practice, I frequently utilize color psychology not only to influence viewer emotions but also to enhance branding. Color choices play an integral role in establishing a brand's identity, as they can evoke feelings that align with the brand's values. For example, a financial institution might use blue to convey trust and security, while a health-focused brand may lean toward greens to symbolize vitality and well-being. When working on branding projects, I carefully curate a color palette that encapsulates the essence of the brand, ensuring that it is consistently applied across various platforms and materials. This consistency not only strengthens recognition but also fosters a deeper connection between the audience and the brand.

Utilizing Canva's tools to create color palettes is an essential part of this process. The platform's palette generator allows me to create a harmonious set of colors that can be easily applied to different design elements. When developing a palette, I often select a primary color that embodies the brand or design's core message, followed by secondary and accent colors that complement it. I experiment with shades and tints of these colors, allowing me to maintain flexibility while ensuring coherence across various applications. This careful curation of color sets serves as a foundation for my designs, enabling me to approach each project with a clear visual strategy.

Another useful aspect of Canva's color tools is the ability to extract color schemes from images. This feature allows me to maintain visual consistency by selecting colors directly from photographs or graphics I intend to use in my designs. By sampling colors from a compelling image, I can create a cohesive palette that reflects the mood and atmosphere of that image. This technique is particularly effective in creating designs where imagery plays a central role, such as event flyers or social media graphics. The extracted colors help create a unified look that ties the design together, ensuring that every element feels interconnected.

As I apply these principles, I pay close attention to the balance between color vibrancy and visual harmony. Overly bright or saturated colors can be overwhelming if not used judiciously, while too many muted tones may result in a lack of energy and engagement. I strive to create a palette that offers visual contrast without sacrificing cohesiveness. A well-balanced design often incorporates a mix of both vibrant and subdued colors, allowing for areas of emphasis while maintaining an overall sense of harmony. This balance is essential in guiding the viewer's eye through the design, emphasizing key information without overwhelming them.

Gradients, which I previously touched upon, also serve as a valuable tool in achieving this balance. By transitioning between colors, I can create depth and dimension that adds visual interest to my designs. Gradients can be particularly effective in backgrounds, offering a dynamic yet soft visual that allows text and images to stand out. I often experiment with gradient placement and direction, adjusting them to complement the overall layout. For instance, a diagonal gradient might convey movement and action, while a vertical gradient can create a more serene and stable feel. The flexibility of gradients allows me to express nuanced emotions through color transitions, enriching the storytelling aspect of my designs.

I am also acutely aware of the importance of testing my color choices across various mediums and devices. What looks good on a computer screen may not translate well to print, and vice versa. I often print out samples of my designs to evaluate how colors appear in physical form. This evaluation helps me identify any adjustments needed to ensure that the design remains effective regardless of the medium. In an increasingly digital world, the ability to create designs that translate well across different formats is paramount. This adaptability not only enhances the professionalism of my work but also ensures that my designs reach the widest audience possible.

Throughout this process, I maintain a commitment to continuous learning and experimentation. Color theory is a vast field, and staying current with trends and new insights allows me to evolve as a designer. I often engage with design communities, attend workshops, or read literature on color psychology to expand my understanding of how color can be leveraged effectively. This ongoing education feeds my creativity and inspires me to push the boundaries of my designs.

As I reflect on my journey through color theory, I recognize the importance of intuition combined with informed decision-making. While guidelines and principles provide a solid foundation, trusting my instincts often leads to the most rewarding creative outcomes. When I allow myself the freedom to experiment and explore unexpected combinations, I frequently discover unique palettes that resonate on a personal level and speak to my audience in profound ways.

Ultimately, the integration of color theory into my design practice enriches not only my work but also my understanding of visual communication. The ability to convey emotion, enhance readability, and create visual appeal through color is a powerful skill that I continually strive to refine. With each project, I embrace the challenge of crafting color schemes that are not only beautiful but also meaningful, using color as a tool to tell stories and engage viewers on multiple levels. As I look ahead, I am eager to continue this exploration, ready to harness the transformative power of color in my designs.

CHAPTER 8: CREATING SOCIAL MEDIA GRAPHICS

In the realm of social media, the ability to create visually striking graphics is essential for capturing attention and fostering engagement. As I embark on the journey of designing social media graphics, I am acutely aware of the unique considerations that come into play. Each platform has its own specifications and audience expectations, which necessitates a tailored approach to design. Understanding these nuances not only enhances the effectiveness of my graphics but also ensures they resonate with the target audience.

The first step in creating compelling social media graphics involves understanding the specific dimensions and format requirements for each platform. For instance, Instagram prioritizes square images for posts, while stories benefit from vertical formats that maximize screen real estate. Facebook often uses horizontal images, particularly for cover photos. I find it essential to consult Canva's preset dimensions for various social media graphics, as these templates streamline the process and help me avoid the pitfalls of incorrectly sized images. By adhering to these specifications, I ensure that my graphics display properly and maintain their intended impact, regardless of where they are viewed.

Once I have established the correct dimensions, I turn

my focus to the design itself. Eye-catching graphics often incorporate bold visuals, striking colors, and clear messaging that captures attention instantly. I pay careful attention to the visual hierarchy within my designs, ensuring that key elements stand out. Using large, legible fonts for headlines is crucial; I want the primary message to be immediately clear to viewers who may be scrolling quickly through their feeds. In social media, the first few seconds of a viewer's attention are critical, so I aim to communicate the essence of the content through compelling imagery and succinct text.

Color choice plays a significant role in creating standout graphics. The colors I select not only contribute to the overall aesthetic but also evoke specific emotions and reactions. I often leverage contrasting colors to enhance visibility and draw attention to important elements. For instance, if I am promoting an event, using a vibrant color for the call-to-action can create urgency and encourage immediate engagement. Additionally, I am mindful of the emotional associations different colors carry, ensuring that my palette aligns with the tone of the message. Warm colors may convey excitement, while cooler tones can evoke calmness and professionalism. This strategic selection of colors enhances the overall effectiveness of my designs.

Incorporating high-quality images is another key component in creating visually appealing social media graphics. I often source images from Canva's extensive library or upload my own to ensure they are relevant and resonate with the intended audience. The quality of the images I choose is paramount; low-resolution or poorly composed images can detract from the professionalism of the design. I take the time to edit and enhance these images using Canva's built-in photo editing tools, making adjustments to brightness, contrast, and saturation to ensure they complement the overall design aesthetic. When images are clear, vibrant, and well-integrated, they significantly enhance the overall impact of the graphic.

In addition to images, I recognize the importance of incorporating design elements that foster engagement. This could include the use of icons, shapes, or borders that help to delineate different sections of content. For example, using icons to represent different features or benefits in a promotional graphic can create visual interest and make the information more digestible. I often utilize lines and shapes to create frames around text or images, enhancing organization and guiding the viewer's eye through the design. These elements not only contribute to the visual appeal but also facilitate a clearer understanding of the content being presented.

As I delve into the specifics of creating social media posts, I also explore the nuances of designing for stories, which offer a unique opportunity for dynamic engagement. Story graphics need to be visually captivating and deliver information quickly, as they typically only last a few seconds on-screen. I focus on bold visuals and minimal text, ensuring that key messages are clear and easily readable in a fleeting format. The use of animations or subtle motion can also enhance the appeal of stories, drawing viewers in and encouraging interaction. Canva's templates for stories provide a solid foundation, allowing me to customize and adapt existing designs to fit my brand and message.

When creating banners or cover images for social media profiles, I find that consistency is key. These graphics often serve as the first impression for potential followers or customers, so maintaining a cohesive brand identity is essential. I ensure that the colors, fonts, and overall aesthetic align with my established brand guidelines. By creating a strong and recognizable visual presence across all platforms, I can enhance brand recognition and build trust with my audience. This consistency extends beyond mere aesthetics; it reflects the values and mission of the brand, creating a deeper connection with viewers.

Throughout the design process, I engage in a continuous cycle of review and refinement. After creating an initial draft, I take a step back to evaluate the overall effectiveness of the graphic. I consider whether the design effectively communicates the intended message and whether the visual elements work together harmoniously. Seeking feedback from colleagues or peers is invaluable during this stage; their fresh perspectives can highlight strengths and reveal areas for improvement that I might have overlooked. This iterative approach not only strengthens my designs but also fosters collaboration and shared creativity.

In conclusion, the art of creating social media graphics in Canva is a nuanced process that requires an understanding of platform-specific dimensions, emotional color choices, engaging imagery, and consistent branding. By leveraging the design tools available within Canva and applying the principles of color theory, I can craft graphics that not only capture attention but also foster engagement and convey clear messages. This exploration into social media design enhances my overall skill set as a designer, empowering me to create visually compelling and impactful content that resonates with audiences across various platforms. As I continue to hone my skills in this area, I remain excited about the possibilities that social media graphics present, ready to push the boundaries of creativity and engagement in my design endeavors.

As I continue to explore the intricacies of creating social media graphics, I find that understanding the audience's preferences and behaviors is just as crucial as mastering design techniques. Each social media platform hosts a unique user demographic and content consumption style, which influences how I approach my designs. For instance, platforms like Instagram are highly visual and prioritize striking

INTRODUCTION TO CANVA: CREATE STUNNING DESIGNS

images and aesthetics, whereas Twitter emphasizes concise messaging with impactful visuals. This understanding allows me to tailor my designs to meet the expectations of users on each platform, ensuring that my graphics are not only eye-catching but also relevant to the audience.

When designing for Instagram, I prioritize creating vibrant, high-quality visuals that capture attention instantly. The platform thrives on imagery that stands out amidst a sea of posts. I often choose bold colors and dynamic compositions that leverage the full square format of the feed. Using Canva's extensive library of templates, I can quickly find design layouts that resonate with the current aesthetic trends, whether they involve minimalistic styles or more eclectic, collage-like presentations. These templates provide a solid foundation that I can customize to fit the specific theme of my content, whether it's for personal branding, a product launch, or a lifestyle post.

In crafting graphics for Instagram Stories, I recognize the need for immediacy and engagement. Stories are ephemeral and often viewed quickly, so I ensure that my designs are visually striking and convey the message within seconds. I typically incorporate large, bold text that is easy to read, paired with impactful visuals that resonate with the narrative. Utilizing Canva's animation features can also enhance the engagement factor, as subtle motion can capture attention more effectively than static images. When designing stories, I often include interactive elements such as polls, questions, or links, prompting users to engage directly with the content. This interactive approach not only enriches the viewer experience but also encourages them to take action, whether it's visiting a website or participating in a survey.

As I move to designing for Facebook, I adapt my approach to account for the platform's unique characteristics. Facebook allows for a mix of text and imagery, so I focus on creating designs that balance visual elements with concise messaging. When crafting cover photos or promotional posts, I ensure that the text is legible even in smaller formats, as users may view these graphics on mobile devices. I often leverage Canva's grid system to organize elements effectively, ensuring that the design feels cohesive while still directing attention to key messages. Additionally, I pay attention to Facebook's guidelines regarding text overlay on images, as excessive text can lead to reduced reach in advertising. This understanding of platform-specific nuances enables me to optimize my designs for maximum visibility and engagement.

For Twitter, where brevity is key, I focus on creating graphics that convey messages quickly and clearly. I often incorporate striking visuals that accompany succinct text, allowing users to grasp the message in an instant. The fast-paced nature of Twitter means that my graphics must stand out while being easily digestible. I find that using bold typography paired with contrasting colors can create a striking effect, drawing attention as users scroll through their feeds. Additionally, I utilize Canva's features to create infographics or data visualizations that can succinctly convey complex information in a visually appealing manner. By combining effective design with concise messaging, I can ensure that my graphics resonate with the fast-moving Twitter audience.

As I explore the creation of banners for social media profiles, consistency becomes a focal point in my design approach. Profile banners serve as a branding opportunity, and I take care to ensure that the colors, fonts, and overall aesthetic align with my established brand identity. Canva's template library provides a variety of options that I can customize to reflect my brand's visual language. By maintaining a cohesive style across all platforms, I strengthen brand recognition and create a unified presence that enhances credibility and trust.

Another critical aspect of creating engaging social media

graphics involves incorporating user-generated content. This approach not only fosters a sense of community but also encourages engagement. I often design templates for followers to use, allowing them to share their experiences with my brand. For example, if I run a fitness program, I might create a visually appealing template for users to post their progress photos. By providing these templates, I not only promote user interaction but also create a sense of belonging within the community. This strategy encourages users to become advocates for the brand, effectively expanding its reach through organic engagement.

In addition to visual elements, I consider the strategic use of hashtags and captions. The graphic itself is just one part of the equation; the accompanying text can enhance the message and encourage interaction. I ensure that captions are concise yet engaging, often posing questions or calls to action that invite users to engage with the content. This combination of compelling visuals and thoughtful text can create a more robust interaction and encourage followers to share the content, amplifying its reach.

As I finalize my social media graphics, I embrace the iterative process of design. I routinely review my work to assess whether it aligns with my initial goals and resonates with the intended audience. This reflection allows me to identify strengths and areas for improvement, leading to stronger outcomes in future designs. Additionally, I actively seek feedback from colleagues or peers, whose insights can provide fresh perspectives on my graphics. This collaborative approach enriches the design process, fostering a creative environment where innovative ideas can flourish.

In the ever-evolving landscape of social media, staying current with trends and best practices is crucial. I regularly engage with design communities, participate in webinars, and follow thought leaders in the field to remain informed about emerging trends in social media design. This commitment to continuous learning not only enhances my skills but also ensures that my designs remain relevant and impactful in a competitive digital environment.

Ultimately, the creation of effective social media graphics in Canva involves a multifaceted approach that considers platform specifications, audience engagement, and cohesive branding. By mastering these elements, I can produce visually compelling designs that capture attention, foster engagement, and effectively communicate messages. As I continue to refine my skills in this area, I eagerly anticipate the creative possibilities that await, ready to explore new dimensions of expression and engagement through the art of social media design.

As I delve further into the nuances of creating social media graphics, I recognize that the visual components must be complemented by strategic thinking about audience engagement and content scheduling. Timing plays a pivotal role in how graphics are received, particularly on fast-moving platforms where trends shift rapidly. Understanding the optimal times to post on various platforms allows me to maximize visibility and engagement. I often analyze analytics data from previous posts to identify when my audience is most active, tailoring my content release schedule accordingly to ensure that my designs reach their intended audience when they are most likely to be online.

Additionally, I embrace the importance of storytelling through my social media graphics. Each post is an opportunity to convey a narrative that resonates with followers. I aim to create a visual journey that captivates viewers from the moment they see the graphic. This might involve using a series of images or graphics that tell a cohesive story over several posts or a carousel format that encourages users to swipe through multiple visuals. By creating a narrative arc within my designs, I encourage deeper engagement, prompting viewers to reflect on the content and share their thoughts, thereby fostering community interaction.

Utilizing Canva's diverse template options allows me to streamline the storytelling process. Many templates are designed specifically for sequential posts or campaigns, providing a cohesive look and feel that can be adapted across multiple pieces. I often customize these templates to fit my specific messaging while maintaining the visual consistency necessary for brand recognition. For instance, if I am promoting a series of educational posts, I might choose a template with a consistent header style and color scheme, ensuring that each post feels part of a larger educational initiative.

In addition to visual consistency, I consider the emotional resonance of the graphics I create. Each element within the design contributes to the overall mood, whether it be through color choice, imagery, or typography. I strive to evoke the desired emotions in my audience—whether it's excitement for a new product, nostalgia for a campaign that aligns with personal experiences, or inspiration from motivational quotes. This emotional connection can significantly enhance engagement, as viewers are more likely to interact with content that resonates with them on a personal level.

I also explore the power of user-generated content in my social media strategies. Encouraging followers to share their own images or experiences related to my brand not only fosters community but also creates a wealth of authentic content that can be re-shared. This strategy enriches my brand narrative, as real users provide testimonials and endorsements through their own stories. When I incorporate user-generated content into my graphics, I often ensure to highlight their contributions creatively, whether by placing their photos within a stylish frame or designing a dedicated post that celebrates their involvement. This approach not only enhances brand loyalty but also amplifies reach, as followers are likely to share graphics that feature their own contributions, expanding visibility to their networks.

The incorporation of calls to action is another critical component of my social media graphics. These prompts are essential for guiding viewer behavior and encouraging interactions, whether it's to visit a website, participate in a poll, or share a post. I often design buttons or highlighted text areas that stand out within the graphic, using contrasting colors to draw attention. Crafting clear, compelling calls to action can significantly impact engagement rates, prompting viewers to take the desired steps. I find that phrasing is also crucial; using action-oriented language such as "Join us," "Discover more," or "Share your story" can create a sense of urgency and invitation that resonates with viewers.

In designing for social media, I remain ever-mindful of the evolving nature of digital communication. Trends in design, user preferences, and platform algorithms shift frequently, requiring me to stay agile and responsive. I actively engage with industry news, follow design influencers, and participate in webinars to remain current on best practices. This ongoing education is vital for enhancing my skills and keeping my designs relevant. When I notice emerging trends, such as the rise of minimalistic designs or specific color palettes, I experiment with incorporating these elements into my graphics, ensuring that my work reflects contemporary tastes and preferences.

As I finalize my graphics for various social media platforms, I meticulously review each design to ensure that all elements work harmoniously together. I assess whether the imagery, typography, and color choices effectively convey the intended message. I often step back and view the design as a whole, considering whether it evokes the right emotions and prompts the desired interactions. This reflective practice enables me to identify any areas that might need refinement or adjustment before the graphics are published.

Finally, I embrace the iterative nature of design, acknowledging that feedback is invaluable in enhancing my work. After launching a new campaign or series of posts, I closely monitor audience reactions and engagement metrics. By analyzing which graphics resonate most with viewers, I can gather insights that inform future designs. This responsiveness allows me to adapt and evolve my strategies over time, ensuring that my graphics continue to engage and captivate my audience.

In conclusion, creating effective social media graphics is a multifaceted endeavor that requires a thorough understanding of platform specifications, audience engagement, storytelling, and emotional resonance. By leveraging Canva's design tools and applying the principles of color theory, I can craft compelling visuals that not only capture attention but also foster interaction and convey meaningful messages. As I continue to refine my skills in this area, I am excited to explore new avenues of creativity and engagement, ready to push the boundaries of social media design and connect with audiences in innovative ways.

CHAPTER 9: DESIGNING PRINT MATERIALS

In the realm of design, transitioning from digital to print requires a nuanced understanding of various technical considerations that ensure the final product is not only visually appealing but also professionally executed. As I delve into the process of designing print materials, I find that factors such as resolution, bleed, and margins are critical elements that must be meticulously addressed to achieve optimal results.

To begin with, resolution is a fundamental aspect of print design that directly influences the quality of the finished product. Unlike digital screens, which can display images clearly at lower resolutions, print materials require higher resolutions to ensure that every detail is crisp and clear. The standard resolution for print designs is 300 dots per inch (DPI). This specification guarantees that images and text appear sharp and well-defined when printed. As I create my designs in Canva, I make it a point to check the resolution of images I use, opting for high-quality graphics that meet or exceed this standard. Utilizing images that are too low in resolution can lead to pixelation and blurriness, ultimately compromising the professionalism of the print material.

Another vital consideration in print design is bleed, which refers to the area of the design that extends beyond the trim edge. Including bleed in my designs is crucial for preventing any unintentional white borders from appearing after trimming, which can occur if the cutting process is slightly misaligned. Typically, a bleed of 0.125 inches on each side is recommended. In Canva, I can easily set this up by extending background colors or images to the bleed area, ensuring that the design flows seamlessly to the edges. This attention to detail not only enhances the visual impact of the final product but also demonstrates a commitment to quality.

Margins are similarly important in print design, serving as a safety zone that protects essential elements of the design from being cut off during the trimming process. When designing materials such as business cards, flyers, or brochures, I establish clear margins to ensure that text and images remain well within the boundaries. A typical margin might be around 0.25 to 0.5 inches, depending on the overall size of the print material. This practice is crucial for maintaining legibility and aesthetic balance, preventing critical information from being inadvertently trimmed away. When I set up my design in Canva, I frequently utilize the grid and ruler features to create visual guides that help me adhere to these margins consistently.

When designing print materials, I also consider the choice of paper and printing methods, as these factors can significantly influence the final appearance of the design. Different types of paper, such as matte, glossy, or textured finishes, can affect color perception and overall aesthetic. For example, glossy paper often enhances the vibrancy of colors, making it an ideal choice for promotional materials that require bold visuals. On the other hand, matte finishes may impart a more sophisticated, subdued look that works well for business cards or professional brochures. When I select the appropriate paper type, I also factor in the printing method, whether digital or offset, as this can further influence color fidelity and overall quality. Canva allows me to explore various options and considerations, ensuring that I make informed decisions that align with my design goals.

Color management is another essential aspect of print design that requires careful consideration. Colors can appear differently when printed compared to how they look on a digital screen due to variations in color profiles and ink application. To mitigate discrepancies, I pay close attention to the color mode I am using; CMYK (cyan, magenta, yellow, black) is the preferred color mode for print designs, as it reflects the way colors are mixed in the printing process. When working in Canva, I ensure that my designs are set to the appropriate color mode to achieve the most accurate representation of colors in the final printed product. This diligence in color management is key to producing professional and visually cohesive materials.

As I explore specific print materials, I recognize that each type requires its own unique approach. For instance, designing business cards demands a focus on concise messaging and impactful visuals that reflect the brand's identity. The limited space necessitates a careful selection of typography and imagery, ensuring that essential information—such as name, title, and contact details—is clearly presented. I often choose fonts that are legible at smaller sizes, opting for a clean and professional look. Canva's templates for business cards provide an excellent starting point, allowing me to customize layouts and styles that align with my brand while maintaining the necessary functionality.

Similarly, when designing flyers, I aim to create eye-catching visuals that communicate key information effectively. Flyers often serve promotional purposes, so I incorporate vibrant images and bold headlines that capture attention and encourage engagement. I prioritize creating a clear visual hierarchy, using varying font sizes and styles to guide the viewer through the content. Canva's design tools enable me to experiment with different layouts, ensuring that the final design is not only visually appealing but also informative and actionable.

When it comes to brochures, the design becomes even more intricate due to the need for organized content across multiple panels. I focus on creating a logical flow that guides the reader through the information presented. Using Canva's grid and layout tools, I can create sections that categorize content, ensuring that each panel serves a specific purpose while contributing to the overall narrative. The use of images, icons, and color coding helps to distinguish different sections, enhancing readability and engagement.

As I finalize my print materials, I engage in a thorough review process to ensure that every aspect meets the highest standards of quality. I check for typos, verify that all images are appropriately sized and positioned, and confirm that colors appear as intended. This meticulous attention to detail reflects my commitment to professionalism and quality, ensuring that the final products not only look great but also convey the right message effectively.

In conclusion, designing print materials in Canva requires a comprehensive understanding of technical specifications, color management, and audience engagement. By considering factors such as resolution, bleed, margins, and color modes, I can create high-quality graphics that translate seamlessly from screen to print. This exploration of print design enhances my skills as a designer, empowering me to produce visually stunning and effective materials that resonate with my audience. As I continue to refine my craft, I remain excited about the opportunities that print design presents, ready to translate my creative visions into tangible realities.

As I delve deeper into the intricacies of designing print materials, I find myself grappling with the relationship between content and design elements. The interplay of text, images, and other graphic elements is crucial for achieving a harmonious and effective layout. In print design, the arrangement of these components must be deliberate and thoughtful to ensure that the viewer can easily navigate the information being presented. For example, in a flyer, I strive to create a balance between text and visuals, using images to draw attention while ensuring that the written content remains clear and concise. This careful consideration allows me to craft materials that are not only visually appealing but also informative and engaging.

When designing business cards, I recognize the importance of making a strong first impression. The limited space on a business card necessitates that I prioritize the most essential information, such as my name, title, and contact details. I often select a font that is legible at small sizes, avoiding overly decorative styles that can detract from readability. The design must convey professionalism, so I typically lean toward clean lines and a simple layout that reflects the brand's identity. I also consider the use of negative space; a well-balanced design with adequate breathing room can enhance clarity and prevent the card from feeling cluttered.

In Canva, I frequently utilize templates specifically designed for business cards, as these provide a solid starting point while allowing for customization. By selecting a template that aligns with my brand's aesthetic, I can modify colors, fonts, and images to create a cohesive look that represents my professional identity. The ability to visualize the design in the context of the card's dimensions helps me make informed decisions about the placement of each element. I pay particular attention to the orientation—whether the card is horizontal or vertical—as this can affect how information is prioritized and perceived.

As I transition to designing flyers, I recognize the need for a slightly different approach. Flyers typically contain more information than business cards, allowing for greater creative expression while still necessitating clarity. I focus on creating a visual hierarchy that guides the viewer's eye through the content, emphasizing key messages while still providing supporting information. Using contrasting font sizes and weights, I establish clear distinctions between headlines, subheadings, and body text. For instance, I might use a large, bold font for the main headline to capture attention, while employing a smaller, lighter font for additional details.

In Canva, I take advantage of the layering capabilities to create depth within my flyer designs. By placing images in the background and overlaying text, I can create a dynamic composition that draws the viewer in. I often experiment with transparency settings to blend images with text seamlessly, allowing the visual elements to complement rather than compete with one another. This approach not only enhances aesthetic appeal but also reinforces the overall message. For example, if I am promoting a community event, using a vibrant background image of the location can evoke excitement while the overlay text provides essential details.

When it comes to brochures, the complexity increases, requiring a more intricate design process. Brochures often consist of multiple panels that must work together to convey a cohesive message. I begin by mapping out the content, ensuring that each panel serves a distinct purpose while contributing to the overall narrative. Utilizing Canva's grid system, I can create structured layouts that facilitate organization, making it easier to categorize information and guide the viewer through the content.

As I design the individual panels, I pay close attention to the flow of information. Each panel should naturally lead to the next, maintaining a logical progression that keeps the viewer engaged. I often incorporate visual elements such as icons or images that reinforce the content, providing visual cues that enhance understanding. This approach is particularly effective in brochures that aim to inform or educate, as the combination of visuals and text can make complex information more digestible.

While designing these print materials, I am also mindful of the importance of consistency in branding. I strive to ensure that the colors, fonts, and overall style align with the brand's identity. Consistency not only strengthens recognition but also conveys professionalism and reliability. In Canva, I often create a brand kit that includes specific color codes, font styles, and logos. This kit serves as a reference point throughout the design process, ensuring that my work remains cohesive and true to the brand's visual identity.

The choice of imagery in print materials is another critical consideration. High-quality images that resonate with the audience can significantly enhance the impact of the design. I source images from Canva's extensive library or upload my own, ensuring that they are relevant and appropriately sized for print. When integrating images, I consider how they complement the text and overall composition. I often opt for images that evoke the desired emotions and align with the message being communicated. For instance, using images of happy customers can instill trust and encourage potential clients to engage with the brand.

Throughout the design process, I emphasize the importance of proofing and revision. Once I have completed a draft, I conduct a thorough review to ensure that all elements align with my initial objectives. I look for any typographical errors, check that images are properly aligned, and confirm that colors are consistent. Additionally, I seek feedback from colleagues or peers to gather insights on the design's effectiveness. This collaborative approach not only strengthens the final product but also fosters a sense of community and shared creativity.

As I prepare to print my designs, I take the time to consider the printing method and paper choice. Different paper types can affect the final appearance of the design, and I select options that best reflect the intended use. For example, glossy paper may enhance vibrant colors for promotional materials, while matte finishes can provide an elegant touch for business cards. Understanding these nuances allows me to make informed decisions that enhance the quality of the printed product.

In conclusion, the process of designing print materials involves a thoughtful blend of technical knowledge and creative expression. By focusing on elements such as resolution, bleed, margins, and consistency, I can create print designs that not only look professional but also effectively communicate their intended messages. This exploration into print design enhances my skills and empowers me to produce high-quality materials that resonate with audiences, paving the way for deeper connections and engagement. As I continue to refine my craft, I remain excited about the opportunities that print design presents, ready to bring my creative visions to life in tangible forms.

As I refine my approach to designing print materials, I increasingly recognize the importance of selecting the right printing method, as this decision profoundly affects the final output. Different printing techniques, such as digital printing, offset printing, and letterpress, each have their unique advantages and limitations. Understanding these methods allows me to choose the best option based on the project's requirements, budget, and desired outcome. For instance, digital printing is often preferred for smaller runs due to its quick turnaround and cost-effectiveness, while offset printing is advantageous for larger quantities because it offers superior color accuracy and quality at scale. When I am tasked with producing business cards or promotional flyers in bulk, I carefully weigh these factors to ensure that my choice aligns with both the practical and aesthetic goals of the project.

Equally important is the choice of paper stock, which can significantly influence the look and feel of the final product. The weight, texture, and finish of the paper contribute not only to the aesthetic quality but also to the tactile experience of the piece. I often consider options such as glossy, matte, or uncoated paper, depending on the desired effect. For example, glossy paper enhances vibrant colors and is ideal for eye-catching flyers aimed at grabbing attention. In contrast, matte finishes impart a sophisticated feel and are often better suited for business cards, where a more understated presentation is desirable. By selecting the appropriate paper stock, I can enhance the visual impact of my designs while aligning them with the intended audience and purpose.

When designing for print, I also emphasize the importance of testing proofs before committing to the final print run. Proofing allows me to evaluate how the design translates from screen to paper, revealing any potential issues such as color discrepancies or alignment errors. In Canva, I take advantage of the ability to create high-resolution PDFs, which I can use for proofing. This process involves reviewing the physical proofs closely, checking for consistency in color, sharpness, and layout. If discrepancies arise, I make necessary adjustments in my design before proceeding with the final print. This careful attention to detail ensures that the end product meets the highest standards of quality and professionalism.

As I explore the specifics of different print materials, I find that brochures require a distinct approach to content organization. Given their multi-panel format, I must be intentional about how information flows from one panel to another. I often start by outlining the content hierarchy, determining which messages are most critical and how they will be presented across the panels. This planning phase is crucial, as it allows me to create a narrative that guides the reader seamlessly through the information. I utilize Canva's grid and alignment features to ensure that the design remains cohesive and visually balanced, allowing for a logical progression of ideas.

When it comes to the use of images in brochures, I carefully select visuals that complement the text and reinforce the overall message. I prioritize high-quality images that resonate with the audience and enhance the storytelling aspect of the brochure. The placement of these images must be deliberate; I often consider how they interact with the text and whether they contribute to or distract from the overall message. By ensuring that images support the content rather than overwhelm it, I create a more effective and engaging design.

Typography also plays a pivotal role in print materials. I strive to select fonts that enhance readability while aligning with the brand's personality. For instance, a playful font might be appropriate for a children's event flyer, while a clean, sans-serif font may suit a corporate brochure better. I often employ a hierarchy of font sizes and weights to guide the reader's attention, using larger, bolder fonts for headlines and smaller, lighter fonts for body text. This hierarchy not only improves readability but also emphasizes key messages, ensuring that critical information stands out.

As I finalize my print designs, I remain cognizant of the importance of feedback. Sharing my work with colleagues or peers can provide valuable insights and highlight aspects that may need refinement. Their perspectives can help identify whether the design effectively communicates the intended message and resonates with the target audience. I find that engaging in this collaborative process not only enhances the quality of my work but also fosters a sense of community and shared creativity, allowing for an exchange of ideas that can lead to innovative solutions.

Moreover, I appreciate the significance of integrating branding elements into all print materials. Each design should reflect the brand's identity and values, creating a cohesive visual language across various touchpoints. This includes consistent use of colors, fonts, and logos, which reinforce brand recognition. I often create a style guide that outlines these elements, serving as a reference to ensure consistency across different print materials. By adhering to these guidelines, I create a unified brand presence that enhances credibility and fosters trust among the audience.

I also recognize the role of storytelling in print materials. Each flyer, brochure, or business card is an opportunity to convey a narrative that resonates with the audience. By crafting compelling messages and pairing them with appropriate visuals, I create a more engaging experience for the viewer. This narrative approach helps foster a connection between the brand and its audience, making the information presented more memorable and impactful.

As I conclude my work on print materials, I remain aware of the broader context of design within the digital age. While digital platforms continue to dominate, print materials retain a unique value in creating tangible connections and experiences. I find that well-designed print materials can leave a lasting impression, serving as a physical reminder of the brand's message. This appreciation for the distinct qualities of print informs my design approach, guiding me to create materials that not only look exceptional but also convey meaningful narratives.

In summary, the process of designing print materials is multifaceted, involving a keen understanding of technical specifications, content organization, and branding consistency. By considering elements such as resolution, bleed, margins, and material choices, I can create professional-grade designs that effectively communicate messages. This exploration of print design enhances my skills as a designer, empowering me to produce high-quality materials that resonate with audiences and create lasting impressions. As I continue to refine my craft, I remain excited about the possibilities that print design presents, ready to bring my creative visions to life in tangible forms.

CHAPTER 10: CRAFTING PRESENTATIONS

As I embark on the process of crafting presentations in Canva, I quickly realize that the art of effective slide design involves not only aesthetic considerations but also strategic communication of information. The primary goal of any presentation is to convey ideas clearly and engage the audience, which necessitates a careful balance between visuals and text. The way I approach this task sets the tone for how the content will be received and understood.

In designing slides, I often begin by establishing a clear narrative structure. Each presentation should follow a logical flow that guides the audience from one idea to the next, allowing them to grasp the overarching message without confusion. I typically outline my key points before diving into design, ensuring that each slide serves a specific purpose within the broader context. This pre-planning phase helps me determine how to allocate information across multiple slides, allowing for a clear division of topics while avoiding overcrowding any single slide with too much content.

When I open Canva to create my presentation, I am greeted by a wealth of templates tailored for various purposes. I find that selecting a template that resonates with the theme of my presentation can significantly enhance the design process. Templates provide a framework that not only saves time but also ensures a level of professionalism and coherence throughout the slides. For instance, if I am preparing a presentation for a corporate setting, I might choose a sleek, minimalistic template with a color scheme that aligns with the company's branding. Conversely, if my presentation is for a creative project, I might opt for a more vibrant template that allows for a playful use of colors and graphics.

As I begin to fill in the template with content, I pay close attention to slide layouts. A well-structured layout can dramatically impact the effectiveness of the presentation. I often utilize a combination of text boxes, images, and graphic elements to create visual interest while ensuring clarity. The hierarchy of information is paramount; I employ larger fonts for headings to signal importance and smaller fonts for supporting details. By varying font sizes and weights, I establish a visual hierarchy that guides the audience's eye and emphasizes key points.

Multimedia elements also play a crucial role in making presentations engaging. Integrating images, videos, and audio clips can help illustrate points and provide a richer context for the information being presented. I frequently utilize Canva's built-in tools to insert high-quality images that align with the message of each slide. Visuals serve not only as decorative elements but also as powerful aids that can reinforce the spoken message. For example, if I am discussing statistics, incorporating a relevant infographic can help clarify complex data and make it more accessible to the audience.

When I include video clips, I ensure they are short and directly related to the content being discussed. A well-placed video can capture attention and break up the monotony of text-heavy slides. However, I remain mindful of pacing; introducing multimedia should enhance the presentation rather than detract from it. I often test these elements beforehand to ensure they work seamlessly during the actual presentation, avoiding technical glitches that could disrupt the flow of my message.

In addition to these considerations, I prioritize the use of consistent branding throughout my presentation. This includes maintaining a uniform color palette, font selection, and visual style that reflects my personal or organizational brand. Consistency helps create a cohesive look, allowing the audience to focus on the content rather than being distracted by varying styles. In Canva, I frequently refer to my established brand guidelines as I design my slides, ensuring that each element aligns with my overall branding strategy.

The aspect of transition and animation is another powerful tool in my presentation design arsenal. Subtle animations can add an engaging dynamic to the slides, drawing attention to specific elements as they appear. However, I exercise restraint; excessive animations can lead to distraction and diminish the professionalism of the presentation. I typically use simple transitions, such as fade-ins or slide-ins, that enhance the viewing experience without overwhelming the audience.

As I approach the final stages of my presentation design, I emphasize the importance of rehearsal and refinement. A presentation is not merely a series of slides; it is a performance that requires practice and polish. I often run through the entire presentation multiple times, assessing the pacing and flow of information. This rehearsal allows me to identify areas that may need adjustment, whether it's revising text for clarity or refining the timing of multimedia elements. Practicing in front of colleagues can provide valuable feedback, helping me gauge how effectively I communicate my message.

After finalizing the design and content, I prepare to export the presentation for delivery. Canva offers multiple export options, allowing me to save the presentation in various formats, including PDF and PowerPoint. I typically choose the format that best suits my delivery method, ensuring compatibility with the equipment I will be using. If I am presenting in person, I might opt for a PDF to avoid any compatibility issues with software. Conversely, if I am presenting remotely, I may save it as a PowerPoint file to utilize its features during the presentation.

Ultimately, the process of crafting presentations in Canva combines creativity with strategic communication. By focusing on layout, multimedia integration, and branding consistency, I can design slides that are visually appealing and effective in conveying my message. Each presentation is an opportunity to connect with an audience, and I embrace the challenge of creating engaging designs that resonate and inspire. As I continue to refine my skills in presentation design, I look forward to exploring new techniques and strategies that enhance my ability to communicate effectively through visual storytelling.

As I delve deeper into the nuances of crafting presentations, I become increasingly aware of the psychological aspects of audience engagement. The way information is presented can greatly influence how it is received, understood, and retained. I focus on establishing an emotional connection with my audience, as this can significantly enhance the impact of my message. One effective strategy is to start my presentation with a compelling story or an interesting fact that relates to the topic. This approach not only grabs attention but also sets the stage for the content that follows. By invoking emotions through storytelling, I create a more memorable experience for my audience, which can lead to greater retention of the information presented.

In addition to storytelling, I pay close attention to the pacing of my presentation. A well-timed delivery can enhance engagement and maintain audience interest. I strive to vary my speech tempo and tone to emphasize key points and keep the audience engaged. This variation helps prevent monotony, especially during longer presentations. I often practice my delivery in front of a mirror or record myself, allowing me to assess my pacing and make adjustments as necessary. Incorporating pauses can also be powerful; a brief pause after presenting a critical point gives the audience time to digest the information before moving on.

As I finalize my slides, I carefully consider the use of whitespace, which is often an overlooked yet vital aspect of effective presentation design. Whitespace, or negative space, provides breathing room around elements, allowing the content to stand out and making it easier for the audience to absorb information. I aim for a clean layout that avoids overcrowding, as this can lead to confusion and diminish the effectiveness of the message. By strategically placing elements and ensuring adequate whitespace, I create a more visually appealing and professional presentation that facilitates understanding.

In terms of font selection, I recognize that readability is paramount, especially when presenting to larger audiences. I often choose sans-serif fonts for their clarity, especially in headings and subheadings, as they tend to be more legible from a distance. Additionally, I maintain consistency in font styles and sizes throughout the presentation to create a cohesive visual identity. This attention to detail not only enhances professionalism but also reinforces the overall branding of the presentation. When utilizing Canva, I take advantage of the font pairing suggestions available, which can help me select complementary fonts that align with my design goals.

As I incorporate multimedia elements into my presentation, I understand that these components should enhance the narrative rather than serve as distractions. Video clips, for example, can be a powerful way to illustrate points and provide context, but I am careful to select clips that are brief and directly relevant to the content. If a video serves to support a specific argument or provide a real-world example, it can significantly bolster the impact of my message. I also consider the technical aspects of incorporating multimedia, ensuring that all files are compatible with the equipment I will be using during the presentation to avoid any last-minute technical issues.

In addition to videos, I often include audio clips and music to create an immersive experience. This auditory element can evoke emotions and reinforce the themes presented. However, I exercise discretion when using sound; it should enhance the presentation rather than overshadow my spoken words. I find that using background music during transitions or pauses can create a more dynamic atmosphere, but it must be at a volume that does not interfere with the clarity of my speech.

As I work with data and statistics in my presentations, I aim to present this information in a way that is visually engaging and easy to understand. I often utilize charts, graphs, and infographics to simplify complex data. In Canva, I can easily create visually appealing representations of data that highlight key trends or insights. By employing these visual tools, I not only make the data more accessible but also engage the audience's interest. A well-designed infographic can convey a wealth of information in a fraction of the time it would take to explain through text alone.

Feedback becomes an invaluable component in the crafting of my presentations. Once I have a draft ready, I often share it with colleagues or trusted peers to gather their insights. This collaborative process allows me to identify areas for improvement that I might not have considered. Constructive criticism can help refine my slides, ensuring that the design effectively communicates the intended message. I also appreciate the value of rehearsing in front of a live audience, as this can provide real-time feedback on the effectiveness of my delivery and engagement strategies.

As I prepare for the actual presentation, I consider the environment in which I will be presenting. Factors such as lighting, seating arrangement, and available technology can significantly impact the delivery of my message. I ensure that my materials are compatible with the presentation equipment, whether I am using a projector, screen, or even presenting on a digital platform. Familiarizing myself with the setup in advance helps to alleviate potential technical issues and allows me to focus on delivering my message with confidence.

Finally, I remind myself of the importance of concluding my presentation effectively. A strong closing reinforces the key points and leaves a lasting impression on the audience. I often summarize the main takeaways and provide a clear call to action, inviting the audience to reflect on what they have learned or encouraging them to engage further with the topic. This concluding segment is crucial in solidifying the information and motivating the audience to act or think critically about the subject matter.

In summary, crafting presentations in Canva involves a thoughtful blend of design principles, audience engagement strategies, and practical considerations. By focusing on storytelling, pacing, typography, and multimedia integration, I can create presentations that captivate and inform. This exploration into the art of presentation design enriches my skills as a communicator and empowers me to deliver messages effectively. As I continue to refine my approach, I look forward to the ongoing opportunities for growth and creativity in the world of presentations.

As I immerse myself in the final stages of crafting my presentation, I pay close attention to the details that can elevate my work from simply functional to truly impactful.

The choice of transitions and animations, for example, can significantly influence the flow and pacing of my presentation. I find that subtle animations, such as fade-ins or slide transitions, can help to maintain the audience's interest without becoming a distraction. Each transition should serve a purpose, either to introduce new content smoothly or to emphasize a point as I move through the slides. I am mindful to avoid overly flashy or complex animations, as these can detract from the professionalism of the presentation and disrupt the audience's focus.

In preparing for the delivery of my presentation, I ensure that I am familiar with the technology I will be using. This includes checking the compatibility of my Canva presentation with the equipment available at the venue. I often download my presentation in multiple formats, such as PDF and PowerPoint, to ensure that I have options should any technical issues arise. Familiarizing myself with the setup allows me to feel more confident and reduces the chances of encountering unexpected problems. I also arrive early to test the equipment and get a sense of the space, adjusting my content and delivery as needed based on the environment.

Another essential aspect of presentation delivery is engaging the audience through eye contact and body language. I strive to connect with my audience members, making them feel involved in the conversation rather than passive recipients of information. By scanning the room and making eye contact with different sections of the audience, I foster a sense of connection and engagement. I also utilize open and confident body language to convey my enthusiasm and conviction regarding the content. This non-verbal communication plays a critical role in reinforcing the message and encouraging audience engagement.

As I present, I pay close attention to audience reactions, adapting my delivery based on their engagement levels. If I notice signs of distraction or disinterest, I may adjust my tone or pacing to recapture their attention. Incorporating rhetorical questions or brief moments of interaction, such as asking for a show of hands, can reinvigorate the audience and encourage participation. This responsiveness to the audience enhances the overall experience and reinforces the connection between the content and the viewers.

After the presentation, I often invite questions and discussions, recognizing that this interaction can deepen the audience's understanding of the material. Addressing questions not only clarifies points but also fosters a collaborative atmosphere where ideas can be shared and explored. I find that these discussions can lead to valuable insights and perspectives that enhance my own understanding of the topic, further enriching the experience for everyone involved.

Reflecting on the presentation process, I acknowledge the importance of continuous improvement. After each presentation, I take the time to evaluate what worked well and what could be refined for future endeavors. I often solicit feedback from peers or mentors, asking them to share their observations on my delivery and design choices. This constructive feedback serves as a foundation for growth, allowing me to identify areas where I can enhance my skills and approach.

In addition to direct feedback, I also analyze audience engagement metrics when available. If I share the presentation on digital platforms, I review analytics to see which slides received the most interaction or where viewers may have dropped off. This data-driven approach informs my future presentations, enabling me to make evidence-based adjustments to my content and delivery.

Ultimately, the experience of crafting presentations in Canva has expanded my understanding of effective communication through design. By integrating visual elements with narrative techniques, I create presentations that are not only informative but also memorable. I embrace the challenge of designing slides that encapsulate my ideas while engaging the audience in a meaningful way. The skills I have honed in presentation design—whether it be through storytelling, strategic use of multimedia, or responsive delivery—empower me to connect with audiences and convey messages that resonate deeply.

As I look forward to future opportunities for presenting, I remain committed to exploring new techniques and refining my approach. The world of presentation design is ever-evolving, and I am excited to experiment with innovative strategies that can enhance my effectiveness as a communicator. Each presentation is not just a reflection of my ideas but also an opportunity to engage, inspire, and inform those who experience it. This ongoing journey of growth and discovery fuels my passion for design and presentation, reminding me that the art of effective communication is both a skill and a creative endeavor.

CHAPTER 11: ENHANCING YOUR DESIGNS WITH ANIMATIONS

As I delve into the world of animations within Canva, I quickly discover how these dynamic elements can breathe life into my designs. Animation has the power to transform static images and text into engaging, interactive experiences that capture the viewer's attention and enhance the overall message. However, I understand that while animations can be captivating, they must be used judiciously to avoid overwhelming the audience. The key lies in striking a balance between creativity and clarity, ensuring that the animations complement the content rather than detract from it.

Canva offers a variety of animation features that allow me to animate text, images, and various design elements with ease. When I begin incorporating animations into my designs, I typically start with the text. Text animations can be particularly effective for emphasizing key messages or creating a sense of movement that draws the viewer's eye. For instance, I might choose to animate a heading with a fade-in effect, which creates a smooth entrance that allows the audience to focus on the text as it appears. This subtle introduction not only enhances visual interest but also provides a moment for the audience to absorb the information before moving on to the next point.

I also explore the various animation styles available in Canva, each offering a unique way to present content. Options like "Slide," "Breathe," and "Pop" can add distinct personality to my designs. The "Slide" animation can give the impression of text or elements entering the scene from a specific direction, which can create a narrative flow as I guide the viewer through the content. On the other hand, the "Pop" animation adds a playful touch, making elements seem as though they are bouncing onto the screen. I find that the choice of animation style should align with the tone of the content; for a formal presentation, I might opt for more subdued animations, while a creative project could benefit from more whimsical effects.

In addition to animating text, I realize that images and graphic elements can also be animated to create an engaging visual experience. For example, if I'm designing a promotional video or an advertisement, I can animate product images to draw attention to specific features or calls to action. A subtle zoom-in effect can emphasize a product's details, while a slide-in effect can guide the viewer's attention toward important information. This level of dynamism not only makes the content more visually appealing but also enhances the storytelling aspect, allowing me to convey messages in a more immersive way.

As I integrate animations into my designs, I remain mindful of timing and pacing. The duration of each animation plays a crucial role in how effectively the audience perceives the content. If animations are too fast, viewers may miss critical information; if they are too slow, attention may wane. Canva allows me to adjust the timing of animations, enabling me to find the sweet spot that maintains audience engagement without feeling rushed. I often preview the animations in real-time to ensure that the flow feels natural and coherent. This attention to pacing is particularly important in presentations, where I want to maintain the audience's focus and guide them through the narrative smoothly.

In addition to individual animations, I also consider how elements work together on the slide. Coordinating animations across multiple elements can create a cohesive and synchronized effect that enhances the overall visual impact. For example, if I animate a heading to appear first, I might follow it with a corresponding image that slides in shortly after. This sequencing creates a dynamic interplay that reinforces the connection between text and visuals, making the content more cohesive. I often experiment with different sequences, observing how the timing and order of animations affect the audience's understanding and engagement.

While animations can be a powerful tool for enhancing designs, I recognize the importance of restraint. Overusing animations can lead to a cluttered and distracting experience that detracts from the message. I strive to maintain a sense of clarity in my designs, ensuring that each animated element serves a specific purpose. I often ask myself whether an animation adds value to the content or simply serves as embellishment. By prioritizing meaningful animations, I can create a more polished and professional appearance that aligns with my overall design goals.

In exploring the use of animations in social media graphics, I find that these elements can significantly enhance engagement rates. Social media users are accustomed to dynamic content, and incorporating animations into posts can help capture their attention in a crowded feed. I experiment with animated GIFs or short video clips that highlight key messages or showcase products in action. These dynamic visuals not only draw viewers in but also encourage them to interact with the content, whether by liking, sharing, or commenting. Canva's animation features enable me to create these engaging graphics effortlessly, allowing me to stand out in the fast-paced world of social media.

As I finalize my designs, I ensure that all animations are appropriately integrated and functioning as intended. I conduct a thorough review of each slide, checking for smooth transitions and coherent animations. I also consider the context in which the presentation or graphic will be viewed. For instance, if I am designing a presentation for a formal business meeting, I might opt for more subtle animations that enhance professionalism. Conversely, if the design is intended for a creative showcase, I might embrace bolder, more dynamic animations that reflect the artistic intent.

Ultimately, the journey of incorporating animations into my designs has deepened my understanding of how to engage and captivate an audience. By utilizing Canva's animation features thoughtfully, I can create presentations and graphics that not only communicate messages effectively but also evoke emotional responses. This exploration of animated design enhances my overall skill set, empowering me to push the boundaries of creativity and interaction in my work. As I continue to refine my approach, I look forward to discovering new techniques and strategies for leveraging animation to enhance my designs and connect with audiences in meaningful ways.

As I further explore the intricacies of using animations in my designs, I begin to appreciate the strategic placement of these animated elements and how they can guide the audience's focus throughout the presentation. When deciding which parts of a slide to animate, I consider the key messages I want to convey and how to emphasize them effectively. For instance, if I am presenting a critical statistic, I might choose to animate that number so that it appears larger or with a dramatic effect, drawing immediate attention. This approach not only makes the information more engaging but also highlights its importance in the overall narrative of the presentation.

In Canva, I can easily apply various animation effects to different elements within my slides. For example, when I animate images, I often use effects such as "Zoom" or "Fade" to create a sense of depth. When an image zooms in, it captures the audience's attention and allows them to absorb the details more fully. Conversely, a fade effect can create a smooth transition that feels more subtle and professional, especially when moving from one piece of content to another. I find that selecting the right animation type is crucial for maintaining the intended tone of the presentation. For a formal business context, I lean towards more understated animations, whereas for a creative project, I might embrace more vibrant, eye-catching effects.

Another crucial aspect of incorporating animations is timing. In presentations, the duration and sequencing of animations can significantly affect how information is processed. I often adjust the duration of animations to ensure that they provide enough time for the audience to absorb each element before moving on to the next. Canva allows me to control these timings, which enables me to synchronize my speaking pace with the animations on the screen. For example, if I introduce a new point, I may time the animation so that the corresponding text appears as I begin to discuss it. This synchronization helps reinforce my message and ensures that the audience remains engaged with the content.

I also pay close attention to how animations work in conjunction with transitions between slides. Transitions can set the stage for what comes next, creating a seamless flow from one idea to another. I often use transitions that complement the animations I've chosen for individual elements within the slides. For instance, if I have animated a bullet point to appear with a "Slide In" effect, I might follow that with a "Dissolve" transition to the next slide, creating a cohesive visual narrative. This thoughtful combination of animations and transitions enhances the storytelling aspect of my presentation, making it easier for the audience to follow along and understand the overall message.

In addition to text and images, I explore how to animate other design elements, such as charts and infographics. Presenting data effectively is vital, and animations can help to clarify complex information. For example, if I have a bar chart depicting growth over time, I might animate each bar to rise sequentially, allowing the audience to visually track the progress as I discuss the data. This step-by-step approach not only makes the data more digestible but also reinforces the narrative I am presenting. By animating infographics, I can create dynamic visuals that captivate the audience and enhance their understanding of the information being shared.

As I delve into the use of animations for social media graphics, I discover that these elements can significantly enhance engagement rates. In a crowded digital landscape, animations can make my posts stand out and capture attention quickly. For instance, an animated post featuring a product can show it in action, demonstrating its features in a way that static images cannot. Canva's tools allow me to create short, looped animations that can easily be shared across platforms, maximizing visibility and interaction. By experimenting with these animated graphics, I can create compelling content that resonates with my audience and encourages them to share it further.

When integrating animations into social media content, I maintain a focus on brevity and impact. Given that social media users often scroll quickly through their feeds, I aim to convey messages as succinctly as possible. This means that my animations should be brief yet impactful, capturing attention without overwhelming viewers. I often choose animations that highlight key messages or calls to action, ensuring that they prompt engagement. For example, if I am promoting an event, I might animate the date and location to draw attention, reinforcing the urgency of the invitation.

As I explore the process of creating presentations that incorporate animations, I also consider the technical aspects of the presentation format. If I plan to present my slides in a setting where internet connectivity may be unreliable, I ensure that all animations are compatible with offline modes. Canva allows me to download presentations in formats that preserve animations, so I can confidently present without worrying about technical glitches. I often conduct final checks to confirm that all elements function smoothly, allowing for a seamless delivery of my message.

Finally, as I prepare to share my designs, I remind myself of the importance of adaptability. Different audiences may respond differently to animations, and being receptive to this feedback allows me to refine my approach continually. After a presentation, I often seek input from attendees regarding their engagement levels and perceptions of the animations used. This feedback helps me gauge what resonated and what might require adjustment for future presentations. By remaining flexible and open to change, I can continuously improve my designs and enhance the effectiveness of my communication.

In conclusion, the journey of enhancing my designs with animations has revealed the profound impact that these dynamic elements can have on audience engagement and message delivery. By thoughtfully incorporating animations into text, images, and other design elements, I can create presentations that are not only visually captivating but also effective in conveying complex information. This exploration of animations within Canva equips me with valuable skills and insights, empowering me to craft presentations that resonate deeply with my audience. As I continue to refine my design process, I am excited to explore new possibilities for integrating animations, ready to elevate my presentations to new heights of creativity and engagement.

As I continue to explore the world of animations in my designs, I delve into the specifics of timing and sequencing, recognizing that these factors can greatly enhance the viewer's experience. The way animations are timed can dictate the rhythm of the presentation, affecting how easily the audience absorbs the information. I often experiment with different timings for each animated element to create a flow that feels natural and intuitive. For instance, when presenting a list of points, I might animate each point to appear one after the other, allowing the audience to focus on one idea at a time. This approach prevents them from becoming overwhelmed by too much information at once and helps maintain engagement throughout the presentation.

In Canva, I appreciate the ability to adjust the duration of animations, which allows me to customize the pace of my presentation according to the content being delivered. I typically opt for quicker animations for less critical elements, as these can serve as visual cues without demanding too much attention. Conversely, I use slower animations for key messages or significant transitions, enabling the audience to process important information thoroughly. This attention to timing enhances the overall coherence of the presentation, ensuring that each animated element serves its intended purpose.

I also consider the impact of layering animations. By staggering the animations of various elements, I create a sense of depth and dimension within the presentation. For example, if I have a slide with both an image and accompanying text, I might animate the image to fade in first, followed by the text that slides in shortly after. This sequencing creates a visual narrative that draws the audience's eye and reinforces the connection between the elements. In my experience, layering animations not only adds visual interest but also enhances storytelling by guiding the audience through the content in a logical manner.

Another important aspect of using animations is understanding the context in which the presentation will be delivered. Different settings, whether in-person or virtual, require adjustments to how I approach animations. In a live setting, I may opt for more subtle animations to maintain a professional tone, while in a virtual environment, I might embrace more dynamic effects to counterbalance the inherent distance of online interactions. This adaptability allows me to connect with my audience in a manner that feels authentic and engaging, regardless of the medium.

In the context of social media, the application of animations takes on a new dimension. Users on these platforms are accustomed to rapid consumption of content, and animations can serve as a powerful tool to capture attention quickly. I often create short, looping animations that highlight key messages or product features. The ability to convey a message in just a few seconds makes animations particularly effective in this environment. I leverage Canva's features to design engaging social media graphics that are both eye-catching and informative, often incorporating animated text or elements that draw viewers in and encourage them to interact with the content.

While creating these social media graphics, I remain mindful of the importance of maintaining brand consistency. Each animated graphic should reflect the established visual identity of the brand, using colors, fonts, and styles that align with previous content. This consistency reinforces brand recognition and builds trust with the audience. I often refer back to my brand guidelines when designing animations to ensure that they not only stand out but also fit seamlessly within the broader narrative of my brand's message.

As I explore the creative possibilities of animations, I also embrace the importance of analytics in evaluating their effectiveness. After publishing animated graphics or presentations, I often review engagement metrics to assess how well they resonated with the audience. For instance, I analyze whether certain animations led to increased click-through rates or improved retention during presentations. This data-driven approach allows me to refine my animation strategies continually, making informed decisions about which styles and techniques yield the best results.

The integration of audience feedback is equally valuable in enhancing my use of animations. After delivering a presentation, I solicit input from attendees regarding their experiences with the animations. Their insights can reveal whether the animations added value or if certain elements felt excessive or distracting. This collaborative feedback process helps me hone my skills and ensures that my future designs align more closely with audience expectations.

As I finalize my designs, I place significant emphasis on testing animations in the context in which they will be viewed. For presentations, I rehearse in front of colleagues or friends to simulate the experience of delivering to an audience. This practice allows me to gauge how effectively the animations complement my speaking and whether they enhance or hinder the overall delivery. In social media, I might preview animations across different devices to ensure they maintain their visual integrity and appeal regardless of how they are viewed.

Ultimately, the experience of enhancing my designs with animations has expanded my creative toolkit, empowering me to engage audiences in new and exciting ways. By thoughtfully incorporating animations, I can create dynamic presentations and graphics that not only convey information but also evoke emotional responses. This exploration of animated design enriches my understanding of effective communication, enabling me to connect with my audience on a deeper level. As I continue to refine my approach and explore new techniques, I look forward to the endless possibilities that animations offer, ready to push the boundaries of creativity and interaction in my work.

CHAPTER 12: ADVANCED DESIGN TECHNIQUES

As I embark on the exploration of advanced design techniques, I find myself captivated by the transformative power of layering, transparency, and blending modes. These concepts can significantly elevate the sophistication of my projects, allowing for a level of depth and complexity that can make designs stand out. Understanding how to effectively utilize these techniques not only enhances my aesthetic sensibility but also broadens my creative toolbox, enabling me to approach design challenges with greater versatility and innovation.

Layering is one of the fundamental techniques that I employ to build visual interest and depth in my designs. By stacking various elements, I can create a sense of dimensionality that draws the viewer's eye and encourages exploration of the composition. For example, when designing a promotional poster, I might place a vibrant background image beneath semi-transparent text boxes that highlight key information. This layering approach creates a visually engaging contrast, allowing the text to pop while still showcasing the background image. As I work in Canva, I can easily arrange and group these layers, manipulating their order to achieve the desired effect.

In mastering layering, I also pay attention to the relationship between foreground and background elements. A well-executed design ensures that the viewer can easily distinguish between different layers while still appreciating how they interact with one another. I often experiment with the placement of elements, adjusting their positions to create a cohesive visual flow. For instance, if I am designing a website banner, I may layer images of products in the foreground while placing a subtle gradient overlay in the background. This technique not only enhances the visual hierarchy but also ensures that the primary focus remains on the product images, which are the centerpiece of the design.

Transparency is another powerful tool that I leverage to add sophistication and nuance to my designs. By adjusting the opacity of elements, I can create a sense of depth and harmony that elevates the overall composition. For instance, if I want to emphasize a specific image while maintaining background details, I may reduce the opacity of the background layer, allowing it to recede while keeping the focus on the foreground subject. This technique can evoke a sense of subtlety and elegance, inviting the viewer to engage with the design more intimately.

In Canva, adjusting transparency is a straightforward process that allows for real-time visualization of changes. I often experiment with different opacity levels to find the right balance that enhances the design without compromising clarity. This flexibility encourages experimentation; I may layer multiple elements with varying levels of transparency to create intriguing visual effects. For example, when designing an event flyer, I can overlay a color wash with reduced opacity over a photo, giving it a cohesive look while also conveying the event's theme through color.

Blending modes introduce yet another layer of complexity to my design practice. These modes determine how layers interact with each other in terms of color and light, producing unique visual effects that can transform an ordinary design into something extraordinary. I often find myself experimenting with different blending modes to see how they alter the appearance of overlapping elements. For instance, using the "Multiply" blending mode can create rich, dark colors by blending two layers together, ideal for creating shadows or adding depth to a design. Conversely, the "Screen" mode lightens colors, which can be effective for highlighting or creating glowing effects.

To gain a deeper understanding of blending modes, I often engage in hands-on experimentation. I might take an image and apply different modes to a colored shape layered on top of it, observing how the interaction alters the overall aesthetic. This exploratory process not only enhances my skills but also inspires new design ideas that I may not have considered initially. I find that blending modes can create a unique visual language in my projects, adding texture and intrigue that engage viewers on multiple levels.

As I apply these advanced techniques, I also consider the importance of cohesiveness in my designs. It's essential that all elements work together harmoniously, regardless of how complex the design becomes. I regularly refer back to my overarching design principles, ensuring that my color palette, typography, and imagery align seamlessly. This alignment is critical in maintaining a unified look and feel, which reinforces the message I aim to convey. For example, when using transparency and layering, I ensure that the colors remain complementary and that the overall composition does not become visually chaotic.

Moreover, I am mindful of the context in which my designs will be viewed. Understanding the medium—be it print, digital, or social media—helps guide my decisions regarding layering, transparency, and blending. For instance, designs intended for social media might benefit from bolder colors and more pronounced layering effects to stand out in a fast-scrolling environment. Conversely, print materials may require more subtlety, with careful attention to how colors and transparency interact when printed.

As I finalize my projects, I take the time to evaluate the effectiveness of the advanced techniques I've employed. This reflective practice allows me to assess whether the use of layering, transparency, and blending has enhanced the overall design and communicated the intended message. I often seek feedback from peers or colleagues, whose insights can reveal whether the design resonates with its intended audience. This collaborative feedback loop is invaluable, as it informs my future work and encourages continuous improvement.

In conclusion, the exploration of advanced design techniques—specifically layering, transparency, and blending modes—has significantly enriched my understanding of visual composition. By applying these techniques thoughtfully, I can create designs that not only engage viewers but also convey messages with clarity and impact. This journey into the realm of advanced design has empowered me to push the boundaries of my creativity and elevate my skills as a designer. As I continue to refine my approach and experiment with new techniques, I am eager to discover how these elements can enhance my work and engage my audience in innovative ways.

As I further immerse myself in the world of advanced design techniques, I realize that the successful integration of layering, transparency, and blending modes requires a keen eye for detail and a strong understanding of visual composition. Each element in a design can serve multiple purposes, and the way I manipulate these elements can drastically change the viewer's perception and emotional response.

Layering is not merely about stacking elements on top of one another; it's about creating a hierarchy that guides the viewer's eye through the design. I often start by considering the focal point of my design—what do I want the audience to notice first? By strategically placing my most important elements in the foreground and allowing supporting details to recede into the background, I create a natural flow that makes it easy for viewers to navigate the content. For instance, when designing a poster for an event, I might feature the event title prominently at the top, using a large, bold font, while layering supporting images and text below in smaller, lighter fonts. This creates a sense of clarity and organization, making the key message unmistakable.

In my exploration of transparency, I begin to appreciate the subtleties that come with varying opacity levels. Transparency can transform the visual weight of elements, allowing me to create a sense of depth without overcrowding the design. When I adjust the opacity of a background image, for example, I can create a soft, muted backdrop that allows foreground text to stand out without competing for attention. This technique works particularly well in creating contrast; by fading the background, I ensure that the main message remains clear and legible. In Canva, I can easily manipulate the opacity of each layer, allowing for real-time adjustments that help me see how changes affect the overall composition.

I often experiment with overlapping elements to see how they interact when transparency is applied. For instance, I might layer two colored shapes and adjust their opacities to create new colors where they overlap. This method not only adds visual complexity but also introduces a playful element to my designs. Such effects can evoke emotions or convey themes effectively; for example, warm colors may suggest energy and vibrancy, while cooler tones can evoke calmness and professionalism. I find that the ability to create these nuanced interactions deepens the emotional impact of my designs.

Blending modes serve as a powerful extension of these layering and transparency techniques, enabling me to manipulate how colors interact between different layers.

Each blending mode affects the colors and brightness of overlapping elements in unique ways, which can lead to stunning visual effects. I frequently use the "Multiply" blending mode to deepen colors in my designs, especially when I want to create shadows or a more dramatic feel. This mode multiplies the color values of the top layer with those of the bottom layer, resulting in darker colors that can enhance depth.

On the other hand, I find the "Screen" blending mode particularly useful for lightening colors and creating a sense of brightness. This mode can be effective when I want to overlay light-colored text on top of a darker image without losing readability. By experimenting with various blending modes, I can achieve effects that I might not have considered initially. For example, I might layer a textured graphic over a solid background and use different blending modes to see how they alter the overall aesthetic, often leading to unexpected and captivating results.

As I refine my designs, I remain cognizant of the importance of maintaining cohesiveness. Advanced techniques can easily lead to complexity, and I must ensure that my designs do not become visually chaotic. A coherent design relies on a unified color palette, consistent typography, and harmonious element interactions. When I use blending modes, for instance, I pay close attention to how the resulting colors work together, ensuring they align with the overall theme and message of the project. I often create a mood board prior to starting my design, collecting colors, textures, and fonts that evoke the desired emotions and themes. This reference point helps me stay focused on my vision as I explore advanced techniques.

Throughout this creative process, I find that iteration plays a crucial role in refining my designs. Each project presents an opportunity to experiment, learn, and adapt. I frequently take breaks to step back and view my work from a distance, which allows me to assess the overall balance and composition more effectively. Sometimes, I may think a particular animation or layered element looks great up close, but from a distance, it may not serve the overall message as intended. This distance provides a fresh perspective and often reveals areas for improvement that I might have overlooked while engrossed in the details.

Moreover, I value the feedback from peers as an essential part of my design journey. Sharing my work with colleagues not only exposes me to different viewpoints but also invites constructive criticism that can elevate the final product. During collaborative sessions, I often receive suggestions on how to enhance visual clarity or simplify complex elements. This dialogue fosters a creative environment where ideas can flourish, and the exchange of insights significantly enriches my design practice.

As I finalize my projects, I take the time to test how different formats and mediums affect the design. Designs intended for print may require different considerations than those meant for digital platforms. I ensure that all layering and transparency effects translate well in both mediums, adjusting my approach accordingly. For instance, a design that looks stunning on a screen may need tweaking to ensure the same impact when printed, as colors often appear differently in print. This attention to detail reinforces my commitment to quality, ensuring that my designs are effective across various applications.

The mastery of advanced design techniques allows me to elevate my creative work significantly. Layering, transparency, and blending modes not only enhance the visual appeal of my designs but also deepen my understanding of how to communicate effectively through visuals. By integrating these techniques thoughtfully, I can create designs that are not only beautiful but also meaningful and impactful. This exploration empowers me to push the boundaries of my creativity, fostering a continual desire to learn and experiment in my craft. As I navigate this journey of design, I look forward to uncovering new possibilities that further enrich my skills and enhance my artistic expression.

As I deepen my understanding of advanced design techniques, I become increasingly aware of the role that texture plays in enhancing visual depth and interest. Texture can be both a physical and a visual component that adds richness to designs, creating an immersive experience for the viewer. I often experiment with incorporating various textures into my projects to evoke specific feelings or themes. For example, using a rough, grunge texture can convey a sense of ruggedness and authenticity, making it perfect for designs related to adventure or nature. Conversely, a smooth, polished texture can impart a sense of elegance and professionalism, ideal for corporate presentations or formal invitations.

In Canva, I have access to a library of textures that I can apply to my designs. When integrating textures, I focus on how they interact with the other elements on the page. For instance, if I apply a textured background to a poster, I ensure that the overlaying text remains legible. To achieve this balance, I often adjust the transparency of the texture, allowing the underlying colors to shine through while still adding depth. This nuanced approach ensures that the texture enhances rather than overwhelms the design.

Moreover, layering textures is a technique I frequently employ to create a more dynamic visual effect. By combining multiple textures and adjusting their blending modes, I can produce intricate designs that draw the viewer in. For example, I might layer a subtle fabric texture over a solid color background, using a soft blending mode to create a unique tactile quality. This layering approach adds complexity and sophistication to my designs, allowing me to create a visual language that resonates with the intended audience.

As I explore these advanced techniques, I am also drawn to the concept of asymmetrical design, which breaks traditional design rules to create unique and striking compositions. Asymmetry can generate a sense of movement and intrigue, making a design feel more dynamic. I often experiment with placing elements off-center or using unexpected alignments to create tension and visual interest. For instance, in a flyer, I might place a bold image on one side while balancing it with text that flows around it in a non-linear fashion. This approach challenges conventional layouts and invites the viewer to engage more actively with the design.

In Canva, I take advantage of grid systems and alignment tools to experiment with asymmetrical layouts effectively. While I embrace the freedom that asymmetry provides, I also remain attentive to balance within the composition. Even in asymmetrical designs, it's essential to create a visual equilibrium that prevents the layout from feeling chaotic. I often step back and assess the overall composition, ensuring that the arrangement of elements feels intentional and cohesive.

Another advanced technique that I find particularly captivating is the use of gradients. Gradients can introduce color transitions that add depth and dimension to designs. I often use gradients to create backgrounds that evoke specific emotions or themes. For instance, a warm gradient transitioning from orange to yellow can evoke feelings of warmth and positivity, making it suitable for designs related to summer or joy. On the other hand, cooler gradients transitioning from blue to purple can create a sense of calmness and serenity, ideal for wellness or meditation themes.

When using gradients, I pay close attention to the direction and intensity of the transition. In Canva, I can customize gradients to achieve the desired effect, whether I want a subtle blend or a more dramatic transition. I also experiment with layering gradients over images, utilizing blending modes to create a harmonious interaction between colors and visuals. This technique can elevate the aesthetic quality of the design, providing a polished and professional look.

As I continue to refine my skills in these advanced techniques, I also recognize the importance of contextualizing my designs. Understanding the intended medium—whether it's print, digital, or social media—can significantly influence how I apply these techniques. For example, designs intended for social media may benefit from bold colors and high contrast, capturing attention quickly in a fast-scrolling environment. In contrast, print materials may require more subtlety and refinement, as colors often appear differently when printed. Being aware of these distinctions allows me to tailor my approach, ensuring that my designs resonate with their intended audiences.

I also place significant value on the role of storytelling in design. Advanced techniques like layering, transparency, and blending can all contribute to the narrative that my designs communicate. Each element should work together to tell a cohesive story that engages the viewer. When crafting a visual narrative, I consider how the arrangement of elements, the use of color, and the application of texture all contribute to the overarching theme. For instance, if I am designing a poster for an environmental campaign, I might use earthy tones, organic textures, and layered images of nature to create a design that reinforces the message of conservation and awareness.

As I finalize my projects, I engage in a thorough review process to assess the effectiveness of the advanced techniques I have employed. I evaluate whether the layering and blending have enhanced the overall design and whether the textures add depth and interest without causing confusion. I also consider how well the design aligns with the intended message and whether it resonates with the target audience. This reflective practice is essential for my growth as a designer, allowing me to learn from each project and continuously improve my skills.

In summary, the exploration of advanced design techniques has empowered me to elevate my creative work significantly. By mastering concepts such as layering, transparency, blending modes, and texture, I can create designs that are not only visually captivating but also meaningful and impactful. This journey into advanced design techniques enriches my understanding of visual communication, enabling me to connect with audiences on a deeper level. As I continue to refine my craft, I am eager to uncover new possibilities that further enhance my designs and inspire innovative approaches to visual storytelling.

CHAPTER 13: UTILIZING CANVA'S DESIGN ELEMENTS

As I begin to explore the diverse range of design elements available in Canva, I quickly recognize their potential to transform my projects into visually compelling compositions. Shapes, lines, and frames are not just functional components; they are foundational tools that can help establish structure, guide the viewer's eye, and create a sense of harmony within the design. My understanding of how to effectively use these elements will significantly enhance my design capabilities, allowing me to create layouts that are both unique and professional.

Starting with shapes, I appreciate their versatility in adding visual interest and structure to my designs. Shapes can be used to create backgrounds, highlight text, or frame images. For example, when designing a flyer, I might incorporate a semi-transparent rectangle behind the main text to ensure legibility against a busy background. This simple addition not only enhances readability but also adds depth to the design. In Canva, I can easily adjust the color, size, and transparency of shapes, allowing me to tailor them to fit the overall aesthetic of my project.

I often experiment with combining shapes to create more complex designs. By layering different shapes and adjusting their sizes and orientations, I can achieve a dynamic composition that draws the viewer's attention. For instance, I might overlay circular shapes in varying sizes to create an abstract background pattern, adding a sense of movement and texture. This layering technique can produce a visually rich environment that invites exploration and enhances the storytelling aspect of my designs.

Lines are another powerful design element that I utilize frequently. They serve multiple purposes, from creating divisions between sections to leading the viewer's eye through the layout. For instance, I might use horizontal lines to separate content blocks in a brochure, providing a clear visual structure that guides the reader through the information. Vertical lines can create a sense of height and elegance, often used effectively in invitations or elegant flyers. I also explore the use of dashed or dotted lines to add a playful touch, which can be particularly effective in designs aimed at younger audiences or creative themes.

In addition to their structural capabilities, lines can also convey movement and energy. I might incorporate diagonal lines to create a sense of dynamism in a design. For example, in a promotional poster for a sports event, using slanted lines can evoke a feeling of speed and excitement. This intentional use of lines helps to establish a mood that aligns with the content, further engaging the audience.

Frames are an additional design element that I find invaluable in my creative process. They can be used to contain images, add structure to layouts, or create a focal point within the design. When I use frames, I often choose ones that complement the overall aesthetic; for instance, a clean, modern frame can enhance a minimalist design, while an ornate frame might be suited for a vintage-themed project. Canva offers various frame styles, allowing me to experiment with how images are presented and how they interact with other elements in the layout.

One of the key advantages of using frames is that they allow for easy integration of images into my designs. By dragging and dropping images into frames, I can achieve a polished and professional look without needing extensive editing skills. I find that this functionality streamlines my workflow, enabling me to focus on the creative aspects of design rather than getting bogged down in technical details.

When I combine these design elements—shapes, lines, and frames—I am able to craft unique layouts that capture the viewer's attention and convey the intended message effectively. I often think of these elements as part of a visual language that communicates ideas and emotions. By considering the interplay between different elements, I can create compositions that are not only aesthetically pleasing but also meaningful.

As I work with these design components, I am constantly reminded of the importance of applying design principles such as balance, contrast, and alignment. Balance is crucial in creating a harmonious layout; whether through symmetrical arrangements or asymmetrical designs that feel visually stable, achieving balance ensures that the viewer's eye moves comfortably through the composition. I often experiment with different placements of shapes and lines, adjusting their sizes and orientations until I find a balance that feels right.

Contrast also plays a pivotal role in my design process. By juxtaposing elements with varying colors, sizes, and shapes, I can draw attention to key messages or create visual interest. For instance, I might use a bright, bold shape against a muted background to highlight important information or calls to action. This contrast not only makes the design more engaging but also ensures that critical content is easily noticed and understood.

Alignment is another principle that I prioritize in my designs.

Proper alignment of elements creates a sense of order and professionalism. I often use Canva's alignment tools to ensure that shapes, text, and images are positioned correctly, creating a cohesive look. Whether aligning elements to the left, right, or center, I am intentional about how these decisions affect the overall composition and clarity of the design.

Throughout this exploration of design elements, I also value the iterative nature of the creative process. I frequently revisit and revise my designs, experimenting with different combinations of shapes, lines, and frames until I achieve the desired effect. This willingness to iterate not only enhances the quality of my work but also fosters a deeper understanding of how each element contributes to the whole. By engaging in this process, I can uncover new possibilities and approaches that may not have been apparent at the outset.

As I continue to refine my skills in utilizing Canva's design elements, I am excited about the potential for creating visually stunning and impactful designs. The combination of shapes, lines, and frames, when used thoughtfully, can elevate my projects to new heights, enabling me to communicate messages effectively and engage audiences in meaningful ways. This exploration enriches my design practice, encouraging me to push the boundaries of creativity and explore new techniques that enhance my overall design capabilities.

As I continue to explore the capabilities of design elements within Canva, I find myself increasingly fascinated by how they can be utilized to create a sense of movement and flow within a composition. Movement in design refers to the way the viewer's eye is guided through the layout, and it can significantly impact the viewer's experience and understanding of the content. By strategically employing shapes, lines, and frames, I can create designs that not only capture attention but also maintain engagement.

One of the most effective ways to instill movement in a design is through the use of directional lines. These lines can guide the viewer's eye along a specific path, helping to emphasize key points or lead them toward a call to action. I often incorporate lines that converge towards important information, such as a product feature or a promotional offer. For instance, if I'm creating a marketing flyer, I might use diagonal lines that point toward the product image, effectively drawing attention to it and encouraging the viewer to explore further. By considering the direction of these lines, I can create a visual hierarchy that enhances the clarity of the design.

In addition to lines, the arrangement of shapes can also contribute to a sense of movement. I often utilize overlapping shapes to create a dynamic composition. By positioning shapes at different angles or layering them in a way that suggests depth, I can produce a design that feels alive and engaging. For example, when designing an event poster, I might place circular shapes in various sizes and orientations around the central text, creating an energetic layout that invites the viewer to explore all areas of the design. This technique not only adds visual interest but also reinforces the overall theme, making the design more cohesive.

Frames, too, can be manipulated to enhance movement. By choosing frames with unique shapes or arrangements, I can create a visual pathway that guides the viewer's eye across the layout. For instance, I might use a series of rectangular frames arranged in a zigzag pattern, allowing images or text to flow from one frame to the next. This not only encourages exploration of the content but also creates a rhythm within the design. Canva's versatility in allowing me to customize frame sizes and orientations further enhances my ability to experiment with movement in my compositions.

While creating a sense of movement is essential, I also pay

close attention to the balance of the design. Effective design is about harmony, and I strive to ensure that the elements work together cohesively. As I layer shapes and images, I regularly assess whether the arrangement feels visually balanced. This often involves adjusting the sizes of shapes or repositioning elements to maintain equilibrium. For instance, if one side of the design feels too heavy due to a large image, I might add a smaller shape or text element to the opposite side to create a counterbalance. By prioritizing balance, I can enhance the overall professionalism of my designs.

As I delve deeper into the creative possibilities offered by Canva's design elements, I become increasingly aware of the importance of color in enhancing my layouts. Color can evoke emotions, convey meaning, and add depth to designs. I often experiment with color schemes to find the right combinations that align with the message I want to communicate. For instance, using warm colors like reds and oranges can create feelings of excitement and urgency, while cooler colors such as blues and greens can evoke calmness and trust. When applying color to shapes and frames, I ensure that my choices complement the overall design, reinforcing the intended mood and theme.

I also recognize the impact of contrasting colors in drawing attention to key elements within my design. By utilizing contrasting colors, I can make important information stand out, guiding the viewer's eye toward the focal points. For example, if I have a dark background, I might use bright, light-colored shapes or text to ensure visibility and create a striking visual effect. This technique is particularly effective when creating call-to-action buttons or highlighted messages, where I want to ensure that the viewer cannot miss critical information.

Incorporating texture into my designs further enhances visual interest and depth. Texture can provide a tactile quality that engages viewers on a different level. I often experiment with textured backgrounds, such as subtle patterns or gradients, to add richness to my compositions. For instance, using a textured paper background can lend an organic feel to a design, making it appear more inviting and relatable. Canva's library includes various textures that I can easily apply to shapes or backgrounds, allowing me to enhance my designs without extensive graphic design experience.

As I integrate these design elements, I remain focused on the principles of unity and consistency. A successful design should feel cohesive, with each element working together to support the overall message. I strive to maintain a consistent style throughout my projects, whether it's through the use of similar colors, shapes, or typography. This consistency reinforces brand identity and enhances recognition, making the design more effective in communicating its purpose. When creating a series of promotional materials, for instance, I ensure that the visual elements align across all pieces, creating a unified brand presence.

Throughout my design process, I embrace the iterative nature of creativity. Each project is an opportunity to experiment with different combinations of elements and techniques. I find that stepping back to evaluate my work allows me to see what's working and what might need adjustment. I often share my designs with peers to gather feedback, as their perspectives can offer valuable insights that refine my approach. This collaborative spirit not only enriches my work but also fosters a sense of community among fellow designers, enhancing my growth and understanding of effective design practices.

As I continue to navigate the possibilities offered by Canva's design elements, I am excited about the potential for crafting unique and impactful designs. By mastering the use of shapes, lines, frames, and color, I can create layouts that resonate with viewers and effectively communicate messages. This journey into the realm of advanced design techniques empowers me to push the boundaries of creativity and elevate my skills as a designer, ready to embrace new challenges and explore innovative solutions in my projects.

As I delve deeper into the utilization of design elements within Canva, I find that combining shapes, lines, and frames in innovative ways can yield unexpected and exciting results. One of the key strategies I employ is to create a layered composition that invites the viewer to explore the design. Layering elements thoughtfully allows me to guide the viewer's eye, creating a sense of depth that adds interest to otherwise flat designs.

To begin with, I experiment with overlapping shapes to create a dynamic background. For instance, when designing a newsletter, I might use various geometric shapes in different colors, overlapping them to form a vibrant collage. By adjusting the opacity of each shape, I can achieve a harmonious blend that makes the background visually appealing while ensuring that the text remains legible. This technique not only adds visual interest but also establishes a unique identity for the newsletter, setting it apart from more conventional layouts.

In conjunction with layering, I often explore the use of lines as structural elements in my designs. Lines can help to delineate different sections, providing a visual framework that guides the viewer's eye from one element to the next. When creating an infographic, for example, I might use horizontal lines to separate distinct categories of information, ensuring clarity and organization. I also play with the thickness and style of the lines; thicker lines can denote significance, while dashed or dotted lines may introduce a playful element to the design. This versatility allows me to tailor the design to the intended message, whether I aim for a formal presentation or a more casual vibe.

Framing is another powerful technique I incorporate to enhance my designs. Frames not only contain elements but also draw attention to them, providing a focal point that can enhance storytelling within the composition. When designing a social media post, I might use a frame to highlight a key image, creating a visually striking contrast with the surrounding elements. By experimenting with the shapes and styles of frames, I can create borders that either blend seamlessly with the design or stand out as decorative features. For instance, a rounded frame might evoke a softer, more inviting feel, while a sharp-edged frame could lend a modern and sleek appearance.

As I continue to refine my approach, I recognize the importance of color in unifying the various design elements. A well-chosen color palette can create a cohesive look and evoke specific emotions. I often draw inspiration from nature, art, or brand guidelines to establish a color scheme that resonates with the message I want to convey. For example, warm colors such as reds and oranges can evoke feelings of excitement and passion, while cooler tones like blues and greens can create a sense of calm and tranquility. In Canva, I can easily test different color combinations, allowing me to see how they interact with the shapes, lines, and frames within the design.

When layering elements, I also pay careful attention to the contrast between colors and shapes. High contrast can enhance legibility and draw attention to key messages, while low contrast can create a more subtle and sophisticated feel. For example, if I am using a dark background, I will opt for lighter colors for my text and shapes to ensure they stand out effectively. Conversely, when working with a lighter background, I may choose darker colors for contrast. This attention to detail helps me create designs that are not only aesthetically pleasing but also functional and easy to navigate.

I find that applying the principles of design—such as balance, alignment, and repetition—plays a critical role in achieving a polished look. Balance can be achieved through symmetrical arrangements or asymmetrical designs that feel visually stable. As I layer shapes and lines, I often evaluate the distribution of visual weight across the composition, making adjustments as needed to ensure a harmonious balance. Alignment is equally important; I utilize Canva's alignment tools to ensure that elements are properly positioned, enhancing the overall professionalism of the design.

Repetition of elements—whether through the use of consistent shapes, colors, or fonts—creates a unified visual identity that reinforces brand recognition. I often develop a style guide for each project, outlining key elements that should be repeated throughout the design. This approach not only ensures consistency but also makes it easier for viewers to navigate the information. When creating a series of marketing materials, for instance, I use the same color palette and fonts across all pieces to establish a cohesive brand presence.

As I finalize my designs, I place great importance on reviewing each element to ensure that they all work harmoniously together. This process involves scrutinizing the relationships between shapes, lines, and frames to confirm that they contribute positively to the overall composition. I frequently step back from my work to evaluate the design from a distance, allowing me to assess the visual impact and identify any areas that may require adjustment.

Another valuable aspect of utilizing Canva's design elements is the opportunity for experimentation. I view each project as a chance to push the boundaries of my creativity. By playing with different combinations of shapes, lines, and frames, I often stumble upon unexpected results that can inspire new ideas. This willingness to experiment fosters a spirit of innovation that enhances my design practice and encourages me to explore new techniques and styles.

As I continue to engage with Canva's design elements, I am constantly reminded of the significance of storytelling in visual communication. Each element serves a purpose in conveying the intended message, and I strive to ensure that my designs tell a cohesive story. Whether creating a presentation, flyer, or social media post, I aim to create a narrative that resonates with the audience, inviting them to engage with the content on a deeper level. The interplay of shapes, lines, and frames not only supports this storytelling but also enhances the emotional impact of the design.

In conclusion, my exploration of Canva's design elements has equipped me with a robust set of tools to create visually engaging and professional compositions. By mastering the use of shapes, lines, and frames, I can craft unique layouts that effectively communicate messages and engage viewers. This journey into the realm of advanced design techniques has enriched my understanding of visual communication, empowering me to connect with audiences in meaningful ways. As I continue to refine my skills and embrace new challenges, I am excited about the endless possibilities that await in the world of design.

CHAPTER 14: CREATING INFOGRAPHICS AND DATA VISUALIZATIONS

As I delve into the creation of infographics and data visualizations, I quickly recognize their unique ability to distill complex information into easily digestible and visually appealing formats. Infographics serve as a bridge between data and understanding, transforming numbers, statistics, and textual information into compelling visual narratives. The art of crafting these visualizations lies not only in the aesthetics but also in the clarity of the information presented.

In Canva, I begin by exploring the various templates specifically designed for infographics. These templates provide a foundational structure that helps me organize information logically while also offering a visually engaging layout. I often choose a template that aligns with the theme of the data I am presenting, whether it be corporate statistics, educational content, or health-related information. The right template can set the tone for the entire infographic and guide my choices regarding colors, fonts, and visual elements.

As I work with the template, I focus on the hierarchy of

information. This involves identifying the key points I want to communicate and determining how best to present them visually. I prioritize the most important data, ensuring that it is easily identifiable and immediately engaging. For instance, I may use larger font sizes or bold text to highlight critical statistics or findings. I also consider how to group related information, using visual separators such as lines or shapes to create distinct sections within the infographic. This structure allows the viewer to navigate the content intuitively, leading them through the narrative I am constructing.

Incorporating charts and graphs into my infographics is a crucial step in visualizing data effectively. These elements provide a clear representation of numerical information, making trends and comparisons immediately apparent. Canva offers various chart types, including bar charts, line graphs, and pie charts, each of which serves a different purpose depending on the data being presented. For example, when displaying changes over time, I often opt for a line graph, as it effectively illustrates trends and fluctuations in the data. Conversely, for showcasing proportions or percentages, pie charts can be particularly effective.

When integrating charts and graphs, I ensure that they are not only visually appealing but also informative. I carefully select colors that are consistent with the overall color palette of the infographic, maintaining a cohesive look. Additionally, I always include clear labels and legends to enhance understanding. Data visualization should aim to eliminate confusion, and well-labeled charts ensure that viewers can grasp the information at a glance. I often find myself iterating on these elements, adjusting colors and layouts until I achieve a balance that feels both informative and engaging.

Icons and graphics play a pivotal role in enhancing the visual appeal of my infographics. These elements can serve as visual shorthand for complex concepts, making the information

Feedback plays a crucial role in my design process. After completing an infographic, I often share it with colleagues or peers for their input. This collaborative approach provides me with fresh perspectives and constructive criticism that can help refine the final product. I value the insights that others bring, as they often notice details that I may have overlooked during the design process. This feedback loop fosters a culture of continuous improvement, enabling me to elevate my work and enhance my skills as a designer.

I also take time to analyze the performance of my infographics once they are published or shared. If the infographic is intended for digital platforms, I monitor engagement metrics such as shares, comments, and click-through rates. This data helps me gauge the effectiveness of my design choices and informs my future projects. Understanding which elements resonated with the audience allows me to make data-driven decisions that enhance my design practice.

The process of creating infographics and data visualizations has not only expanded my technical skills but has also deepened my appreciation for the art of visual communication. By effectively combining text, imagery, and data, I can craft compelling narratives that inform and engage viewers. This journey has reinforced the idea that design is not merely about aesthetics; it is about conveying information in a way that is both engaging and accessible. As I continue to refine my craft and explore new techniques, I look forward to the opportunities that lie ahead in the realm of infographics and data visualization, eager to share meaningful stories through compelling design.

As I continue my exploration of creating compelling infographics and data visualizations, I delve into the intricate balance of aesthetics and functionality. Each design choice I make plays a crucial role in how the information is perceived, and I must navigate the line between engaging visuals and clear communication. I find that every element, from the choice of colors to the arrangement of text and graphics, contributes to the overall effectiveness of the infographic.

One of the most significant aspects of effective infographics is the careful selection of a cohesive color palette. The colors I choose not only serve to enhance the visual appeal but also convey specific emotions and themes. For example, using vibrant colors such as reds and yellows can evoke feelings of excitement and urgency, which might be appropriate for marketing materials. In contrast, softer blues and greens can create a calming effect, making them ideal for health and wellness topics. I often begin my design process by selecting a color scheme that aligns with the subject matter, utilizing tools like Canva's color wheel to identify complementary colors that will enhance the visual hierarchy.

In addition to color, typography plays a pivotal role in how the information is communicated within the infographic. I carefully select fonts that reflect the tone of the content, ensuring they are both legible and aesthetically pleasing. For instance, I prefer sans-serif fonts for their modern and clean appearance, especially in data-heavy sections where clarity is paramount. However, for headings and key points, I may choose a bolder or more decorative font to draw attention and create visual contrast. It is crucial to maintain consistency in font choices throughout the infographic, as this contributes to a cohesive look and reinforces the visual identity of the design.

As I integrate charts, graphs, and icons into my infographics, I focus on ensuring that each element serves a clear purpose. Each chart must not only present data accurately but also do so in a way that is easy for viewers to understand at a glance. I often opt for bar graphs when comparing quantities, line graphs for trends over time, and pie charts for illustrating proportions. By carefully labeling each chart and providing context, I ensure that viewers can quickly grasp the significance of the data presented.

Incorporating icons is another effective strategy for enhancing visual communication. Icons serve as visual metaphors that can convey complex concepts succinctly. For instance, when discussing environmental statistics, I might use an icon of a tree to represent forestry data or a water droplet to symbolize water conservation efforts. This use of familiar symbols aids in immediate recognition, allowing the viewer to connect with the information on a deeper level. In Canva, I find a vast library of icons that I can customize in terms of color and size, ensuring they align perfectly with my overall design.

As I assemble my infographics, I am keenly aware of the importance of whitespace. Often underestimated, whitespace serves as a visual breathing room that prevents the design from feeling cluttered. By incorporating adequate spacing between elements, I create a layout that feels balanced and organized. This clarity is vital, especially when presenting complex data. Whitespace allows key points to stand out, guiding the viewer's eye naturally through the information without causing confusion. I often adjust the margins and padding of elements to achieve the desired level of clarity and openness in the design.

Feedback is an integral part of my design process, and I value the insights of others when refining my infographics. After completing a draft, I often share it with colleagues or mentors to gather their perspectives. This collaborative approach provides me with fresh eyes that can identify areas of improvement that I may have overlooked. I ask for their thoughts on the clarity of the information presented, the effectiveness of the visuals, and whether the overall narrative flows well. This constructive criticism helps me make necessary adjustments to enhance the final product, ensuring that it effectively communicates the intended message.

I also recognize that the effectiveness of an infographic can be measured by its ability to engage and inform the audience. To evaluate this, I consider the context in which my infographic will be presented. If it's for a presentation, I anticipate the questions the audience may have and ensure that the design addresses those inquiries proactively. Conversely, if it's intended for social media, I focus on creating eye-catching elements that will encourage shares and interactions. Understanding the audience and the medium allows me to tailor my designs for maximum impact.

Once the infographic is complete, I take time to test it across various platforms to ensure that it maintains its visual integrity. This is particularly important for digital infographics, as elements may render differently depending on the device or screen size. I preview my designs on mobile devices, tablets, and desktops to ensure that all components are clear and effective regardless of where they are viewed. This thoroughness reflects my commitment to quality and attention to detail, reinforcing the professionalism of my work.

Creating infographics and data visualizations has not only improved my technical skills but has also deepened my understanding of visual storytelling. The process of transforming complex information into accessible visuals has taught me the importance of clarity and engagement in communication. Each infographic I design represents an opportunity to convey messages that resonate with viewers, encouraging them to reflect on the information presented.

As I continue to refine my approach to infographic design, I look forward to exploring new techniques and innovations that can enhance my work. The ability to visualize data effectively and create compelling narratives is a valuable skill in today's information-driven world. With each project, I am excited to push the boundaries of creativity, ready to embrace the challenges and opportunities that lie ahead in the realm of infographics and data visualization. This ongoing journey not only enriches my design practice but also equips me to share meaningful stories through the power of visual communication.

CHAPTER 15: DESIGNING FOR SOCIAL MEDIA

As I embark on the journey of designing for social media, I quickly realize that each platform presents its own unique set of requirements and best practices that must be considered. Social media is not just a channel for broadcasting information; it is a dynamic environment where visual content plays a crucial role in capturing attention and engaging audiences. Understanding the nuances of each platform allows me to tailor my designs effectively, ensuring that they not only fit the technical specifications but also resonate with the target audience.

When beginning a design project for social media, the first step is to familiarize myself with the specific dimensions and formats required by each platform. For instance, Instagram thrives on visually striking images and typically utilizes a square format for posts, while stories are best suited for vertical designs. Facebook, on the other hand, supports a variety of formats, from shared images and videos to cover photos and event banners. Twitter focuses on horizontal images for tweets but also requires attention to the overall aesthetic of the profile page, including header images. LinkedIn emphasizes professionalism, necessitating designs that align with corporate branding and networking norms.

With this understanding, I often start by creating templates for each platform in Canva. By setting the correct dimensions from the outset, I can ensure that my designs will display correctly without requiring significant adjustments later. This initial step saves me time and frustration, allowing me to focus on the creative aspects of the design. Each template serves as a foundation on which I can build tailored graphics that meet the specific demands of each social media platform.

As I work on the design itself, I pay careful attention to the branding elements that need to be consistent across all platforms. Brand identity is crucial in social media, where users are bombarded with visual content. Maintaining consistency in colors, fonts, and logo placement reinforces brand recognition and helps establish a cohesive presence across different channels. I often create a brand guide that outlines these elements, ensuring that I adhere to them in every design. This not only strengthens brand identity but also fosters trust and familiarity with the audience.

When designing for social media, the importance of visual hierarchy cannot be overstated. I must consider how to arrange elements within the graphic to draw attention to the most critical information. For example, when creating an announcement for a product launch, I might use larger fonts for the product name and a contrasting color to make it stand out against the background. Subtext can be smaller and in a more subdued color, guiding the viewer through the information in a logical order. By effectively utilizing visual hierarchy, I can create designs that communicate messages clearly and effectively, even in a fast-scrolling environment.

In addition to layout and hierarchy, I also consider the use of imagery in my social media designs. High-quality images are essential for capturing attention and enhancing engagement. When selecting images, I often choose visuals that are not only relevant to the content but also evoke the desired emotions. For instance, if I am promoting a wellness program,

I might opt for images that depict serene landscapes or people engaging in healthy activities. This alignment between imagery and content helps reinforce the message and creates a more compelling visual narrative.

Furthermore, incorporating text into social media graphics requires careful consideration. Text should be concise and impactful, as viewers may only glance at the graphic for a few seconds. I often use catchy headlines or taglines that encapsulate the message while ensuring they are easy to read. This is where the choice of typography comes into play; I prefer bold, legible fonts that can stand out against the background. Additionally, I utilize contrast effectively to ensure that text is readable, avoiding overly complex fonts that may be difficult to decipher, especially on smaller screens.

Another crucial element of social media design is adaptability. Given the diverse range of devices on which users access social media, I must ensure that my graphics are optimized for both desktop and mobile viewing. This involves testing how designs appear across different screen sizes and making adjustments as necessary. For instance, I might simplify a design for mobile viewing by reducing the amount of text or streamlining the visual elements. Canva's preview feature allows me to see how my designs will look on various devices, which is invaluable in ensuring a consistent user experience.

As I refine my social media graphics, I also consider the call to action (CTA). Every graphic should encourage some form of engagement, whether that be visiting a website, signing up for a newsletter, or sharing the content. I often incorporate clear and compelling CTAs, using buttons or highlighted text to draw attention. The placement of these CTAs is strategic; I generally position them toward the bottom of the graphic or in a prominent location where they naturally follow the flow of information. This positioning ensures that the audience knows exactly what action to take after viewing the content.

Finally, I continually seek feedback on my designs, understanding that fresh perspectives can provide insights that I may have missed. I share my social media graphics with colleagues or peers, asking for their thoughts on clarity, engagement, and visual appeal. This collaborative approach not only enhances the quality of my work but also fosters an environment of learning and growth within my design practice. Constructive criticism helps me refine my skills and encourages me to push the boundaries of creativity in my designs.

In conclusion, designing for social media requires a careful blend of creativity, technical skill, and strategic thinking. By understanding the unique requirements of each platform, maintaining brand consistency, and employing effective design principles, I can create compelling graphics that resonate with audiences. The journey into social media design has not only expanded my technical abilities but has also deepened my appreciation for the power of visual communication. As I continue to develop my skills and adapt to the ever-changing landscape of social media, I look forward to creating impactful designs that engage and inspire.

As I dive deeper into the intricacies of designing for social media, I recognize that understanding audience behavior is essential to crafting effective graphics. Each platform attracts different demographics, and tailoring my designs to resonate with these audiences can significantly enhance engagement. For instance, Instagram is heavily visual and popular among younger audiences, making vibrant and eye-catching designs essential. In contrast, LinkedIn caters to professionals, where the emphasis is often on clean, polished graphics that convey credibility and expertise. This distinction influences not only the design elements I choose but also the tone and style of the content.

In approaching platforms like Instagram, I am mindful of

the importance of the first impression. A scroll-stopping graphic must not only attract attention but also convey the message quickly. I often employ bold visuals and dynamic compositions to capture the viewer's eye. Using high-quality images and striking colors helps ensure that the design stands out in a crowded feed. I also take advantage of Instagram Stories, where I create engaging, temporary content that utilizes a combination of animations, text overlays, and interactive elements, such as polls or questions, to foster viewer engagement. These elements not only make the content more interactive but also encourage audience participation, which can significantly increase visibility and reach.

Moving to Facebook, I consider the platform's diverse functionalities and the types of content that perform well. Facebook supports a variety of formats, including shared images, videos, and carousel posts. This versatility allows me to experiment with different layouts and designs. For a carousel post, I might create a series of graphics that tell a story or present a sequential argument. Each graphic is designed to stand alone while also fitting cohesively into the overall narrative. I ensure that there is a consistent visual style throughout, using similar colors, fonts, and imagery, to enhance brand recognition and maintain a professional look.

In terms of technical specifications, I ensure that my images are optimized for each platform's requirements. Facebook allows for higher resolution images, so I often design graphics at a larger size to ensure clarity when viewed on various devices. Additionally, I take advantage of the cover photo feature by creating a visually striking header that encapsulates the essence of the brand. I often include essential information, such as a tagline or call to action, directly in the cover photo, ensuring that it is instantly recognizable.

Twitter presents unique challenges and opportunities as a

fast-paced platform where brevity is key. I focus on creating graphics that are clear and to the point, given that users often scroll quickly through their feeds. I usually design for Twitter using concise messaging, opting for sharp, bold visuals that convey the intended message at a glance. The use of vibrant colors and bold typography helps draw attention amidst the noise of constant updates. I also utilize Twitter's image preview feature, ensuring that important details are visible even before the post is clicked on.

When designing for LinkedIn, my approach shifts to align with the platform's professional ethos. I prioritize clean, sophisticated designs that convey authority and trustworthiness. The graphics I create for LinkedIn often reflect industry standards and the professional branding of the company or individual. I frequently use a limited color palette, incorporating shades that reflect the brand's identity while maintaining a polished appearance. Infographics and data visualizations perform well on this platform, as they can effectively summarize complex information in a visually appealing way that is relevant to professionals.

Maintaining brand consistency across all social media platforms is paramount to ensuring a cohesive identity. I often create a style guide that outlines the specific colors, fonts, and graphic styles that represent the brand. This guide serves as a reference to maintain consistency, regardless of the platform or the specific project at hand. Consistent branding builds familiarity and trust with the audience, making them more likely to engage with the content and recognize the brand in various contexts.

As I refine my designs, I also embrace the importance of analytics in evaluating their effectiveness. After publishing graphics on social media, I monitor engagement metrics, such as likes, shares, and comments, to assess which designs resonate most with the audience. This data provides valuable insights that inform future projects, helping me understand what works and what needs improvement. For instance, if I notice that posts featuring certain colors or styles generate higher engagement, I may incorporate those elements more frequently in my designs.

Another key aspect of designing for social media is adaptability. Social media is constantly evolving, with new features and trends emerging regularly. I stay informed about these changes and trends, adapting my designs to fit the latest practices. For example, the rise of video content on social media has prompted me to incorporate animated graphics or short video snippets into my posts. By being adaptable and responsive to these trends, I can keep my content fresh and relevant, ensuring that it captures attention in an ever-changing landscape.

As I reflect on the process of designing for social media, I find that it is a blend of creativity, strategy, and adaptability. Each platform requires a tailored approach that considers audience preferences, technical specifications, and branding. By leveraging Canva's powerful tools and templates, I can create engaging graphics that effectively communicate messages and build connections with viewers. This exploration into social media design has not only enhanced my technical skills but has also deepened my understanding of visual communication in a digital age. I look forward to continuing this journey, eager to discover new ways to engage audiences and tell compelling stories through design.

As I further refine my approach to designing for social media, I find that engaging with the audience extends beyond merely creating visually appealing graphics. It involves understanding the context in which these graphics are consumed and leveraging social media's interactive features to foster connection and conversation. This realization shapes the way I conceptualize my designs, making me consider how to invite user engagement right from the outset.

One of the key strategies I employ is incorporating interactive elements into my designs, particularly on platforms like Instagram and Facebook, where user engagement is highly encouraged. For example, I create eye-catching graphics that include prompts for the audience, such as "Share your thoughts in the comments!" or "Tag a friend who needs to see this!" This call to action not only encourages engagement but also creates a community feel, making viewers feel like they are part of a conversation rather than passive observers. Designing with this interactive mindset allows me to craft content that invites participation, which is essential in building a loyal audience.

Moreover, the use of hashtags is another element that plays a crucial role in increasing the visibility of my social media graphics. I carefully select relevant hashtags that align with the content and the target audience. These hashtags not only categorize the content but also increase its reach by making it discoverable to users interested in specific topics. When designing graphics, I often include hashtags in a visually appealing way, perhaps by integrating them into the design without cluttering the overall layout. This attention to detail ensures that the hashtags enhance rather than detract from the primary message of the graphic.

As I navigate the specific requirements of each platform, I also pay close attention to timing and frequency of posts. Each social media platform has its own optimal posting times based on user activity patterns. I conduct research to identify when my target audience is most active and schedule my posts accordingly. For instance, I have found that Instagram engagement peaks during weekends and early evenings, while LinkedIn tends to see higher activity during weekdays, especially in the morning. This understanding informs my planning process and helps ensure that my graphics reach the audience when they are most likely to engage with them.

I also recognize the significance of storytelling in social media design. Each graphic should tell a story that resonates with the audience on a personal level. When creating a series of posts for a campaign, I often develop a narrative arc that progresses over multiple images. This might involve a sequence that begins with an introductory post, followed by posts that build on the theme, culminating in a final call to action. By constructing this narrative, I can keep the audience engaged over time, encouraging them to follow along and interact with each new installment. This technique not only enhances engagement but also builds anticipation and excitement around the campaign.

Incorporating user-generated content into my social media designs is another effective strategy. By encouraging followers to share their experiences or interpretations related to my brand, I can create a sense of community and authenticity. I often design graphics that highlight user submissions, showcasing their creativity while reinforcing the message of the campaign. This not only fosters a sense of inclusivity but also generates fresh content that resonates with the audience. Canva's templates allow me to easily incorporate these user-generated visuals into my branded posts, maintaining consistency while celebrating the contributions of my community.

Furthermore, analytics play a pivotal role in shaping my ongoing strategy. After posting graphics on social media, I closely monitor engagement metrics to assess the performance of each design. This data provides insights into what types of visuals resonate most with the audience. For instance, if I notice that posts featuring certain colors or styles generate higher engagement, I take note and consider integrating those elements into future designs. Analyzing audience interactions helps me fine-tune my approach, allowing me to craft more effective content over time.

I also prioritize mobile optimization in my designs, as a significant portion of social media users access platforms through their smartphones. This requires me to consider how my graphics will appear on smaller screens. I ensure that text is legible and that important elements are not lost in the transition from desktop to mobile. Testing my designs across various devices allows me to confirm that they maintain their visual integrity and effectiveness, regardless of how they are viewed.

In the realm of social media, staying updated on current trends and emerging formats is crucial. Social media platforms continuously evolve, introducing new features and content formats that can enhance engagement. I make it a point to stay informed about these developments, adapting my designs to leverage new opportunities. For example, the increasing popularity of short-form video content on platforms like TikTok and Instagram Reels has prompted me to explore ways to incorporate animated elements or dynamic storytelling into my graphics, ensuring that my content remains fresh and relevant.

As I continue to engage with the ever-changing landscape of social media design, I find that flexibility and adaptability are essential traits for success. The ability to pivot and experiment with new ideas is critical in maintaining audience interest and relevance. I remain open to exploring different design styles, formats, and approaches, continuously seeking inspiration from other creators and industry trends. This creative exploration fuels my passion for design and enhances my ability to connect with audiences in meaningful ways.

The journey of designing for social media has profoundly impacted my understanding of visual communication. It has taught me that effective design is not solely about aesthetics but is also about connecting with the audience and conveying messages that resonate. By leveraging the unique features of each platform and employing strategic design principles, I can create impactful graphics that capture attention, engage viewers, and foster community. This ongoing exploration inspires me to innovate and experiment, driving my growth as a designer and storyteller in the vibrant world of social media.

CHAPTER 16: CUSTOMIZING CANVA TEMPLATES

As I begin to explore the art of customizing Canva templates, I am immediately struck by the balance between utilizing a ready-made design and infusing my own unique vision into the project. Templates serve as valuable foundations, providing a structured starting point that can significantly reduce the time and effort required to create professional graphics. However, the true power of these templates lies in their adaptability; they are a canvas that invites creativity and personal expression. To fully realize this potential, I delve into advanced customization techniques that transform standard templates into distinctive designs that resonate with my brand and message.

The first step in the customization process involves thoroughly understanding the template's layout. Each template is designed with a specific arrangement of elements, which often includes predefined sections for images, text, and graphics. As I evaluate the layout, I consider how it aligns with the content I intend to present. If the existing arrangement does not suit my needs, I explore ways to modify it without losing the overall coherence of the design. This might involve shifting elements, resizing sections, or even removing unnecessary components. For instance, if I find that a template has too many text boxes for my message, I can consolidate the information into fewer sections, creating a cleaner and more impactful presentation.

Once I have adjusted the layout to my satisfaction, I turn my attention to the color scheme. The colors I choose play a critical role in conveying the mood and tone of the design. Canva provides a range of color palettes, but I often prefer to customize the colors to ensure they align with my brand identity. I may reference my brand guide, which outlines the specific colors associated with my brand, to maintain consistency across all my materials. By incorporating these brand colors into the template, I create a cohesive look that reinforces my identity and helps the audience immediately recognize the content as part of my brand.

In adjusting the color scheme, I also consider the psychological effects of colors. Different colors evoke different emotions and responses, and I am intentional about selecting hues that support the message I want to convey. For instance, if I am creating a promotional graphic for a wellness program, I may choose soft greens and blues to evoke feelings of calmness and health. Conversely, for a campaign aimed at boosting sales, I might select vibrant reds or yellows to instill a sense of urgency and excitement. This thoughtful approach to color enhances the overall effectiveness of the design, ensuring that it resonates with the target audience.

The next layer of customization involves integrating custom elements that further personalize the design. While Canva offers a wealth of built-in images, icons, and graphics, I often seek to incorporate unique elements that reflect my style or the specific content of the project. This might include uploading original graphics, custom illustrations, or even photographs that I have taken. By incorporating these personalized touches, I create designs that stand out and reflect my individuality. I appreciate that Canva's user-friendly interface allows me to seamlessly upload and position these elements within the template, ensuring they complement the existing design rather than disrupt it.

In addition to integrating custom visuals, I often experiment with the typography in the template. The choice of font can dramatically affect the tone of the design. I consider the readability and style of the typefaces used in the template, making adjustments as needed to align with my brand's voice. For example, if the template uses a playful font that does not resonate with my professional brand, I may switch to a more formal serif or sans-serif font. I also ensure that the hierarchy of text is clear; headings should be distinguishable from body text, allowing viewers to navigate the information easily. By applying consistent font choices across the design, I enhance the overall professionalism of the piece.

As I customize the template, I am mindful of the principle of visual balance. It is essential to create a harmonious composition where no single element overwhelms the others. This involves assessing the visual weight of various components and making adjustments to ensure that the design feels cohesive. If one side of the graphic feels heavier due to an oversized image, I might balance it by adjusting the placement of text or adding smaller visual elements on the opposite side. This attention to balance helps me achieve a polished and professional look, making the infographic or graphic more effective in conveying its message.

In the process of customization, I also leverage Canva's grouping and alignment tools. These features streamline my workflow and ensure that elements are positioned accurately. By grouping related elements together, I can move them as a single unit, which is particularly useful when adjusting layouts. Alignment tools help me maintain a structured look, ensuring that elements line up neatly and enhancing the overall visual appeal. I find that these tools significantly reduce the time I spend fine-tuning the layout, allowing me to focus on the creative aspects of the design.

As I finalize my customized template, I take a step back to evaluate the design in its entirety. I review it from the perspective of the target audience, asking myself whether the design effectively communicates the intended message and engages viewers. This self-assessment often reveals areas for improvement that I may have overlooked during the customization process. I may also seek feedback from peers or mentors, as their insights can provide valuable perspectives that enhance the final product.

Ultimately, the process of customizing Canva templates empowers me to transform standard designs into unique representations of my vision and brand. By skillfully modifying layouts, adjusting color schemes, and integrating custom elements, I can create compelling graphics that resonate with audiences and convey meaningful messages. This journey into the realm of advanced customization enhances my design capabilities and deepens my understanding of visual communication, equipping me with the skills to produce impactful and professional designs that stand out in a crowded digital landscape. As I continue to explore and refine my approach, I look forward to uncovering new techniques and insights that will further enrich my design practice.

As I continue to refine my approach to customizing Canva templates, I recognize that the journey is about exploring the full potential of the design tools at my disposal. One of the essential aspects of customization is the manipulation of template layouts to better fit the specific content I am working with. While a pre-designed layout may offer a solid foundation, it is crucial to adapt it in a way that enhances the message and engages the audience effectively.

When I first analyze a template, I look for opportunities to modify its layout to suit the unique demands of my content. I consider the information hierarchy and how best to guide the viewer's eye through the design. For instance, if a template features several sections that feel cramped, I might redistribute the elements to create a more spacious and inviting layout. This could involve moving text blocks to different areas of the canvas, resizing images, or even introducing additional whitespace to enhance readability. By thoughtfully restructuring the layout, I ensure that the most important information is prominently displayed and that the overall design feels balanced and cohesive.

In the process of modifying layouts, I often take advantage of Canva's grid and alignment tools. These features are invaluable for ensuring that elements are positioned accurately and consistently. I can create a grid system that provides a visual structure for my design, allowing me to align text and images seamlessly. This precision not only enhances the aesthetics of the graphic but also reinforces a sense of professionalism. I frequently use the alignment guides that appear as I move elements around, which helps maintain uniform spacing and ensures that my design adheres to established visual standards.

Another critical component of customization is adjusting the color scheme of the template. Color has a profound impact on visual communication, influencing mood, readability, and brand perception. When I modify a template's colors, I often start by selecting a palette that aligns with my brand identity or the message I want to convey. I make use of color theory principles, considering how different colors interact and what emotions they evoke. For instance, using warm colors can create a sense of energy and excitement, while cooler tones can evoke calmness and professionalism.

In Canva, I appreciate the ability to create and save custom color palettes, which streamlines the process of applying consistent colors across different elements. When customizing a template, I may adjust not just the background color but also the colors of individual shapes, text, and icons. This level of detail allows me to create a harmonious design that reflects my brand's visual identity. I often find that subtle adjustments, such as changing a text color to enhance contrast against a background, can make a significant difference in the overall effectiveness of the graphic.

As I customize a template, I also focus on integrating custom elements that reflect my unique style and enhance the message of the design. While Canva provides a rich library of stock images, icons, and illustrations, I find that incorporating original elements can elevate the design and set it apart. Whether it's using my own photography or custom illustrations, these personalized touches add authenticity and originality to the project. The process of uploading and integrating these custom elements is straightforward in Canva, allowing me to drag and drop my assets into the design seamlessly.

In addition to integrating custom visuals, I often experiment with textures and patterns to add depth and interest. By layering textures behind shapes or using patterns within specific design elements, I can create a multi-dimensional look that captures the viewer's attention. For example, if I am designing a promotional flyer for a creative event, I might use a textured background that conveys a sense of artistry while allowing the foreground elements to stand out clearly. This approach not only enhances visual appeal but also reinforces the thematic elements of the design.

Typography is another critical aspect of customization that I prioritize. The font choices I make can significantly influence the overall tone of the design. I assess the default fonts in the template and determine whether they align with my brand identity. If the template uses a font that feels too casual or too formal, I am not hesitant to make changes. I often mix and match fonts for different sections, using one font for headings and another for body text. This approach not only adds visual variety but also helps establish a clear hierarchy within the design.

As I refine my typography choices, I consider aspects such as kerning, line spacing, and text alignment. Small adjustments can dramatically improve the readability and overall aesthetic of the graphic. I often take the time to experiment with different configurations, ensuring that text is easy to read and visually pleasing. By aligning text to the left or center, I create a clean and organized appearance that enhances the design's professionalism.

Once I have made substantial modifications to the template, I take a step back to assess the design as a whole. This self-review process is essential for ensuring that all elements work harmoniously together. I evaluate whether the layout feels balanced, if the color scheme enhances the content, and whether the typography is legible and aligned with the brand's voice. This reflective practice often leads to additional tweaks, ensuring that the final design meets my standards of quality and effectiveness.

I also find it beneficial to seek feedback from peers or colleagues at this stage. Fresh perspectives can provide insights that I might not have considered, helping to identify areas for improvement. I share my customized designs with trusted individuals who can offer constructive criticism, asking them specific questions about clarity, visual appeal, and engagement. This collaborative feedback loop not only enhances the quality of my work but also fosters a culture of learning and growth within my design practice.

As I finalize the customized template, I prepare for its intended application, whether for print or digital use. This requires ensuring that the design is properly formatted and optimized for its specific purpose. For print materials, I double-check that the resolution meets the required standards to prevent pixelation or blurriness. For digital graphics, I optimize file sizes to ensure fast loading times without compromising quality. By attending to these technical details, I can deliver designs that not only look great but also function effectively across various platforms.

In conclusion, customizing Canva templates offers a rich opportunity for creative expression and professional branding. Through careful modification of layouts, strategic adjustments of color schemes, and the integration of custom elements, I can transform pre-designed templates into unique graphics that reflect my vision and brand identity. This journey into advanced customization techniques enhances my design skills and deepens my appreciation for the art of visual communication. As I continue to explore and refine my approach, I look forward to uncovering new techniques and insights that will further enrich my design practice.

As I dive further into the intricacies of customizing Canva templates, I begin to appreciate the subtleties that can transform a generic design into a personalized masterpiece. The process is not merely about altering existing elements; it is about infusing my vision and creativity into a framework that facilitates effective communication. Each decision I make, from layout adjustments to the integration of unique visuals, plays a crucial role in crafting a design that is not only functional but also resonates deeply with its intended audience.

One of the essential techniques I explore in this customization process is the strategic modification of layout components. While a template provides a solid structure, I often find that adapting it to better suit my content leads to a more impactful design. I start by analyzing the visual flow of the template, identifying areas where I can enhance or simplify the arrangement. For instance, if a template features multiple columns but my content is primarily text-based, I might choose to consolidate information into fewer sections. This approach not only reduces visual clutter but also improves readability, allowing the viewer to absorb the message more effortlessly.

In addition to simplifying layouts, I also experiment with the spatial relationships between elements. I take into account the balance of negative space, or whitespace, which can dramatically influence how a design is perceived. By thoughtfully placing elements, I can create an inviting and organized composition. For example, when working on a promotional poster, I might leave ample space around the main image to allow it to breathe, drawing attention without overwhelming the viewer. This practice reinforces the idea that less can often be more, allowing critical information to stand out.

The next area I focus on is the color scheme, which serves as a vital component of any design. The colors I select not only establish the mood but also enhance brand recognition. I make it a point to align the color palette with my brand identity or the specific emotional response I want to evoke in the viewer. Utilizing Canva's color tools, I explore various combinations, often referencing color theory principles to ensure that the colors I choose harmonize well. For instance, complementary colors can create a striking contrast that draws attention, while analogous colors provide a more serene and cohesive look.

As I adjust the color scheme, I am mindful of the psychological effects different colors can have on the audience. For example, warm colors like reds and oranges can evoke feelings of excitement and urgency, making them suitable for sales promotions. On the other hand, cooler colors like blues and greens often convey tranquility and trust, which can be ideal for brands in the health and wellness sectors. By deliberately choosing colors that align with the intended message, I enhance the overall effectiveness of the design.

Integrating custom elements into my designs further allows me to differentiate my work from standard templates. While Canva offers a vast library of images, icons, and graphics, I frequently upload my original visuals to add a personal touch. This might include custom illustrations, photos I've taken, or graphics designed in other software. The integration of these elements allows me to tell a more authentic story, reinforcing my brand's unique identity. Canva's user-friendly interface simplifies this process, enabling me to position and modify my uploaded assets seamlessly within the template.

I also take the opportunity to explore the use of textures and patterns in my designs. Adding a textured background can create depth and interest, breaking away from the flatness that some digital designs can exhibit. For example, using a subtle paper texture as a background for a flyer can give it a tactile quality that feels more engaging. Similarly, patterns can be utilized within certain elements to create visual variety without overwhelming the overall design. I often experiment with different textures in Canva, layering them behind shapes or images to create a sense of dimensionality.

Typography, too, is an area where I find significant opportunities for customization. The choice of font can dramatically influence the overall tone of the design. When selecting fonts, I consider not only their aesthetic appeal but also their readability across different platforms and devices. I might choose a bold font for headings to grab attention, while opting for a simpler, sans-serif font for body text to ensure clarity. It is crucial that the typography complements the visual elements and contributes to a coherent overall design.

In addition to font selection, I pay close attention to spacing, line height, and kerning, as these factors can significantly affect legibility and visual appeal. A well-spaced design feels organized and professional, while cramped text can lead to a frustrating viewer experience. I often make adjustments to these settings to find the right balance that enhances the readability of the content.

After I have made extensive customizations, I embark on a thorough review process. This self-assessment is crucial for ensuring that all design elements work harmoniously together. I often step back to view the design as a whole, assessing whether the layout is balanced, the colors are cohesive, and the typography is legible. This reflective practice allows me to make necessary adjustments that elevate the final product.

Collaboration is also an important part of my design process. I often share my customized templates with colleagues or mentors for feedback. This external input provides valuable insights that can enhance my work. Constructive criticism can highlight areas that need improvement and inspire new ideas, making the final design stronger and more effective.

As I finalize the customized template, I ensure that it is prepared for its intended use, whether for digital distribution or print. This involves checking that all elements are properly formatted and optimized for their specific application. For print designs, I confirm that the resolution is adequate to prevent pixelation, while for digital graphics, I optimize file sizes for quick loading times. This meticulous attention to detail underscores my commitment to delivering high-quality designs.

Ultimately, the process of customizing Canva templates empowers me to transform basic designs into unique expressions of my creativity and brand identity. Through thoughtful modifications of layouts, strategic adjustments of color schemes, and the integration of personalized elements, I can create graphics that not only capture attention but also convey meaningful messages. This journey into advanced customization techniques enhances my design skills and enriches my understanding of visual communication, equipping me with the tools to produce impactful and professional designs that stand out in a competitive landscape. As I continue to explore and refine my approach, I look forward to uncovering new techniques and insights that will further enhance my design practice.

CHAPTER 17: COLLABORATING WITH TEAMS

As I delve into the realm of collaborating with teams using Canva, I quickly recognize the power of collective creativity and the efficiency that comes from seamless communication. In today's fast-paced digital landscape, collaboration is essential for producing high-quality designs that meet the diverse needs of various stakeholders. Canva offers a suite of collaborative features that facilitate teamwork, allowing members to contribute their unique perspectives and skills while maintaining a streamlined workflow.

The first step in harnessing the collaborative capabilities of Canva involves sharing designs with team members. I appreciate the intuitive interface that allows me to easily invite colleagues to view or edit projects. When I create a new design, I can simply click on the "Share" button, which provides options for inviting team members via email or generating a shareable link. This flexibility ensures that I can collaborate with both internal team members and external partners without unnecessary barriers. As I share designs, I often include a brief message outlining the purpose of the project and any specific areas where I seek feedback, creating clarity from the outset.

Once I have shared a design, I find that Canva's commenting feature becomes invaluable for fostering meaningful dialogue among team members. Each collaborator can leave comments directly on the design, allowing for context-specific feedback that is easy to understand. I encourage my team to provide constructive criticism and suggestions, as this open exchange of ideas often leads to more innovative outcomes. The ability to tag specific team members in comments ensures that the right people are alerted to relevant feedback, which streamlines communication and keeps discussions organized. I often remind my colleagues to be specific in their comments, addressing particular elements of the design, whether it's about color choices, typography, or layout adjustments.

In addition to comments, I can track the changes made by team members in real time. This feature is particularly beneficial when multiple collaborators are working on a project simultaneously. I often find myself in brainstorming sessions where we collectively refine a design, and the ability to see edits as they happen fosters a dynamic and collaborative environment. As we make adjustments, I encourage my team to communicate their thought processes, sharing insights on why certain changes are made. This not only enhances the design but also cultivates a culture of transparency and shared ownership over the project.

Managing team roles and permissions is another crucial aspect of effective collaboration in Canva. I can assign specific roles to team members, determining who has editing capabilities and who may only view the design. This functionality is particularly useful when I am working with clients or stakeholders who need to provide input without altering the design directly. By setting permissions appropriately, I can maintain control over the creative process while ensuring that all relevant parties can contribute their feedback. I often take time to discuss these roles with my team before starting a project, clarifying expectations and ensuring everyone understands their responsibilities.

As the design progresses, I frequently revisit the shared designs to assess how they align with our original objectives. Regular check-ins allow us to stay on track and ensure that we are meeting deadlines. I find that scheduling periodic reviews, where we gather to discuss the design and evaluate progress, keeps the project moving forward. During these meetings, I encourage open discussion about what is working well and what may need further refinement. This collaborative reflection is essential for maintaining momentum and achieving our goals.

In addition to verbal feedback, I also emphasize the importance of visual feedback in the design process. Using the presentation mode in Canva, I can showcase the design to the team, allowing everyone to see it in a more polished format. This mode creates an immersive experience, enabling us to visualize how the final product will appear to the audience. As we review the design together, I encourage team members to share their reactions and impressions, which often leads to insightful discussions about potential improvements.

The flexibility of Canva's collaboration tools extends to the ability to create design templates for recurring projects. This functionality allows my team to maintain consistency across various designs while streamlining our workflow. By creating a standardized template that includes brand colors, fonts, and layout structures, we can save time and reduce redundancy in the design process. I often emphasize the importance of adhering to these templates, as they reinforce brand identity and ensure that our work remains cohesive, even when multiple team members are contributing.

Another aspect of collaboration I find beneficial is the ability to create shared folders within Canva. By organizing our designs into specific folders, I can ensure that all relevant materials are easily accessible to the team. This organization reduces the time spent searching for assets and fosters a more efficient workflow. I make it a practice to label folders clearly, categorizing designs by project, campaign, or client. This clarity helps everyone quickly locate the resources they need, enabling us to focus on the creative aspects of our work.

As we finalize designs, I emphasize the importance of preparing for presentation or delivery. Collaborating in Canva allows us to gather input and make adjustments in real time, ensuring that we are all aligned before the final product is shared externally. I often create a checklist of final steps that we collectively review to confirm that all elements are polished and ready for distribution. This process instills a sense of accountability among team members, as we all have a stake in the success of the project.

In conclusion, collaborating with teams in Canva opens up a world of possibilities for enhancing the design process. By leveraging the platform's sharing capabilities, commenting features, and role management tools, I can foster a collaborative environment that promotes creativity and innovation. As I continue to navigate this collaborative landscape, I look forward to refining my approach and uncovering new strategies that will further enhance our collective design efforts. The journey of collaboration not only enriches my own skills as a designer but also strengthens the bond within the team, ultimately leading to more impactful and successful design outcomes.

As I continue to explore the intricacies of collaborating with teams in Canva, I find that fostering a strong sense of teamwork is essential for maximizing the potential of the platform's collaborative features. A well-functioning team not only produces higher-quality designs but also nurtures an environment where creativity can thrive. One of the key elements in this collaborative dynamic is effective communication, which I strive to maintain throughout the design process. Clear communication channels help ensure that everyone is on the same page regarding project goals, timelines, and individual responsibilities.

I often begin by establishing a shared understanding of the project's objectives with my team. This initial discussion lays the groundwork for our collaboration, enabling us to clarify expectations and outline our desired outcomes. During this phase, I encourage team members to voice their ideas and insights, as diverse perspectives can lead to more innovative solutions. I find that when everyone feels heard and valued, the team is more motivated to contribute actively, resulting in a more dynamic and productive workflow.

Once we have aligned on our objectives, I utilize Canva's sharing features to distribute access to our design files. I am particularly mindful of managing permissions based on the roles and responsibilities of each team member. Some may need full editing capabilities, while others may only require commenting access. This granularity in permissions allows me to maintain control over the design while still empowering my colleagues to contribute effectively. I often reiterate the importance of respecting these roles to avoid confusion and ensure that the project moves forward smoothly.

As our collaboration progresses, the ability to provide real-time feedback within Canva proves invaluable. When team members can comment directly on specific elements of the design, it creates an efficient feedback loop that enhances our creative process. For example, if someone notices that a color choice doesn't align with our brand identity, they can leave a comment on that particular element. This immediate feedback helps me make adjustments on the spot, ensuring that the design evolves in response to input from the team. I encourage everyone to be constructive in their comments, focusing on how to enhance the design rather than simply pointing out issues. This approach fosters a supportive environment where the goal is to improve the work collaboratively.

I also appreciate the transparency that comes with Canva's version history feature. As we make changes and incorporate feedback, I can easily review previous iterations of the design. This capability allows me to track the evolution of our work and to revert to earlier versions if necessary. It provides a safety net that encourages experimentation, knowing that we can always fall back on a previous design if an adjustment doesn't yield the desired effect. I find this feature particularly useful during brainstorming sessions, where we may try various styles or layouts before settling on the final direction.

Another essential aspect of successful collaboration is keeping the lines of communication open beyond the comments within Canva. I often supplement our design discussions with regular meetings or check-ins, where we can discuss progress, address any concerns, and brainstorm new ideas. These meetings allow for deeper conversations about the design, fostering a sense of camaraderie among team members. I utilize video conferencing tools or chat platforms to facilitate these discussions, ensuring that everyone has the opportunity to contribute regardless of their location.

When working on larger projects, I also find it beneficial to break the work into manageable tasks. By assigning specific roles for different aspects of the design, such as content creation, layout design, or visual elements, I can ensure that everyone has a clear understanding of their responsibilities. This task-oriented approach not only enhances efficiency but also allows each team member to play to their strengths. For instance, if someone excels at writing engaging copy, I will encourage them to take the lead on that aspect while others focus on visual design. This collaborative division of labor creates a sense of ownership and accountability, motivating team members to deliver their best work.

As the project progresses, I continually emphasize the importance of flexibility and adaptability in our collaborative efforts. Design is inherently iterative, and it is crucial that we remain open to new ideas and changes. I encourage my team to experiment with different concepts and to not be afraid of taking creative risks. When someone proposes an unconventional idea, I ensure that we explore it, as it could lead to breakthrough moments that elevate the overall design. This culture of exploration not only strengthens our collaboration but also enriches the final output.

In the final stages of the design process, I focus on refining our graphics to ensure they meet our original objectives and standards. I encourage team members to conduct a final review of the designs, checking for consistency in branding, visual appeal, and clarity of message. This collaborative review process often highlights areas that may need further adjustments, ensuring that the final product is polished and cohesive. I find that a collective final assessment strengthens our sense of accomplishment and reinforces our shared commitment to delivering high-quality designs.

Once we have finalized our designs, I make it a point to celebrate our achievements as a team. Recognizing individual contributions and the collective effort reinforces a sense of camaraderie and motivates team members to continue collaborating in the future. I often send out a team-wide message expressing gratitude for their hard work and creativity, highlighting specific contributions that made a significant impact on the project. This acknowledgment fosters a positive team culture and encourages everyone to continue striving for excellence in our future collaborations.

In summary, the experience of collaborating with teams in Canva has deepened my understanding of the creative process. By utilizing the platform's robust collaborative features and fostering an environment of open communication, I can maximize the potential of my team's collective creativity. Through effective role management, real-time feedback, and a commitment to flexibility, we can produce outstanding designs that resonate with our audiences. This journey into teamwork and collaboration enriches my design practice, equipping me with the skills and insights needed to thrive in a dynamic and collaborative creative landscape. As I continue to engage with these collaborative practices, I look forward to the innovative solutions and impactful designs that await us in our future projects.

As I delve deeper into the dynamics of collaborating with teams using Canva, I come to appreciate the importance of establishing a structured yet flexible workflow that encourages creativity while ensuring that everyone stays on track. A well-defined process helps to minimize confusion and enhance productivity, allowing team members to contribute effectively to the design project. This begins with setting clear expectations and guidelines from the outset, which includes establishing timelines, assigning tasks, and defining the objectives for the collaboration.

I often initiate projects by holding a kickoff meeting where the team can gather to discuss the goals and vision for the design. During this meeting, I outline the project scope and any key deliverables, inviting team members to share their insights and suggestions. This collaborative brainstorming session not only fosters a sense of ownership among team members but also allows us to leverage each other's strengths. I find that when team members feel invested in the project from the beginning, they are more likely to engage actively throughout the design process.

One of the standout features of Canva's collaboration tools is the ability to set up team folders. By organizing our designs into shared folders, I can streamline access to all relevant materials, ensuring that everyone has the resources they need at their fingertips. I make it a point to label these folders clearly, categorizing them by project, client, or campaign to enhance navigability. This organization mitigates the risk of team members working from outdated or incorrect files, which can lead to confusion and inefficiencies.

As the project progresses, I actively encourage feedback through comments directly within Canva. This immediate feedback mechanism allows us to address issues or concerns in real time, ensuring that we can pivot quickly if needed. I often remind team members to be constructive in their critiques, focusing on specific elements that could be improved rather than general observations. For example, if someone feels that a particular color scheme is not effective, I encourage them to suggest alternative colors that might better align with our brand identity. This not only fosters a positive atmosphere but also drives the design toward its best possible outcome.

In addition to real-time commenting, I leverage the ability to conduct design reviews within the platform. As we approach key milestones in the project, I organize sessions where the team can collectively assess our progress. This collaborative review allows us to take a step back and evaluate how well our designs align with our initial objectives. During these meetings, we discuss what is working well and what may need further refinement, encouraging open dialogue and creative brainstorming. I find that these sessions often spark new ideas and solutions that can elevate the design beyond our original vision.

Managing roles and responsibilities within the team is another crucial aspect of effective collaboration. I ensure that each member knows their specific tasks and how their contributions fit into the broader project. This clarity helps prevent overlap and confusion, allowing everyone to focus on their assigned responsibilities. For instance, if one team member is in charge of creating graphics while another focuses on copywriting, I emphasize the importance of communication between these roles to ensure that the visuals and text complement each other seamlessly. Establishing these roles early on helps foster accountability and ensures that the project progresses smoothly.

I also recognize the value of utilizing templates that can serve as starting points for specific types of designs. By creating and sharing custom templates within the team, I can maintain consistency across different graphics while allowing each team member the flexibility to add their creative touch. This approach not only saves time but also reinforces our brand identity, ensuring that all designs adhere to established visual standards. I encourage team members to personalize these templates while remaining within the parameters we've set, balancing creativity with brand consistency.

As the design process unfolds, I remain attentive to the importance of adaptability. Collaborative projects can be unpredictable, and being open to changes or adjustments is crucial for success. I foster an environment where team members feel comfortable proposing new ideas or alternative directions, even if it means deviating from our initial plan. This flexibility allows us to respond to feedback and insights that arise during the design process, leading to more innovative and effective outcomes. I often remind my team that creativity thrives in an atmosphere where experimentation is encouraged.

When it comes time to finalize designs, I place great emphasis on conducting a thorough review. This includes checking for consistency in branding, ensuring that all elements align with our established guidelines, and confirming that the content is clear and engaging. I often create a checklist of final steps that we collectively review, ensuring that we address any last-minute adjustments. This collaborative final assessment reinforces our shared commitment to delivering high-quality designs, and I find that it enhances our sense of accomplishment as a team.

As we prepare to share our designs with the public or specific stakeholders, I take time to celebrate our achievements. Recognizing individual contributions not only fosters a positive team culture but also motivates everyone to continue striving for excellence in future projects. I send out a team-wide message expressing gratitude for their hard work and creativity, highlighting specific contributions that made a significant impact on the project. This acknowledgment fosters a sense of community and belonging, essential elements in maintaining a cohesive and effective team.

Finally, as I reflect on the collaborative experience in Canva, I am continually reminded of the importance of fostering a culture of creativity and support within the team. The tools and features available through Canva empower us to work together seamlessly, but it is the relationships we build and the communication we maintain that ultimately drive our success. Through shared goals, open feedback, and a commitment to excellence, we can create designs that not only meet our objectives but also resonate deeply with our audience. This journey into collaborative design has not only enhanced my skills as a designer but has also enriched my understanding of the power of teamwork in the creative process. As I continue to engage with these collaborative practices, I look forward to discovering new ways to leverage the strengths of my team, ultimately leading to even more impactful and successful design outcomes.

CHAPTER 18: DESIGNING PRINT MATERIALS

As I embark on the journey of designing for print, I quickly recognize the fundamental differences between digital and print design. The transition from screen to paper requires a keen understanding of various technical aspects to ensure that the final product is not only visually appealing but also meets industry standards for quality. The first consideration I encounter is the importance of dimensions and layout. Unlike digital designs, which can easily be resized without loss of quality, print materials must be meticulously planned to specific dimensions that adhere to the requirements of the intended printing process.

I start by familiarizing myself with the standard sizes for different print materials. For instance, business cards typically measure 3.5 by 2 inches, while brochures can vary widely in size depending on their layout and purpose. It is crucial that I select the appropriate dimensions from the outset to avoid any issues later in the printing process. Canva provides a variety of templates that cater to common print sizes, which serve as excellent starting points. However, I often prefer to create custom dimensions when necessary, ensuring that my designs perfectly fit the needs of the project.

In addition to dimensions, I must also consider the layout of the design. This involves planning how elements will be arranged within the defined space. When designing for print, I prioritize a clear visual hierarchy that guides the viewer's eye. I often employ techniques such as grouping related elements together and using varying font sizes to delineate headings from body text. This approach not only enhances readability but also makes the design more engaging. I pay special attention to margins and bleed areas, understanding that leaving sufficient space around the edges prevents important content from being cut off during the printing process. The bleed area, typically set at an additional 0.125 inches beyond the trim size, allows for slight variations in cutting and ensures a professional finish.

Another critical aspect of print design is the color mode. In the digital realm, designs are typically created in RGB (Red, Green, Blue) color mode, which is suitable for screens. However, for print materials, I must convert my designs to CMYK (Cyan, Magenta, Yellow, Black) color mode. CMYK is the standard color model used in the printing industry, and understanding its nuances is essential for achieving accurate color representation. I often find myself adjusting the colors in my designs after switching to CMYK, as some vibrant hues that appear bright on a screen can look duller in print. This adjustment is a vital step in ensuring that the final printed product aligns with my original vision.

As I work with color in print designs, I also pay attention to the choice of paper. Different paper stocks can significantly impact how colors appear and the overall feel of the printed material. I take the time to consider whether I want a matte or glossy finish, as this decision influences the texture and appearance of the design. For instance, a glossy finish can enhance color vibrancy and is often used for photographs, while a matte finish can create a more sophisticated look for brochures or business cards. I often request paper samples from printers to see how my designs translate to physical materials, which helps me make informed decisions about my final output.

Once I have finalized the design, I focus on selecting the correct file format for printing. Different printers may have varying preferences for file types, but I generally find that PDF is the most widely accepted format for high-quality printing. PDFs preserve the integrity of the design, ensuring that fonts, colors, and layouts remain consistent. I also make it a practice to export my designs at a minimum resolution of 300 DPI (dots per inch), which is essential for achieving crisp, clear images in print. This resolution prevents any pixelation or blurriness, which can detract from the professional quality of the printed material.

Before sending my designs to print, I conduct a thorough review to catch any potential issues. I examine the design at 100% zoom to ensure that all elements are sharp and that text is legible. Additionally, I review the color settings to confirm that they are set to CMYK, and I double-check the bleed and margin settings. This meticulous final review helps to prevent any surprises during the printing process and ensures that the final product aligns with my expectations.

I also recognize the value of collaborating with printing professionals during this phase. I often reach out to my chosen printer to discuss my design specifications and any requirements they may have. Their expertise can provide valuable insights into how to optimize my designs for the specific printing process they use, whether it be digital printing, offset printing, or another method. I find that establishing open communication with the printer helps to ensure a smoother workflow and can often lead to recommendations for paper stocks or finishes that I may not have considered.

As I send my designs off for printing, I embrace the excitement that comes with seeing my work come to life on paper. The tactile nature of printed materials adds a dimension to design that digital formats cannot replicate. Whether it's the smooth finish of a business card or the glossy sheen of a brochure, the physicality of print enhances the overall experience for the viewer. I take pride in knowing that my careful attention to detail throughout the design process has contributed to a polished final product.

In conclusion, designing for print requires a nuanced understanding of various technical considerations, from dimensions and layouts to color modes and file formats. By approaching each project with a focus on clarity, organization, and collaboration, I can create high-quality print materials that not only meet industry standards but also resonate with audiences. The journey of mastering print design has enriched my skills as a designer and deepened my appreciation for the artistry involved in bringing ideas to life on paper. As I continue to explore this facet of design, I look forward to further developing my expertise and discovering new ways to create impactful printed materials.

As I continue my exploration of designing print materials, I recognize that understanding the specifics of printing techniques can significantly enhance the quality of my work. Various printing methods, such as digital, offset, and screen printing, each have their own unique characteristics, and knowing these nuances helps me tailor my designs to maximize their effectiveness.

Digital printing is often the go-to choice for smaller runs or projects requiring quick turnaround times. This method allows for high-quality color printing without the need for extensive setup. I appreciate that digital printing can accommodate complex designs and images with numerous colors. However, I must keep in mind that color consistency can vary between prints, so I make sure to proof my designs before proceeding with a large order. This proofing stage allows me to verify that the colors, resolution, and overall design translate well to the final printed piece.

On the other hand, offset printing is typically used for larger print runs, offering a more cost-effective solution for high-volume projects. This method involves creating metal plates for each color, which can lead to more consistent color reproduction and sharper images. However, the setup time and costs can be higher compared to digital printing. As I design for offset printing, I pay particular attention to ensuring that the colors I select can be accurately reproduced. I often consult Pantone color guides to choose colors that will remain true during the printing process. By specifying Pantone colors in my designs, I help ensure that my final products have the desired vibrancy and accuracy.

Screen printing, another technique, is often used for specialty items like t-shirts or promotional materials. This method applies layers of ink directly onto the material, allowing for unique textures and finishes. When designing for screen printing, I take into account the limitations of the method, particularly regarding color complexity. Screen printing works best with a limited color palette, as each color requires a separate screen. Therefore, I focus on creating bold, simple designs that will have a strong visual impact while remaining within the constraints of this printing technique.

As I navigate the printing landscape, I also consider the type of paper that will be used for my designs. The choice of paper can profoundly affect the overall look and feel of the final product. Different types of paper—such as glossy, matte, textured, or recycled—impart distinct characteristics to the printed materials. For instance, glossy paper can enhance color saturation and is often used for vibrant promotional materials, while matte paper lends a more sophisticated and elegant touch. I often request samples from printing companies to physically assess the paper's texture, weight, and finish, allowing me to make informed decisions that align with the project's goals.

When preparing my designs for print, I pay careful attention to the resolution and quality of images used within the design. Print materials require a higher resolution than digital designs; a standard minimum of 300 DPI (dots per inch) is essential for ensuring sharp, clear images. I frequently check the resolution of each image before integrating it into my design. This step prevents pixelation and ensures that the images maintain their integrity when printed. If I discover that an image is too low in resolution, I either source a higher-quality version or adjust my design to use an alternative image that meets the necessary standards.

I also prioritize the importance of bleeds in print design. Bleeds are areas of the design that extend beyond the trim edge, allowing for a seamless finish when the printed piece is cut to its final size. Typically, I include a bleed of at least 0.125 inches on all sides of the design. This precaution ensures that any minor shifts during the cutting process do not result in white edges appearing on the final product. I often add guidelines in Canva to visualize the bleed area, helping me to ensure that important content stays within the safe zone and is not inadvertently cut off.

As I prepare to export my final design for printing, I make sure to select the appropriate file format. While PDF is generally the preferred format for print materials due to its ability to preserve design elements, I sometimes consider other formats based on specific printer requirements. I ensure that I export my files at the correct resolution and with the necessary settings for bleed and crop marks, which guide the printer during the cutting process. I often conduct a final review of the exported file to confirm that everything is in order before sending it off for printing.

Throughout this design process, I find that collaboration with printing professionals is invaluable. Establishing a relationship with my printer allows me to gain insights into best practices for print design, including any specific requirements they may have for file submissions. I often consult with them about paper recommendations, color options, and finishing techniques that can enhance the quality of the printed materials. This collaborative approach ensures that I am aligned with their capabilities and can produce designs that translate beautifully from screen to paper.

After submitting my designs for printing, I eagerly anticipate the moment when they arrive. There is something uniquely satisfying about holding a physical representation of my work, seeing the colors and textures come to life. I make it a point to inspect the final product carefully, checking for quality and consistency. If everything meets my expectations, I feel a sense of accomplishment and pride in the work we have produced.

In summary, designing for print requires a multifaceted approach that encompasses an understanding of printing techniques, paper choices, and file preparation. By navigating these elements with care and attention to detail, I can create high-quality printed materials that effectively communicate my intended message. This exploration into print design has enriched my skills as a designer, deepening my appreciation for the artistry involved in producing tangible creations. As I continue to refine my practice, I look forward to exploring new avenues in print design and discovering innovative ways to bring my ideas to life on paper.

As I delve deeper into the intricacies of designing print materials, I realize that the final touch of a printed piece often lies in its finishing options. The way a design is finished can significantly enhance its aesthetic appeal and functionality. Various finishing techniques can transform an ordinary print job into something extraordinary, and understanding these options allows me to make informed decisions that elevate the final product.

One of the most common finishing techniques is lamination, which adds a protective layer to the printed material. Lamination comes in two primary finishes: gloss and matte. Gloss lamination creates a shiny, reflective surface that enhances color vibrancy, making it ideal for promotional materials where visual impact is crucial. Conversely, matte lamination offers a subdued, sophisticated finish that can impart an elegant touch to business cards or brochures. I consider the purpose of the printed material when choosing between these finishes; for instance, a glossy brochure for a vibrant event might be more appropriate than a matte finish, which could convey a sense of professionalism and restraint.

In addition to lamination, I also explore the possibilities of die-cutting. This technique involves cutting the printed material into custom shapes rather than the standard rectangular format. Die-cutting can create unique and eye-catching designs that stand out in a crowded marketplace. I might use die-cutting to craft business cards in the shape of a logo or promotional materials that feature intricate patterns. This level of customization not only enhances the visual appeal but also creates a tactile experience that can leave a lasting impression on the audience. However, I must consider the added costs and production time associated with die-cutting, ensuring it aligns with the overall project budget and timeline.

Another finishing technique I often consider is embossing or debossing. Embossing creates a raised effect on the printed surface, while debossing results in an indented design. Both techniques add a tactile quality to print materials that can elevate their perceived value. For example, when designing a luxury brand brochure, incorporating embossed elements can convey a sense of sophistication and attention to detail. I find that these finishing touches can significantly enhance the overall design, making it feel more premium and engaging to the audience.

As I finalize my designs for print, I also focus on understanding the proofing process. Proofing is a critical step that allows me to review a physical or digital sample of the printed material before the final run. I often request a printed proof from the printer, which gives me an opportunity to assess color accuracy, resolution, and overall quality. During this stage, I meticulously examine the proof, comparing it to my original design to ensure that everything translates as expected. If I notice any discrepancies—such as colors appearing dull or images not displaying correctly—I address these issues with the printer to make necessary adjustments. This diligence in the proofing stage is essential for achieving a high-quality final product.

In addition to the technical aspects of proofing, I also consider the feedback from others. I often share the printed proof with colleagues or stakeholders for their input. Their fresh perspectives can reveal insights that I might have overlooked during the design process. I encourage constructive feedback, as it can lead to refinements that enhance the final outcome. This collaborative approach fosters a sense of teamwork and collective ownership of the project, ensuring that everyone is aligned on the vision for the printed materials.

As I prepare to finalize the print job, I also reflect on the logistics involved in the production process. Coordinating with the printing company is crucial to ensure a smooth workflow. I often engage in discussions regarding timelines, delivery methods, and quantities. Understanding the printing company's capabilities allows me to make informed decisions about the production schedule, ensuring that I allow ample time for any unforeseen issues that may arise during printing or shipping.

I am also aware of the importance of sustainability in print design. As I select paper stocks, I seek out eco-friendly options that align with my values and those of my clients. Recycled paper and sustainable sourcing practices are essential considerations in today's design landscape, and I strive to incorporate these practices into my work whenever possible. Not only do these choices contribute to environmental conservation, but they also resonate with audiences who prioritize sustainability. I often research local printers who specialize in eco-friendly materials, ensuring that my designs reflect a commitment to responsible practices.

In conclusion, designing print materials requires a comprehensive understanding of various elements that influence the final product. From selecting the right dimensions and color modes to incorporating finishing techniques and engaging in the proofing process, every decision I make plays a crucial role in delivering high-quality printed designs. This journey into print design has not only honed my technical skills but has also deepened my appreciation for the artistry involved in translating ideas into tangible forms. As I continue to explore this realm, I look forward to uncovering new possibilities and techniques that will enhance my practice, ultimately leading to impactful and visually stunning print materials that resonate with audiences.

CHAPTER 19: LEVERAGING CANVA'S BRAND KIT

As I delve into the functionality of Canva's Brand Kit, I find that this feature is instrumental in establishing a cohesive visual identity across all my designs. The Brand Kit allows me to consolidate my branding elements in one accessible location, making it easier to maintain consistency throughout various projects. This is particularly valuable when working on multiple designs that require a unified look and feel, as it ensures that every piece of content I produce aligns seamlessly with my brand identity.

Setting up the Brand Kit begins with uploading essential brand assets, including logos, fonts, and color palettes. I start by gathering my brand's visual identity elements, which have been carefully selected to represent the ethos and values of my organization. The logos I upload serve as the cornerstone of my Brand Kit, as they encapsulate my brand's essence and are crucial for establishing recognition. I make sure to include different variations of the logo, such as full color, black and white, and any specific adaptations for different backgrounds. This range allows me to select the most appropriate logo for each design context, ensuring versatility while maintaining brand integrity.

Next, I focus on defining the color palette that represents my brand. Color is a powerful tool in design, influencing emotions and perceptions, so it is imperative that I choose colors that align with my brand identity. I often refer to my brand guidelines to ensure I select the exact hexadecimal codes for each color. By adding these colors to my Brand Kit, I can easily access them whenever I create new designs. This not only saves time but also reduces the risk of inconsistencies that can arise when colors are manually selected. I emphasize the importance of sticking to the brand palette in all materials, as consistency reinforces brand recognition and trust among my audience.

The selection of fonts is another critical component of my Brand Kit. Typography plays a significant role in how content is perceived, and using consistent fonts across all designs helps to communicate professionalism and coherence. I carefully choose primary and secondary typefaces that complement each other and reflect my brand's personality. For example, a bold sans-serif font may serve as the primary heading typeface, conveying strength and modernity, while a more elegant serif font might be used for body text, adding a touch of sophistication. Once I upload these fonts to my Brand Kit, I ensure that they are applied consistently across all designs, which helps establish a recognizable visual language.

With my Brand Kit established, I turn my attention to applying these brand elements to my designs. Canva makes this process intuitive and straightforward. When I start a new project, I can easily access the Brand Kit from the design panel. This integration allows me to apply my color palette, select fonts, and incorporate logos with just a few clicks. As I design, I consciously choose elements from my Brand Kit to reinforce brand consistency, ensuring that every design reflects the visual identity I have cultivated.

Moreover, I often create templates using my Brand Kit, which further streamlines the design process. By setting up templates with predefined brand elements, I can ensure that future designs will inherently align with my brand's aesthetic. For example, I might create a social media post template that incorporates my color palette, logo placement, and font selections. This not only saves time but also allows other team members to create on-brand content without needing to adjust individual elements manually. I find that this collaborative approach enhances productivity while maintaining a strong brand identity.

As I utilize the Brand Kit feature, I also pay attention to how it can facilitate collaboration with my team. When multiple people are involved in a design project, consistency can sometimes be compromised if everyone has different interpretations of the brand guidelines. By having a centralized Brand Kit, I can provide my team with the tools they need to create cohesive designs. I encourage my colleagues to refer to the Brand Kit when producing materials, ensuring that our collective efforts reinforce the brand identity we have established.

Additionally, I often review and update the Brand Kit as needed. As brands evolve, it is essential to revisit visual identity elements to ensure they still resonate with the audience and reflect current values. If I decide to refresh my color palette or introduce a new logo, I update the Brand Kit accordingly, which allows for a seamless transition across all designs. This adaptability is crucial in today's fast-paced environment, where trends and consumer preferences can shift rapidly.

As I reflect on my experience with Canva's Brand Kit, I recognize that it not only enhances my design workflow but also reinforces the core principles of effective branding. Consistency in visual identity is vital for building brand recognition and fostering trust with audiences. By centralizing my brand assets and making them easily accessible, I am empowered to create designs that are not only aesthetically pleasing but also aligned with my brand's values.

In conclusion, leveraging Canva's Brand Kit is an essential practice for any designer aiming to maintain consistency and professionalism in their work. By carefully uploading and managing logos, color palettes, and fonts, I can streamline the design process while ensuring that every piece of content I produce embodies the visual identity I have cultivated. This focus on cohesion and quality enhances my overall design practice, allowing me to effectively communicate my brand's message and values through compelling visuals. As I continue to utilize these tools, I am excited to explore new ways to strengthen my brand presence and engage my audience through effective design.

As I further explore the functionalities of Canva's Brand Kit, I realize that the effective use of this feature goes beyond simply maintaining consistency in my designs. It also plays a crucial role in streamlining the creative process, enabling me to work more efficiently while ensuring that every design I produce aligns with my brand identity. The ability to have all brand assets organized and easily accessible not only saves time but also fosters a more creative environment where I can focus on ideation rather than the logistics of design.

One of the key advantages of utilizing the Brand Kit is the way it facilitates quick access to essential brand assets, allowing me to make informed design choices instantly. When starting a new project, I can quickly refer to my uploaded logos and color palettes to determine the best fit for the design at hand. This immediacy helps eliminate the guesswork involved in color selection and logo placement, enabling me to make confident decisions that reinforce my brand's visual identity. For example, if I am designing a flyer for an upcoming event, I can easily pull up my color palette to select complementary colors that enhance the overall aesthetic, ensuring that the final product is visually striking and cohesive.

As I incorporate my brand elements into various designs, I find that I often experiment with different combinations of colors and fonts to discover new possibilities within my established brand identity. The flexibility that the Brand Kit provides encourages creativity while still adhering to the foundational elements of my brand. I might decide to test how my primary brand color looks alongside a secondary accent color in different contexts, such as a social media graphic versus a printed poster. This experimentation is essential for ensuring that my brand remains relevant and adaptable to changing trends while still being recognizable.

Moreover, the ability to create and save custom color palettes within the Brand Kit empowers me to maintain color consistency across different projects. I often find that having a set of predefined color combinations makes it easier to adhere to my branding guidelines, particularly when working on large campaigns that require multiple materials. For example, when launching a new product, I can create a cohesive look across various platforms—social media posts, email newsletters, and print advertisements—by using the same color palette. This consistency not only enhances brand recognition but also reinforces the professional appearance of all my materials.

In addition to color palettes, I take great care in selecting and managing fonts within my Brand Kit. Fonts are integral to establishing my brand's voice, and using consistent typography across all designs helps communicate that voice effectively. I typically choose a primary font for headlines and a complementary font for body text, ensuring that both align with my brand's personality. For instance, a modern sans-serif font may convey a sense of innovation and simplicity, while a classic serif font might evoke tradition and reliability. By keeping these font choices centralized in my Brand Kit, I can easily apply them to any new project without needing to remember specific font styles or sizes.

As I work on designs, I also recognize the importance of maintaining a library of templates that adhere to my brand guidelines. By creating templates within Canva that incorporate my brand elements, I ensure that every piece of content I produce remains consistent and on-brand. These templates can be used for various purposes, such as social media graphics, presentations, or marketing materials, and they allow me to save time during the design process. When I start a new project, I can simply select the appropriate template and adjust the content, confident that the design will align with my brand's visual identity.

Another significant benefit of utilizing Canva's Brand Kit is the ease with which I can collaborate with team members or stakeholders. When multiple individuals are involved in the design process, having a centralized Brand Kit ensures that everyone is using the same assets and adhering to the established guidelines. I encourage team members to reference the Brand Kit as they create new designs, which fosters a sense of accountability and shared ownership over our brand identity. This collaborative approach reduces the likelihood of inconsistencies arising from individual interpretations of the brand guidelines.

When I collaborate with clients or partners, I often find that sharing the Brand Kit can enhance our discussions around design preferences and visual identity. By providing access to the Brand Kit, I can clearly communicate the color palettes, fonts, and logos that represent my brand, making it easier for others to understand and align with my vision. This transparency fosters productive conversations about design direction, ensuring that all parties are on the same page and contributing to a cohesive end product.

As I continue to utilize the Brand Kit, I am also mindful of the importance of updating and refreshing my brand assets as needed. Brands evolve over time, and it is essential to periodically review and revise the elements within the Brand Kit to reflect current trends or changes in brand strategy. I take the initiative to reassess my color palette and typography choices regularly, ensuring they still resonate with my audience and effectively communicate my brand's message. If I decide to introduce new colors or fonts, I can easily update my Brand Kit to reflect these changes, ensuring that all new designs maintain the same level of professionalism and consistency.

In conclusion, leveraging Canva's Brand Kit has transformed my approach to design, allowing me to maintain a cohesive and professional visual identity across all my projects. By centralizing my brand assets, I can streamline the creative process, enhance collaboration, and ensure consistency in my designs. The ability to quickly access logos, color palettes, and fonts empowers me to make informed design decisions that align with my brand values. As I continue to refine my use of the Brand Kit, I look forward to exploring new ways to enhance my brand identity and engage my audience through effective design. This journey of leveraging the Brand Kit not only enhances my skills as a designer but also strengthens the overall impact of my work in the ever-evolving landscape of branding and design.

As I continue to navigate the intricate landscape of leveraging Canva's Brand Kit, I realize that the effective application of brand elements is not merely about aesthetic consistency; it extends to the emotional resonance that these elements evoke within the target audience. A well-crafted brand identity communicates values, narratives, and personality, making it essential for me to think critically about how I utilize my Brand Kit to foster these connections.

The first aspect I consider is the psychological impact of colors included in my Brand Kit. Each color has its own connotations and can evoke specific emotional responses. For instance, blue often conveys trust and professionalism, making it a popular choice for corporate branding. In contrast, red can evoke excitement or urgency, often employed in promotional materials to stimulate action. I find myself reflecting on the colors I've chosen for my palette and their alignment with my brand's core messages. By applying these colors consistently across all designs, I ensure that the emotional undertones remain intact, which reinforces the brand's narrative in the minds of the audience.

Furthermore, typography plays a pivotal role in establishing a brand's voice. The fonts I select from my Brand Kit should reflect the essence of my brand—be it modern, playful, or sophisticated. For example, using a clean, sans-serif font can convey a contemporary feel, while a classic serif font might communicate tradition and reliability. I meticulously choose typefaces that align with the tone of my messaging, ensuring that they resonate with the audience I aim to reach. The application of these fonts across various platforms—from social media graphics to printed brochures—ensures a cohesive experience that strengthens brand recognition.

As I create new designs, I prioritize the integration of my brand elements in a way that feels organic and intuitive. Each design serves as an opportunity to showcase the brand identity, and I aim for a seamless flow between visuals and messaging. For instance, when designing a marketing flyer for an upcoming event, I incorporate the brand's logo prominently, ensuring that it captures attention without overshadowing the event details. By balancing the placement of my logo with other elements, such as images and text, I create a visually appealing layout that draws the viewer's eye and facilitates understanding.

Collaboration remains an essential component of my design process, and the Brand Kit significantly enhances team efforts.

When working with colleagues, I encourage them to reference the Brand Kit to ensure alignment with our established brand identity. By integrating the Brand Kit into our collaborative tools, everyone can easily access the same logos, color palettes, and fonts, reducing the likelihood of inconsistencies arising from personal interpretations. This shared resource fosters a sense of unity among the team, as we collectively work toward a common goal of maintaining brand integrity.

Another significant advantage of utilizing the Brand Kit is its role in streamlining the revision process. When feedback is received on a design, having all brand assets organized within the Brand Kit allows for swift adjustments. If a colleague suggests a change in color or font, I can quickly apply these modifications without needing to search for specific assets or color codes. This efficiency not only saves time but also enables us to respond promptly to feedback, ensuring that our designs remain relevant and engaging.

As I implement my Brand Kit, I also focus on the importance of consistency across various channels. With the multitude of platforms available today—social media, websites, printed materials—maintaining a uniform brand presence is crucial. I often create specific templates for different mediums, applying the same brand elements while adjusting layouts and dimensions to fit each format. For example, while a social media post might require a more vibrant and attention-grabbing design, a printed brochure may benefit from a more subdued and sophisticated approach. By tailoring my designs to the platform while adhering to brand guidelines, I ensure that my brand is instantly recognizable, regardless of where it appears.

Moreover, I find that the ability to update my Brand Kit as my brand evolves is invaluable. Brands are not static; they grow and change with time, responding to shifts in audience preferences and market trends. By revisiting my

Brand Kit periodically, I can make necessary adjustments to my color palette, fonts, or logos to reflect this evolution. This adaptability ensures that my branding remains relevant and engaging, allowing me to connect with my audience in meaningful ways. When making updates, I communicate these changes to my team, reinforcing the importance of alignment and consistency in all future designs.

In addition, I understand the significance of aligning my Brand Kit with broader marketing strategies. The visual elements I incorporate must not only resonate with my audience but also support the overall messaging and goals of the marketing campaigns. I regularly review the goals of upcoming campaigns, ensuring that the designs I create using the Brand Kit effectively communicate the intended message. For example, if the campaign emphasizes sustainability, I may choose earth-toned colors and organic shapes in my designs to visually reflect that theme.

As I conclude my exploration of leveraging Canva's Brand Kit, I am reminded of the profound impact that a well-defined brand identity can have on audience perception. By consistently applying my brand elements across all designs, I am able to create a cohesive experience that fosters recognition and loyalty. The Brand Kit not only simplifies my design workflow but also empowers me to communicate my brand's values and personality effectively. This journey of establishing and utilizing my Brand Kit has been instrumental in enhancing my design practice, equipping me with the tools to create impactful visuals that resonate with audiences and convey my brand's message with clarity and confidence. As I continue to develop my skills and refine my branding strategies, I look forward to discovering new opportunities to engage my audience through innovative and consistent design.

CHAPTER 20: EXPLORING CANVA APPS AND INTEGRATIONS

As I delve into the diverse array of apps and integrations available within Canva, I quickly discover how these features can significantly enhance my design capabilities and overall workflow. The platform's versatility extends far beyond traditional design tools, allowing for seamless connections with various applications that facilitate everything from content creation to social media management. This integration not only streamlines the design process but also maximizes productivity, making it easier for me to manage multiple tasks within a single environment.

One of the most compelling aspects of Canva's app ecosystem is its ability to integrate with popular social media platforms. As I work on graphics intended for platforms such as Facebook, Instagram, and Twitter, I find that the direct connection to these services allows me to publish designs instantly without the need to download and re-upload files. For instance, while designing a promotional post, I can easily select the desired dimensions specific to each social media platform. Once the design is complete, I have the option to share it directly to my social media accounts with just a few clicks. This feature eliminates unnecessary steps in my workflow and ensures that my content can be distributed in real time, allowing me to maintain a consistent online presence.

Additionally, Canva's integration with stock photo libraries is another powerful enhancement to my design process. I often rely on high-quality images to enrich my designs, and the ability to access a vast library of stock photos directly within Canva saves me considerable time. Rather than searching through multiple sites for the right image, I can use the built-in search functionality to find the perfect photo, illustration, or graphic element to complement my design. This accessibility ensures that I can create visually engaging content efficiently while also adhering to copyright considerations, as the images available through Canva are often licensed for use within the platform.

Moreover, the ability to connect Canva with productivity and project management tools has revolutionized the way I approach collaborative projects. By integrating platforms like Slack or Trello, I can share designs and updates directly with my team, facilitating communication and feedback without the need for constant back-and-forth emails. For example, if I create a new design for a marketing campaign, I can post it directly into a dedicated Slack channel where my team can review it, provide comments, and suggest changes in real time. This immediate feedback loop fosters collaboration and ensures that everyone involved in the project is aligned on the design direction.

I also find value in the integration with tools such as Google Drive and Dropbox. These services allow me to store and access files seamlessly, providing a centralized location for all design-related assets. When I upload images or documents to Canva from these cloud storage platforms, I can easily incorporate them into my designs without having to switch between applications. This integration is particularly useful when working on projects that require multiple assets, as it minimizes disruptions in my workflow and helps me maintain focus on the creative process.

In addition to these integrations, Canva also offers a variety of built-in apps that expand my design capabilities. For instance, the Animation app allows me to add dynamic elements to my graphics effortlessly. Whether I'm creating a video for social media or an engaging presentation, the ability to incorporate animations enhances the visual appeal of my designs. I can choose from various animation styles and apply them to specific elements, ensuring that my content captures the attention of my audience while maintaining a professional finish.

Furthermore, the Charts app provides a user-friendly way to create data visualizations directly within Canva. As I often need to present data in a visually engaging manner, this feature is invaluable. I can input my data, select from various chart styles, and customize the colors and fonts to match my brand identity. This capability allows me to transform complex information into easily digestible visuals that enhance the overall communication of my message.

Another noteworthy app within Canva is the Content Planner. This feature helps me schedule and plan my social media posts directly from the platform. By integrating my design process with content scheduling, I can streamline my workflow and ensure that I have a consistent posting schedule. I can visualize my social media calendar, drag and drop designs into the appropriate dates, and even set reminders for when posts should go live. This level of organization allows me to manage my online presence effectively, making sure that I capitalize on key marketing moments.

As I continue to explore the breadth of Canva's apps and integrations, I appreciate the extensive customization options available. The ability to connect with third-party applications allows me to tailor my design process to fit my unique needs. For instance, I can integrate email marketing tools like Mailchimp to create visually appealing email campaigns that reflect my brand's identity. By designing email headers and graphics in Canva, I can maintain a consistent look and feel across all marketing channels, enhancing brand recognition.

In my experience, the effectiveness of Canva's integrations is magnified by its user-friendly interface. Navigating between different apps and tools is intuitive, allowing me to focus on creativity rather than getting bogged down by technical details. This simplicity empowers me to experiment with various design elements, styles, and layouts without the fear of complicating my workflow.

As I wrap up my exploration of Canva's app ecosystem, I am invigorated by the potential these features unlock for my design practice. The ability to streamline my workflow, enhance collaboration, and elevate the quality of my designs through integrations transforms how I approach each project. By leveraging these capabilities, I not only improve my productivity but also create designs that resonate more deeply with my audience. This journey into the world of Canva apps and integrations reaffirms my commitment to staying at the forefront of design trends and tools, enabling me to craft compelling visuals that effectively communicate my brand's message across various platforms. As I continue to leverage these features, I look forward to exploring new possibilities that will further enhance my creative endeavors.

As I delve deeper into Canva's suite of apps and integrations, I begin to appreciate how these tools can facilitate not only my design process but also my overall project management. The interplay between design and productivity tools allows me to create a streamlined workflow that enhances my creative capabilities. I find that the integration of various apps enables me to manage multiple aspects of a project without the constant need to switch between different platforms, saving valuable time and mental energy.

One particularly valuable integration is with project management tools like Asana and Trello. By linking these applications with Canva, I can create a cohesive system that allows me to track progress on design projects while keeping all team members informed. For example, if I am tasked with creating a series of social media graphics for an upcoming campaign, I can set specific deadlines and tasks within Trello. As I complete each design in Canva, I can mark it as finished within the project management tool. This synchronization not only keeps everyone on the same page but also instills a sense of accountability within the team. Each member can easily see what has been completed, what remains pending, and who is responsible for each task.

Moreover, the ability to use Canva in conjunction with email marketing platforms such as Mailchimp is another significant advantage. Creating visually appealing email headers and promotional graphics is essential for effective communication with my audience. By designing these elements in Canva and seamlessly importing them into Mailchimp, I maintain a consistent brand identity across all marketing channels. This integration simplifies the process, allowing me to focus on crafting compelling content rather than worrying about the logistics of transferring designs between platforms.

In addition to enhancing my workflow, the integration with social media management tools like Buffer or Hootsuite allows me to schedule posts directly from Canva. After designing a striking social media graphic, I can share it to my connected social media accounts right from the platform. This functionality enables me to plan and execute my social media strategy with precision. I can visualize my content calendar, ensuring that my posts align with marketing campaigns, seasonal promotions, or significant events. This level of organization is crucial in today's fast-paced digital landscape, where timing can significantly impact engagement and reach.

As I create and manage multiple designs across various platforms, I also find great value in Canva's ability to connect with cloud storage services such as Google Drive and Dropbox. This integration allows me to store and retrieve assets seamlessly, ensuring that I have access to all necessary files without the hassle of locating them across different folders or drives. When I need to incorporate images, videos, or other documents into my designs, I can simply pull them from these cloud services, streamlining the design process. This functionality is particularly beneficial for collaborative projects where multiple team members may need to access shared assets.

I also appreciate the insights provided by Canva's analytics features, especially when it comes to social media performance. By integrating with analytics tools, I can monitor the engagement of my posts, track performance metrics, and understand which designs resonate most with my audience. This data-driven approach enables me to refine my design strategies over time, ensuring that I create content that effectively captures attention and drives engagement. By analyzing this feedback, I can make informed decisions about future designs, tailoring my approach to better meet the needs of my audience.

Another significant benefit of using Canva's integrations is the ability to connect with e-commerce platforms like Shopify. This functionality allows me to design product images and promotional materials directly tailored for online stores. By integrating my design efforts with my e-commerce strategy, I ensure that all visuals align with the brand's overall aesthetic and marketing goals. Creating cohesive product visuals is essential for attracting customers and enhancing their shopping experience. By utilizing Canva's design capabilities,

I can easily produce high-quality images that showcase products effectively, which in turn can lead to increased sales and customer satisfaction.

As I explore these integrations further, I also recognize the importance of adaptability in my design approach. The digital landscape is constantly evolving, and new tools and applications emerge regularly. Staying updated on the latest integrations that Canva offers allows me to expand my creative toolkit continually. By being open to new technologies, I can discover additional ways to enhance my design processes and improve efficiency.

I also find that the community surrounding Canva is a rich resource for discovering innovative uses of the platform's integrations. Engaging with other designers and marketers through forums and social media can provide inspiration and insights into best practices. This exchange of ideas often leads to new techniques and strategies that I can incorporate into my own workflow. By sharing experiences and learning from others, I can refine my use of Canva's features to better serve my design needs.

In conclusion, leveraging Canva's apps and integrations significantly enhances my design capabilities and workflow efficiency. By connecting Canva with various project management, social media, and cloud storage tools, I can create a seamless process that empowers me to focus on creativity while maintaining organization and productivity. The ability to quickly access brand assets, collaborate with team members, and analyze performance data provides a comprehensive approach to design that is essential in today's fast-paced environment. As I continue to explore and utilize these integrations, I am excited about the potential they hold for optimizing my design practice and delivering impactful visual content that resonates with my audience. This journey through Canva's ecosystem not only enriches my skills as a designer but also fosters a more collaborative and innovative approach to my work.

As I further immerse myself in the capabilities of Canva's apps and integrations, I become increasingly aware of how these tools can enhance not only the design process but also the strategic planning behind each project. One of the standout integrations that significantly influences my workflow is the capability to connect Canva with marketing automation platforms such as HubSpot or Mailchimp. By linking these services, I can seamlessly create visually engaging email campaigns that reflect my brand's identity and messaging.

When designing email graphics, I take advantage of Canva's templates specifically tailored for email marketing. These templates are optimized for various email formats and allow me to maintain consistency with my branding. Once I create a compelling header or promotional image, I can export it directly to my chosen email platform. This integration eliminates the cumbersome steps of downloading images and then uploading them again, streamlining the entire process and allowing me to focus on crafting compelling copy that accompanies the visuals.

Additionally, the integration with e-commerce platforms such as Shopify enhances my ability to create marketing materials that are directly aligned with sales efforts. By designing product images and promotional banners that reflect the current inventory, I can ensure that my marketing efforts are timely and relevant. When I design these elements in Canva, I have the ability to visualize how they will appear on the online store, which allows me to make adjustments as necessary to optimize the presentation. This integration ensures that my designs are not just visually appealing but also effectively drive sales and engagement.

Incorporating video content into my marketing strategy is another area where Canva's app integrations prove beneficial.

With the rise of video marketing, I find that the ability to create dynamic video content within Canva is invaluable. By utilizing video templates and editing tools, I can craft engaging promotional videos that highlight products or events. The integration with platforms like YouTube allows me to upload my completed videos directly, streamlining the distribution process. This not only saves time but also enhances my ability to engage with my audience through varied content formats.

The ability to access stock video and audio libraries directly within Canva further enriches my video projects. When creating a video, I often incorporate background music or sound effects to enhance the viewer's experience. The integration with audio libraries allows me to select appropriate tracks that align with my brand's tone, ensuring a cohesive auditory experience that complements the visual elements. This holistic approach to content creation helps me produce polished and professional materials that resonate with my audience.

As I continue to explore Canva's integration capabilities, I find that analytics tools also play a crucial role in evaluating the effectiveness of my designs. By connecting Canva with analytics platforms, I can track the performance of my social media posts and marketing campaigns. Understanding metrics such as engagement rates, click-through rates, and audience demographics helps me refine my strategies over time. For instance, if a particular design garners significant engagement, I analyze what elements contributed to its success, whether it be color choices, imagery, or messaging. This data-driven approach informs my future designs and enhances my overall effectiveness as a marketer.

Moreover, I recognize the value of using Canva's integrations for collaborative brainstorming sessions. When working with teams on design projects, I often utilize collaboration tools like Slack or Microsoft Teams. Integrating Canva with these platforms allows me to share designs in real time, enabling team members to provide feedback instantly. This immediate input is invaluable, as it fosters a collaborative atmosphere where ideas can be exchanged freely, ultimately enhancing the creative process. I encourage my team to use the commenting feature within Canva, which facilitates productive discussions about design choices and potential revisions.

The use of Canva's mobile app also allows me to leverage its capabilities on the go. Whether I'm traveling for business or simply away from my desk, having the ability to access my Brand Kit, edit designs, and share content directly from my mobile device ensures that I remain productive regardless of my location. This flexibility is crucial in a fast-paced work environment where quick responses to opportunities or changes in strategy are often necessary.

In the realm of education and training, Canva's apps offer tools that facilitate the creation of instructional materials and resources. By integrating with platforms such as Google Classroom, I can design engaging presentations, infographics, and other educational content that can be easily shared with students. The collaborative features of Canva allow for group projects where students can contribute their ideas and designs, fostering a sense of community and teamwork.

As I delve deeper into Canva's ecosystem, I also discover the importance of continuous learning and staying updated with new integrations. The digital landscape is ever-evolving, and I find it essential to keep abreast of the latest tools and features available within Canva. Regularly attending webinars, participating in community forums, and engaging with other users allows me to learn best practices and discover innovative uses for the platform. This ongoing education enriches my design practice, empowering me to leverage Canva's capabilities to their fullest potential.

In conclusion, exploring Canva's apps and integrations has profoundly enhanced my design workflow and overall productivity. By connecting with various tools and platforms, I have streamlined processes that allow for seamless content creation, effective marketing strategies, and collaborative projects. The ability to access a wide range of resources and functionalities within a single platform empowers me to produce high-quality designs that resonate with my audience. As I continue to leverage these integrations, I am excited about the potential they hold for expanding my creative capabilities and delivering impactful visual content across multiple channels. This journey into Canva's ecosystem not only enhances my skills as a designer but also positions me to navigate the dynamic landscape of marketing and communication with confidence and agility.

CHAPTER 21: DESIGNING EFFECTIVE PRESENTATIONS

As I embark on the journey of designing effective presentations, I recognize that the key to captivating an audience lies not only in the content but also in the way that content is visually communicated. A well-crafted presentation can transform complex ideas into accessible narratives that resonate with viewers, and it is essential to approach the design process with intention and creativity. The foundation of a compelling presentation begins with thoughtful slide layouts, which serve as the backbone of the overall narrative structure.

When I start designing a presentation, I prioritize the layout of each slide. A clear and organized layout enhances readability and allows the audience to easily follow the flow of information. I typically adopt a grid system, which provides a structured framework for positioning elements like text, images, and graphics. This structured approach not only promotes balance but also helps guide the viewer's eye naturally from one point to the next. For instance, I often use a title and content layout for introductory slides, ensuring that the key message is immediately visible. Subsequent slides may utilize a two-column layout to juxtapose text and visuals, allowing for an engaging comparison that reinforces the points being made.

In addition to the structural elements, I place great emphasis on visual storytelling techniques. Storytelling is a powerful tool in presentations, as it creates an emotional connection with the audience. To effectively convey a narrative, I begin by outlining the main message and the supporting points I wish to communicate. I then consider how visuals can complement and enhance this narrative. For example, if I am discussing the impact of a new marketing strategy, I may include graphs that illustrate key metrics, alongside images that evoke the desired emotional response. The interplay between visuals and text is crucial; I strive to ensure that each slide reinforces the narrative, avoiding clutter and ensuring that every element serves a purpose.

One of the features I find particularly useful in Canva is the ability to create custom templates. By designing a template that reflects my brand identity—through color schemes, fonts, and logo placement—I establish a consistent visual style throughout the presentation. This consistency not only enhances professionalism but also aids in brand recognition. I often choose a limited color palette that aligns with my brand's identity, ensuring that all slides maintain a cohesive look. The careful selection of fonts is equally important; I choose legible typefaces that align with the tone of my presentation. For instance, a clean sans-serif font may convey a modern and approachable feel, while a serif font could add a touch of sophistication for more formal presentations.

As I continue to design my slides, I place a strong emphasis on the effective use of images and graphics. High-quality visuals can enhance engagement and understanding, making complex information more digestible. I often incorporate infographics to summarize data or concepts visually, allowing the audience to grasp the information quickly. When selecting images, I ensure they are relevant and resonate with the audience's interests. Canva's extensive library of stock photos and graphics is invaluable in this regard; it allows me to source visuals that complement my message without compromising quality.

Moreover, I find that incorporating animations and transitions can enhance the overall flow of the presentation. Thoughtful use of animations can draw attention to specific points, guiding the audience's focus and keeping their interest piqued. However, I am careful to use animations judiciously, as excessive or distracting effects can detract from the message. For instance, I might use a subtle fade-in effect for key bullet points, allowing them to appear sequentially as I discuss each one. This technique keeps the audience engaged and reinforces the idea that the information is being presented in a clear and organized manner.

Another essential aspect of designing effective presentations is considering the pacing of the delivery. I often rehearse my presentations to ensure that I can convey the information comfortably within the allotted time. This practice allows me to refine my slides, adjusting content as needed to ensure clarity and impact. I find that leaving space for pauses during transitions or when shifting to a new topic can provide the audience with a moment to absorb the information. During rehearsals, I also pay attention to my verbal delivery, ensuring that my tone and pace align with the overall mood of the presentation.

In the context of presenting remotely, which has become increasingly common, I adapt my design strategies to account for the virtual environment. I ensure that my slides are not only visually appealing but also optimized for digital viewing. This involves selecting bold, clear fonts and high-contrast colors to ensure readability on various screens. I often include larger visuals and minimal text to accommodate viewers who may be participating from smaller devices, such as smartphones or tablets. Understanding the dynamics of virtual presentations helps me create an engaging experience, even when I am not physically present with my audience.

The feedback I receive from presentations is invaluable for my growth as a designer and presenter. After each presentation, I take the time to reflect on what worked well and what could be improved. I often solicit feedback from colleagues or mentors, who provide insights into the clarity of my visuals and the effectiveness of my delivery. This iterative process of design and feedback allows me to refine my approach continually, ultimately leading to more effective presentations over time.

In conclusion, creating impactful presentations involves a multifaceted approach that combines thoughtful design principles with effective storytelling techniques. By focusing on slide layouts, visual elements, and engaging delivery, I can craft presentations that captivate and resonate with my audience. The tools and features offered by Canva enhance my ability to execute this vision, enabling me to produce polished and professional presentations that communicate my ideas clearly and effectively. As I continue to hone my skills in this area, I am excited to discover new ways to engage audiences and convey messages through the art of presentation design.

As I delve deeper into the nuances of designing effective presentations, I recognize that the rhythm and flow of the slides play a pivotal role in keeping the audience engaged. The transitions between slides should be as seamless as the ideas being presented, and I often consider how each slide relates to the previous one and the next. By employing a narrative arc—a clear beginning, middle, and end—I can guide the audience through my points, ensuring they remain connected to the overall message. This storytelling approach transforms a series of disparate slides into a cohesive journey, making the information more memorable.

To enhance the narrative structure of my presentations, I typically start with an attention-grabbing opening slide. This could be an impactful image, a provocative question, or a surprising statistic that sets the stage for what's to come. The key is to capture the audience's attention from the outset, encouraging them to invest their focus and interest in the presentation. I often use Canva's extensive library of visuals to find images that not only align with my message but also evoke an emotional response. A well-chosen visual can resonate with the audience on a deeper level, making them more receptive to the information that follows.

Once I have established an engaging opening, I strategically structure the body of the presentation to build upon that initial interest. I like to break down complex ideas into digestible segments, using clear headings and subheadings to delineate each section. This hierarchical structure not only improves comprehension but also helps maintain focus. Each slide becomes a stepping stone toward the conclusion, reinforcing the main points while providing the necessary context. To visually enhance this structure, I often employ consistent color schemes and typography from my Brand Kit, ensuring that each slide feels like part of a unified whole.

Visual storytelling is a crucial technique I leverage throughout the presentation. Instead of overwhelming the audience with dense blocks of text, I focus on key points, using concise bullet points or short phrases to communicate essential information. I find that this minimalist approach keeps the audience engaged and encourages them to listen rather than read. Accompanying these text elements with relevant visuals—such as charts, diagrams, or infographics—further reinforces the message. For example, when discussing trends or statistics, a well-designed chart can convey complex data at a glance, making it easier for the audience to grasp and retain the information.

As I create each slide, I am mindful of the pacing of my delivery. I often rehearse my presentations to determine how long I should spend on each slide, ensuring that I do not rush through important points or linger too long on any one element. Effective pacing allows me to emphasize key takeaways while still keeping the audience's attention. During these rehearsals, I pay attention to my verbal delivery, adjusting my tone and cadence to match the content. For instance, I may slow down my speech when introducing critical concepts to allow the audience to absorb the information fully.

When it comes to integrating multimedia elements, I find that adding audio or video can significantly enhance engagement. For instance, I might include a short video clip that illustrates a key point or provides a real-world example of the concepts being discussed. Canva's integration with video editing tools allows me to incorporate these elements seamlessly into my slides, ensuring a polished presentation. When using videos, I am careful to keep them concise and relevant, ensuring that they serve to enhance rather than detract from the overall message.

Another aspect of presentation design that I take seriously is the consideration of accessibility. As I design my slides, I keep in mind the diverse needs of my audience. This includes using high-contrast color combinations to ensure readability, choosing legible fonts, and avoiding overly complex language. By making my presentations accessible to all audience members, I demonstrate a commitment to inclusivity and ensure that everyone can engage with the content. I often test my designs by asking colleagues for feedback on readability and clarity, allowing me to make necessary adjustments before the final presentation.

In the realm of virtual presentations, I recognize that

additional considerations come into play. With the rise of remote work and online meetings, ensuring that my presentations are effective in a digital format is paramount. I adjust my slide designs to be easily viewable on various screen sizes, keeping text large enough to read and avoiding cluttered layouts. Additionally, I pay special attention to how I present myself on camera, ensuring that I maintain eye contact with the audience and engage with them through the screen. This virtual connection is essential for fostering engagement, even in a digital environment.

As I conclude the presentation, I strive to leave the audience with a strong, memorable message. The final slide should encapsulate the key takeaways, often summarized in a visually compelling way. This could involve a powerful quote, a call to action, or a visual that resonates with the main theme of the presentation. I often ask myself what I want the audience to remember long after the presentation is over and design the closing slide accordingly. This thoughtfulness ensures that my presentation not only informs but also inspires action or reflection.

The importance of follow-up cannot be overstated. After delivering a presentation, I often share the slides with my audience, allowing them to revisit the information and concepts discussed. This practice not only reinforces the message but also opens the door for further engagement. I might include additional resources or links to relevant articles, encouraging audience members to continue exploring the topic. By providing these materials, I enhance the overall impact of my presentation, ensuring that it lives on beyond the initial delivery.

In reflecting on the journey of designing effective presentations, I realize that the process involves a delicate balance of creativity, strategy, and communication skills. By thoughtfully considering slide layouts, incorporating visual storytelling techniques, and utilizing Canva's features to their fullest potential, I am able to craft presentations that captivate and engage my audience. This multifaceted approach ensures that my message is conveyed with clarity and impact, fostering a connection that resonates long after the presentation concludes. As I continue to refine my skills in this area, I look forward to discovering new ways to engage and inspire audiences through the art of presentation design.

As I delve into the final elements of designing effective presentations, I recognize that the delivery of my content is just as important as the visual design itself. Even the most beautifully crafted slides can fall flat if not presented with confidence and clarity. I take great care in preparing not only the slides but also my verbal delivery and body language to ensure that I connect with my audience in a meaningful way.

I begin by considering the importance of practice. Rehearsing my presentation multiple times allows me to refine my timing, smooth out any rough transitions, and ensure that my key points are communicated effectively. During these practice sessions, I focus on vocal variety—modulating my tone and pace to emphasize important points and maintain audience engagement. I often record myself to assess my delivery, allowing me to identify areas for improvement, such as pacing issues or unclear explanations. This self-review process is invaluable in building my confidence and ensuring that I convey my message with authority.

I also pay careful attention to body language during my presentations. Nonverbal cues can significantly influence how my message is received. Maintaining eye contact with the audience fosters a sense of connection and trust, while open gestures can enhance my points and engage the audience visually. I consciously avoid crossing my arms or using closed-off postures, opting instead for relaxed and welcoming gestures that invite participation. This body language helps create an atmosphere of openness, encouraging audience members to feel comfortable asking questions or sharing their thoughts during or after the presentation.

As I consider audience interaction, I find that incorporating questions or prompts throughout my presentation can significantly enhance engagement. Rather than waiting until the end for a Q&A session, I often pause at strategic points to invite questions or encourage discussion. This not only keeps the audience involved but also allows me to gauge their understanding and adjust my delivery as needed. I have found that prompting the audience to reflect on what they have learned or to share their own experiences related to the topic can lead to a more dynamic and memorable presentation.

In terms of visual elements, I recognize the importance of simplicity and clarity in slide design. While I strive for creativity, I also ensure that each slide communicates a single idea clearly. I often utilize white space strategically, allowing the content to breathe and making it easier for the audience to focus on the main message. Cluttered slides with excessive information can overwhelm viewers, leading to disengagement. By adhering to the principle of "less is more," I can create slides that are visually appealing and effective in conveying my points without unnecessary distraction.

Another aspect I focus on is the use of transitions and animations within my presentation. While these features can enhance engagement when used judiciously, I am mindful not to overdo it. I typically choose subtle transitions that help guide the audience's attention without becoming a distraction. For example, using a simple fade-in effect for bullet points allows me to introduce each point sequentially, reinforcing the narrative and helping the audience absorb information more effectively. I strive for a balanced approach where transitions enhance rather than detract from the overall message.

As I approach the conclusion of my presentation, I aim to leave the audience with a strong takeaway. This final impression is crucial; I often summarize the key points discussed and reinforce the main message, ensuring it resonates with the audience. I find that using a compelling quote or a call to action can further emphasize the importance of the material. By articulating what I want the audience to remember and act upon, I enhance the likelihood that my presentation will have a lasting impact.

Following the presentation, I make it a point to engage with the audience further. I welcome questions and discussions, which not only clarifies any uncertainties but also provides an opportunity for deeper engagement. I often encourage audience members to share their perspectives or experiences related to the topic, fostering a collaborative environment where everyone feels valued. This interaction reinforces the idea that presentations are not just one-way communications but rather opportunities for dialogue and exchange.

In addition, I consider the importance of follow-up materials. After concluding my presentation, I typically share the slides and any additional resources with the audience. This not only reinforces the content covered but also provides them with tools to explore the topic further. I often include links to relevant articles, studies, or tools that can help deepen their understanding. By providing these resources, I enhance the overall experience and ensure that my message continues to resonate after the presentation is over.

Lastly, I reflect on the lessons learned from each presentation experience. Gathering feedback from attendees, whether through informal conversations or structured surveys, allows me to identify areas for improvement. I pay attention to comments about clarity, engagement, and overall effectiveness, using this input to refine my future presentations. This continuous improvement mindset is essential in my journey as a designer and presenter, as it empowers me to adapt and grow in response to audience needs and preferences.

As I conclude my exploration of effective presentation design, I recognize that the art of creating impactful presentations is an ongoing journey. Each experience builds upon the last, allowing me to develop my skills and enhance my ability to engage audiences. By focusing on slide layouts, visual storytelling techniques, and the thoughtful integration of design elements, I can create presentations that are not only informative but also inspiring. The tools and features offered by Canva enhance my ability to execute this vision, empowering me to craft compelling presentations that resonate deeply with my audience. This commitment to excellence in presentation design ensures that my messages are communicated with clarity and impact, fostering connections that endure long after the presentation has ended.

CHAPTER 22: CREATING ENGAGING MARKETING MATERIALS

In the realm of marketing, the ability to create engaging materials is essential for capturing attention and communicating effectively with the audience. As I set out to design marketing materials such as flyers, brochures, and posters using Canva, I recognize that the visual aspects of these designs play a pivotal role in not only attracting attention but also conveying a message that resonates with the intended audience. The process begins with a thorough understanding of the target demographic, as this knowledge informs every design decision I make.

The first step in creating impactful marketing materials is selecting the right template. Canva offers a plethora of templates tailored for various purposes and industries, which serves as a valuable starting point. When choosing a template, I consider the overall tone and messaging of my marketing campaign. For example, a vibrant and playful template might be suitable for a children's event, while a sleek and professional design would better suit a corporate workshop. By aligning the template with the campaign's objectives and audience expectations, I set the stage for a cohesive design that communicates the intended message effectively.

Once I have selected a template, I focus on customizing it to reflect my brand identity. This involves incorporating brand elements such as logos, color palettes, and fonts that are consistent with my overall branding strategy. I utilize Canva's Brand Kit feature to ensure that these elements are readily accessible, allowing for a seamless integration into my designs. Maintaining consistency across all marketing materials is crucial, as it reinforces brand recognition and fosters trust with the audience. As I customize the template, I pay careful attention to how each element interacts with the overall design, ensuring that the visual hierarchy is clear and that the most important information stands out.

A significant aspect of designing effective marketing materials is the strategic use of persuasive design elements. I often employ compelling visuals that capture attention and evoke emotions. High-quality images, graphics, and icons play an important role in making materials visually appealing. I select images that not only relate to the content but also resonate with the target audience. For example, if I am creating a promotional flyer for a local health fair, I might choose images of diverse individuals engaging in healthy activities, thus promoting an inclusive and vibrant community atmosphere. These visuals serve to draw the audience in, making them more likely to engage with the content.

In addition to imagery, typography is a critical component of my design. I carefully select fonts that are not only legible but also reflective of the campaign's tone. For example, using bold, modern fonts can convey a sense of urgency and excitement, while more traditional serif fonts might evoke a sense of reliability and trustworthiness. I typically utilize a maximum of two or three font styles within each design to maintain clarity and cohesion. The title should always stand out, drawing the viewer's eye immediately, while the body text should be easy to read at a glance. I often employ contrast

—using darker text on a lighter background or vice versa—to enhance readability and ensure that the key messages are easily digestible.

As I refine the design, I consider the layout and structure of the marketing material. I find that a balanced layout not only enhances visual appeal but also guides the viewer's eye naturally through the content. I utilize grid systems to create an organized structure, ensuring that elements are aligned and spaced consistently. This attention to detail helps convey professionalism and care, which are qualities that audiences often look for in marketing materials. I also ensure that there is sufficient white space around text and images, which allows the design to breathe and prevents it from feeling cluttered or overwhelming.

While crafting the content of my marketing materials, I focus on creating a compelling narrative that resonates with the audience. I aim to articulate a clear message that communicates the value proposition effectively. For instance, when writing the text for a brochure promoting a new product, I emphasize the benefits and unique features that set it apart from competitors. I often use action-oriented language to encourage the audience to take the next step, whether that means visiting a website, signing up for an event, or making a purchase. This persuasive writing style complements the visual elements of the design, creating a cohesive and impactful marketing piece.

Another critical element to consider is the call to action (CTA). A strong CTA is essential for guiding the audience toward the desired action. I ensure that the CTA is prominently displayed, using bold text or contrasting colors to make it stand out. Phrasing like "Sign Up Now," "Learn More," or "Get Your Free Sample" creates a sense of urgency and encourages the audience to respond. I often position the CTA strategically, such as at the end of a flyer or brochure, where it serves as a natural conclusion to the narrative I have built throughout the material.

As I finalize the design, I also ensure that it is optimized for the intended distribution channels. Whether the materials will be printed, shared digitally, or posted on social media, I make necessary adjustments to ensure compatibility. For print materials, I pay careful attention to resolution and file formats to ensure high-quality output. I often export designs in PDF format for printing, ensuring that all elements are crisp and clear. For digital distribution, I consider optimizing images for faster loading times while maintaining visual quality. Understanding the specifications for different platforms—such as social media dimensions—allows me to tailor my designs effectively for their intended use.

Throughout this process, I continuously seek feedback from colleagues or peers. Their perspectives can provide valuable insights and help identify areas for improvement that I may have overlooked. Engaging in collaborative discussions about design choices, content effectiveness, and overall impact can lead to stronger marketing materials. This feedback loop fosters a culture of creativity and refinement, ultimately enhancing the quality of the final product.

In summary, the creation of engaging marketing materials involves a thoughtful and strategic approach. By carefully selecting templates, incorporating persuasive design elements, and ensuring clarity in messaging, I can craft marketing materials that effectively capture attention and communicate key information. The tools available within Canva empower me to execute this vision, allowing for a seamless design process that ultimately enhances the overall effectiveness of my marketing efforts. As I continue to refine my skills in this area, I look forward to exploring new techniques and strategies that will further elevate the impact of my marketing materials.

As I delve deeper into the creation of engaging marketing materials, I find that one of the most critical aspects is understanding the context in which these materials will be used. Different environments and audiences require tailored approaches. For instance, a flyer designed for a local event must not only attract attention but also provide clear logistical details, whereas a brochure promoting a service may focus more on conveying benefits and establishing credibility. By taking into account the context and the specific goals of each marketing piece, I can better align my design choices with the desired outcomes.

To begin this nuanced process, I conduct thorough research on my target audience. I seek to understand their preferences, pain points, and motivations, which informs every design decision I make. For example, if I am creating a flyer for a fitness program targeting young professionals, I might opt for a modern aesthetic with vibrant colors and dynamic imagery that resonates with an active lifestyle. On the other hand, if the audience is retirees interested in a community health fair, a more subdued color palette and accessible fonts may be more appropriate to convey trust and approachability.

Once I have a clear understanding of the audience, I turn my attention to selecting the most suitable template from Canva's extensive library. The template serves as the foundation for my design and can significantly influence the effectiveness of the final product. I evaluate various templates based on their layout, style, and alignment with the brand identity I wish to convey. When I find a template that resonates, I carefully analyze its structure to ensure it can accommodate the content I plan to include without feeling cramped or overwhelming.

After selecting a template, I focus on customizing it to ensure it is unique and reflective of my brand. This process begins with the application of consistent branding elements, including logos, color schemes, and typography. I utilize

Canva's Brand Kit, which allows me to easily access and apply these elements throughout my designs. This consistency is crucial, as it reinforces brand recognition and helps establish trust with the audience. I often adjust the color scheme of the template to align with my brand's colors, ensuring that each element feels cohesive and intentional.

As I customize the design, I prioritize the strategic placement of persuasive design elements that can enhance the effectiveness of the marketing material. Imagery plays a crucial role here; I select visuals that not only complement the content but also evoke an emotional response from the viewer. Whether it's a vibrant photograph of a smiling group participating in an event or a striking graphic that illustrates a key benefit of a product, the right visuals can draw the audience in and encourage them to engage with the content.

Typography is another essential component that I pay careful attention to in my designs. I choose fonts that align with the tone of the marketing material and are legible at a distance, especially for posters and flyers. I often employ a combination of font styles—one for headings and another for body text—to create visual interest while maintaining clarity. The hierarchy established through typography allows the audience to quickly identify key messages and navigate the content effortlessly. For instance, using a bold font for the title alongside a lighter weight for supporting text helps to guide the viewer's attention effectively.

In addition to these design choices, I understand the importance of a compelling call to action (CTA). The CTA is a crucial element that prompts the audience to take the next step, whether it be signing up for an event, visiting a website, or making a purchase. I ensure that the CTA is prominently displayed, often utilizing contrasting colors or larger text to make it stand out. I carefully phrase the CTA to create a sense of urgency or excitement, using action-oriented language that encourages immediate engagement. For example, phrases like "Join Us Today" or "Limited Spots Available" can effectively motivate the audience to respond promptly.

As I continue refining my marketing materials, I prioritize the use of data to inform my design choices. By analyzing metrics from previous campaigns, I gain valuable insights into what resonates with my audience. For instance, if past flyers with certain color schemes or imagery performed significantly better than others, I take this information into account when designing new materials. This data-driven approach not only enhances the effectiveness of my designs but also fosters a greater understanding of the audience's preferences.

Once I have finalized my designs, I take care to prepare them for distribution. If I am creating printed materials, I ensure that the resolution is suitable for high-quality printing, often opting for PDF exports to preserve the integrity of the graphics. I also pay close attention to bleed and margin settings to prevent any important elements from being cut off during printing. For digital marketing materials, I optimize file sizes to ensure quick loading times without sacrificing visual quality. This attention to detail is vital for maintaining professionalism and ensuring that my materials perform well across different platforms.

Additionally, I consider how the marketing materials will be distributed. For instance, if I am designing flyers for a community event, I think about how they will be handed out —whether at local businesses, community centers, or events. This context influences the design, as I may opt for more durable paper stock or a design that accommodates a tear-off section for interested individuals to take with them. Understanding the logistics of distribution allows me to create materials that are not only visually appealing but also practical for real-world use.

Lastly, I place great importance on gathering feedback after the distribution of my marketing materials. This can involve informal conversations with audience members or conducting surveys to understand their reactions and preferences. The insights gained from this feedback loop provide valuable information that I can incorporate into future designs. By remaining open to constructive criticism and continuously learning from each project, I enhance my ability to create effective marketing materials that resonate with my target audience.

In this journey of creating engaging marketing materials, I recognize the powerful impact that thoughtful design can have on communication. By strategically selecting templates, incorporating persuasive elements, and ensuring clarity in messaging, I am able to craft materials that not only attract attention but also drive action. The tools and resources available through Canva empower me to execute this vision effectively, allowing me to create marketing pieces that are both visually compelling and strategically sound. As I continue to refine my skills in this area, I look forward to exploring new techniques and approaches that will further elevate the effectiveness of my marketing efforts.

As I move into the final stages of creating engaging marketing materials, I recognize that effective distribution and evaluation are critical components that can greatly influence the success of my designs. Once the materials are finalized, I shift my focus to how they will be shared and promoted to maximize their impact. This involves strategic planning regarding both the physical distribution of print materials and the digital dissemination of online content.

When preparing to distribute printed marketing materials, I consider the venues and events where my audience is likely to be present. This could include local community events, trade shows, or business expos. Each setting presents unique opportunities for interaction. For instance, when attending a community event, I often create an eye-catching display that not only showcases my flyers and brochures but also invites conversation. By incorporating elements such as a visually appealing tablecloth and promotional items, I can create a welcoming atmosphere that encourages attendees to engage with the materials. I find that an interactive display can enhance the effectiveness of the marketing materials, as it provides an avenue for direct communication with potential customers.

Moreover, the timing of distribution is equally important. I analyze the schedules of events and relevant holidays to ensure that my marketing materials reach the audience when they are most receptive. For example, if I'm promoting a summer festival, I aim to distribute flyers well in advance, allowing potential attendees ample time to make plans. By timing my distribution effectively, I can capitalize on peak interest periods, thereby increasing engagement and attendance.

In addition to print distribution, I also focus on digital channels for disseminating marketing materials. Social media platforms serve as powerful tools for reaching broader audiences, and I strategically adapt my materials for these channels. This often involves resizing graphics to fit platform specifications and creating tailored content for each medium. For instance, a vibrant poster can be transformed into a series of social media posts that highlight different aspects of the event or promotion, thus maximizing the reach of the original design. I take advantage of Canva's scheduling features to plan and automate these posts, ensuring consistent visibility across platforms.

Engagement through digital channels doesn't stop at mere distribution; I actively monitor and interact with my audience online. When I post marketing materials on social media, I encourage my followers to share their thoughts or experiences related to the content. This interaction not only builds community but also provides valuable insights into how my materials are being received. For instance, I may ask questions such as, "What are you most excited about at our upcoming event?" or "How have our services impacted your life?" Engaging my audience in this way fosters a sense of connection and encourages them to feel more invested in my brand.

After distribution, the evaluation of the effectiveness of my marketing materials becomes a priority. I employ various metrics to gauge success, including tracking engagement rates on social media posts, analyzing website traffic generated from specific campaigns, and measuring attendance at events. For instance, if I notice a significant increase in web traffic following the release of a particular brochure, I take that as an indicator that the design resonated with the audience and successfully directed them to learn more. Conversely, if a specific flyer underperformed, I assess what may have contributed to that outcome, such as design elements or messaging. This analysis helps me refine my approach for future campaigns.

Additionally, I make use of feedback mechanisms to gather insights directly from my audience. I often include QR codes on printed materials that link to brief surveys, encouraging recipients to share their thoughts on the design and messaging. This feedback is invaluable, as it provides real-world insights into how the materials are perceived and what improvements can be made. The willingness of my audience to provide input reflects their engagement, and I view this as an opportunity for growth.

In terms of continuous improvement, I also draw inspiration from successful marketing campaigns across various industries. I analyze what elements made those campaigns effective and consider how I can adapt similar strategies to my own materials. For instance, if I observe that a competitor's brochure effectively utilized storytelling techniques, I may experiment with incorporating narrative elements into my designs. This process of exploration and adaptation is essential for keeping my marketing materials fresh and relevant in a competitive landscape.

As I reflect on the design process for marketing materials, I find that collaboration often leads to enhanced creativity. I value the input of colleagues and other creatives who can provide different perspectives on design choices. By involving others in brainstorming sessions or feedback loops, I can generate new ideas and refine existing concepts. This collaborative spirit not only enriches the design process but also fosters a sense of community and shared ownership of the final product.

In conclusion, the creation of engaging marketing materials involves a comprehensive approach that encompasses design, distribution, evaluation, and continuous improvement. By strategically selecting templates, incorporating persuasive elements, and considering the needs and preferences of my target audience, I can develop materials that effectively capture attention and drive engagement. The tools provided by Canva empower me to execute this vision seamlessly, allowing for a cohesive design process that ultimately enhances the impact of my marketing efforts. As I continue to hone my skills in this area, I remain committed to exploring innovative strategies that will elevate the effectiveness of my marketing materials and foster deeper connections with my audience.

CHAPTER 23: DESIGNING FOR MOBILE AND WEB

As I embark on the process of designing for mobile and web platforms, I recognize that the digital landscape is characterized by an ever-increasing variety of screen sizes and resolutions. This diversity poses unique challenges and opportunities that require careful consideration to ensure optimal user experiences across devices. The primary goal in creating responsive graphics is to maintain visual integrity and functionality, regardless of the platform on which the content is viewed. I begin this endeavor by understanding the foundational principles of responsive design and how they apply to both mobile and web environments.

One of the first steps I take is to familiarize myself with the various screen sizes and resolutions that my audience may be using. The proliferation of smartphones, tablets, and desktops means that my designs must adapt to a wide range of dimensions. For mobile devices, I pay particular attention to portrait and landscape orientations, as well as the fact that touch interactions differ from mouse clicks. This means I need to consider the placement of buttons and interactive elements, ensuring they are not only accessible but also easy to tap without causing frustration for the user.

As I begin designing, I typically start with a mobile-first approach. This means I prioritize the mobile layout and then expand to accommodate larger screens. By focusing on mobile design first, I am forced to streamline content and eliminate unnecessary elements, leading to a cleaner and more focused design. This approach is crucial because it helps prioritize the most important information, which is particularly beneficial given the limited screen space available on mobile devices. I often create wireframes to sketch out the layout, ensuring that the essential elements are easily accessible while maintaining an intuitive flow.

When utilizing Canva for my designs, I leverage its ability to create custom dimensions tailored specifically for mobile screens. By selecting the appropriate size from the outset, I can focus on optimizing every element for clarity and impact. I tend to use larger fonts and ample spacing, as smaller text can be difficult to read on mobile devices. The goal is to enhance legibility and make navigation as straightforward as possible. I also find that using contrasting colors for text and backgrounds enhances readability, especially in outdoor settings where glare can be an issue.

In considering the design for web platforms, I aim to create responsive layouts that automatically adjust based on the screen size. This adaptability is crucial as users might access the same content on a desktop, laptop, or tablet. I take advantage of grid systems to organize content effectively, allowing for a fluid design that rearranges itself seamlessly across devices. In Canva, I often use flexible grids and templates that can easily be adjusted, ensuring that images and text adapt without losing their intended message or aesthetic.

Visual hierarchy is another key component I focus on in my designs. It is essential to guide the viewer's eye toward the most important elements of the content, whether they are viewing on a mobile device or a desktop. I utilize size, color, and placement strategically to create a clear path for the audience to follow. For instance, I may use a larger, bold heading at the top of the screen, followed by subheadings that draw attention to the key points. Incorporating visual breaks, such as horizontal lines or spacing, can also help segment information, making it easier for users to digest.

As I continue developing my designs, I consider the role of imagery and graphics. High-quality images that are optimized for web and mobile viewing are critical in maintaining engagement. Canva provides a wealth of stock images and graphic elements that I can incorporate, and I always ensure they are appropriately sized to avoid slow loading times. On mobile, where data usage might be a concern, I often opt for images that are both visually appealing and lightweight to ensure quick loading speeds. In contrast, for web designs, I can utilize higher-resolution images that enhance the visual experience without sacrificing performance.

Another important consideration is the interactivity of my designs. For mobile interfaces, I make sure that buttons and links are appropriately sized and spaced to accommodate touch interactions. A good rule of thumb I follow is to ensure that buttons are at least 44 pixels high, as this size is generally easy for users to tap accurately. I also ensure that any interactive elements have clear visual cues, such as hover effects or color changes, which provide feedback to users, reinforcing their actions.

Furthermore, I recognize the importance of testing my designs on various devices before finalizing them. This testing phase allows me to observe how my graphics behave across different screen sizes and orientations, ensuring that they function as intended. I often use tools that simulate different devices to visualize how the designs will appear in real-world scenarios. By testing for responsiveness, I can identify and address any issues, such as overlapping text or misaligned elements, before they reach the audience.

In addition to visual considerations, I also focus on the emotional impact of my designs. User experience extends beyond mere functionality; it encompasses the feelings and connections that users have with the content. I strive to create designs that evoke the desired emotional response, whether that's excitement, curiosity, or trust. The careful selection of images, colors, and typography plays a vital role in achieving this emotional connection.

Ultimately, the key to effective design for mobile and web platforms lies in understanding the unique characteristics and user behaviors associated with each medium. By adopting a mobile-first approach, utilizing responsive layouts, and prioritizing clarity and engagement, I can create marketing materials that resonate with my audience. The tools available within Canva empower me to execute this vision seamlessly, allowing for a cohesive design process that enhances the user experience across all devices. As I continue to refine my skills in this area, I am excited to explore new techniques and strategies that will further elevate my ability to design effective digital content.

As I continue my exploration of designing for mobile and web platforms, it becomes increasingly clear that user experience (UX) should remain at the forefront of every design decision. A critical aspect of achieving an optimal UX lies in the seamless navigation that allows users to interact with content intuitively. I focus on ensuring that navigation elements—such as menus, buttons, and links—are not only visually appealing but also strategically placed for ease of access. For mobile designs, where screen real estate is limited, I often prioritize a simplified navigation structure that minimizes the number of clicks needed to access critical information.

When designing navigation for mobile platforms, I gravitate toward a hamburger menu or tab bar format. The hamburger menu, which collapses into a single icon, conserves space while still offering access to various sections of the content. This approach allows users to focus on the main content without being overwhelmed by options. Conversely, for desktop designs, I utilize a horizontal navigation bar that clearly displays the primary categories, ensuring that users can quickly find what they are looking for. This dual approach allows me to maintain a cohesive user experience across platforms while catering to the specific needs of each device.

Responsive design requires a deep understanding of fluid grids and flexible images. I implement a grid-based layout that adapts to different screen sizes by utilizing percentages rather than fixed measurements. This technique ensures that the layout adjusts dynamically, maintaining the visual hierarchy and balance regardless of the device. I take care to create breakpoints in my designs, which are specific points where the layout changes to accommodate different screen sizes. For example, a three-column layout on a desktop may shift to a single-column format on mobile, streamlining the presentation of information for users.

Another key consideration in designing for mobile and web is the optimization of images and other visual elements. I focus on file formats that offer a good balance between quality and loading speed. For instance, I often choose to use WebP images for their superior compression capabilities without sacrificing quality, particularly in mobile contexts where users may be concerned about data usage. By optimizing image sizes and leveraging responsive image techniques, I can ensure that visuals load quickly, enhancing the overall user experience. This focus on performance is essential, as slow-loading graphics can lead to increased bounce rates and frustration among users.

I also recognize the importance of accessibility in my designs. A well-designed user experience is inclusive and considers users with varying abilities. I adhere to Web

Content Accessibility Guidelines (WCAG) by ensuring that text contrasts sufficiently with backgrounds, images have descriptive alt text, and interactive elements are navigable using keyboard shortcuts. This inclusivity not only broadens the audience but also reflects a commitment to thoughtful design practices. By designing with accessibility in mind, I create a more welcoming environment for all users, ensuring they can interact with my content seamlessly.

Color choices play a significant role in how users perceive and engage with content. I select colors that not only align with my brand identity but also enhance usability. High contrast between text and backgrounds improves readability, particularly on smaller screens where eye strain can occur more easily. Additionally, I consider the psychological impact of colors on user emotions and actions. For instance, using warm colors like red or orange can evoke urgency, making them ideal for calls to action. Conversely, cooler colors like blue can convey trust and professionalism, making them suitable for more serious contexts. Understanding color theory allows me to create designs that not only look appealing but also elicit the desired responses from users.

As I design for various platforms, I remain acutely aware of the different contexts in which users engage with my content. For instance, mobile users are often on-the-go, seeking quick information and immediate solutions. To cater to this behavior, I focus on concise messaging and clear visuals that communicate key points quickly. I often utilize bullet points or infographics to present information succinctly, ensuring that even a quick glance conveys the essential message. This prioritization of clarity ensures that my marketing materials are effective in capturing attention, even in fleeting moments.

In contrast, web users may be more inclined to engage with content at length, often seeking deeper information. For web designs, I leverage this tendency by incorporating elements such as expandable sections or interactive graphics that allow users to explore content in greater detail. This interactivity keeps users engaged while providing them the freedom to navigate at their own pace. By offering multiple layers of information, I cater to diverse user preferences and enhance overall satisfaction with the experience.

As I finalize my designs, I consider the testing phase to be crucial. Before launching any marketing materials, I often conduct usability tests on different devices. This involves gathering feedback from real users to identify pain points, such as difficult navigation or unclear content. By observing users as they interact with the design, I gain invaluable insights into how to improve the experience. I take note of any areas where users hesitate or express confusion, allowing me to make informed adjustments that enhance usability.

Moreover, I analyze metrics post-launch to understand how my designs are performing in the real world. Tools such as Google Analytics provide data on user interactions, bounce rates, and conversions, which help me gauge the effectiveness of my designs. If I find that users are frequently abandoning a mobile landing page or failing to engage with a call to action, I delve into the specifics to identify the underlying issues. This data-driven approach enables me to iterate on my designs, making continuous improvements that align with user needs and preferences.

In the end, designing for mobile and web platforms is an intricate process that balances aesthetics, functionality, and user experience. By employing responsive design techniques, optimizing visuals, and incorporating accessibility features, I can create marketing materials that effectively engage users across a spectrum of devices. The insights gained from user testing and analytics further refine my designs, ensuring they remain relevant and effective. As I continue to navigate the evolving landscape of digital design, I am excited to explore innovative approaches that enhance user experiences and create lasting connections with my audience.

As I continue to refine my approach to designing for mobile and web platforms, I recognize that user feedback remains an invaluable asset in shaping effective designs. After launching my marketing materials, I actively solicit feedback from users to understand their experiences. This process often involves creating surveys or using feedback tools embedded within the digital content itself. By asking targeted questions about usability, aesthetics, and overall satisfaction, I can gather qualitative insights that complement the quantitative data collected through analytics.

Engagement with users post-launch is not merely about gathering data; it is also an opportunity for connection. When I respond to feedback or clarify doubts, I foster a sense of community around my brand. This engagement can turn casual viewers into loyal advocates, as they appreciate that their voices are heard and valued. I often share updates or improvements made based on their suggestions, reinforcing the idea that the design process is collaborative rather than unilateral.

Another critical consideration in my design process is the incorporation of accessibility features, ensuring that all users, regardless of ability, can engage with my content effectively. I take particular care to implement features such as alternative text for images, which not only aids visually impaired users utilizing screen readers but also enhances SEO. Additionally, I ensure that all interactive elements are keyboard navigable, accommodating users who may have mobility challenges. By incorporating these features from the outset, I create a more inclusive experience that broadens my audience reach.

As I design mobile and web content, I also focus on optimizing loading times. In today's fast-paced digital environment, users expect content to load almost instantaneously. I often compress images and minimize the use of heavy graphics that can slow down performance. Furthermore, I consider the file formats used; for instance, I typically opt for SVG files for logos and icons due to their scalability and small file size. This optimization not only improves the user experience but also enhances the overall performance of the website or application, positively impacting search engine rankings.

An additional aspect I explore is the use of responsive typography. The text must remain legible and aesthetically pleasing across various devices, so I often use relative units such as percentages or ems rather than fixed pixel sizes. This flexibility allows my text to scale appropriately, ensuring that headlines, body text, and calls to action are readable on both mobile and desktop platforms. Moreover, I pay close attention to line height and letter spacing, which can greatly influence readability. A well-proportioned text layout encourages users to read through the content without experiencing fatigue, which is especially crucial for lengthy articles or promotional materials.

With regard to interactive elements, I ensure that buttons and links are clearly defined and accessible. On mobile devices, I make sure that touch targets are large enough to be easily tapped, typically aiming for a minimum size of 44 pixels by 44 pixels. This attention to detail helps reduce user frustration, as it minimizes the likelihood of misclicks. I also employ hover effects and visual cues that provide feedback to users when they interact with these elements, reinforcing a sense of engagement.

I often utilize A/B testing to evaluate different design variations and their impact on user behavior. By presenting two versions of a design to different audience segments, I can analyze which elements drive higher engagement or conversion rates. This data-driven approach allows me to make informed decisions about design choices, ensuring that

I prioritize features that resonate with users. For instance, if one button color consistently results in higher click-through rates, I will consider adopting that color across my marketing materials for better performance.

In addition to testing and feedback, I remain committed to staying abreast of emerging design trends and technological advancements. The digital landscape is constantly evolving, and what works today may not be effective tomorrow. I regularly engage with design communities, attend webinars, and follow industry leaders to gain insights into innovative practices. By continually updating my knowledge, I can ensure that my designs remain relevant and appealing to users.

Furthermore, I recognize the importance of storytelling in digital content. Users are often more engaged when they can connect emotionally with the material. I strive to incorporate narratives into my designs that resonate with the audience. Whether it's through compelling images, relatable anecdotes, or powerful statistics, I aim to create a connection that prompts users to reflect on their own experiences and motivations. This storytelling aspect not only enhances engagement but also fosters a deeper understanding of the content being presented.

Finally, as I refine my designs for mobile and web platforms, I focus on creating a seamless user journey from start to finish. This journey encompasses everything from the first impression of the landing page to the final call to action. I ensure that every touchpoint is cohesive and reinforces the overall message, creating a sense of continuity that guides users through the content. By focusing on user experience holistically, I can create designs that not only look great but also effectively drive user engagement and action.

In conclusion, designing for mobile and web platforms requires a multifaceted approach that prioritizes user experience, accessibility, and performance. By leveraging responsive design techniques, optimizing visual elements, and actively engaging with users, I can create compelling marketing materials that effectively capture attention and drive interaction. The tools available within Canva empower me to execute this vision with ease, allowing for a streamlined design process that enhances the overall effectiveness of my digital content. As I continue to refine my skills in this area, I look forward to embracing new opportunities and techniques that will further enhance my ability to create impactful designs in the ever-evolving digital landscape.

CHAPTER 24: DESIGNING FOR DIFFERENT PLATFORMS**

As I delve into the intricacies of designing for different digital platforms, I realize that understanding the unique requirements and characteristics of each platform is essential for creating visually compelling and effective designs. Each platform presents its own set of constraints and opportunities, from screen sizes to user interactions. This understanding forms the foundation of my design strategy, enabling me to tailor my visuals to suit the specific context in which they will be viewed.

One of the first considerations in this process is recognizing the varying dimensions and resolutions of devices. Designing for a desktop website, for instance, allows for more space to showcase content, whereas mobile applications demand a more compact layout that prioritizes essential information. I often begin by researching the standard dimensions for each platform, ensuring that I design with these specifications in mind. For example, a common resolution for desktop screens might be 1920 x 1080 pixels, while mobile screens can range from 375 x 667 pixels to larger resolutions, depending on the device. This knowledge helps me create designs that not only fit well but also maintain their integrity across different displays.

With the understanding of dimensions established, I then turn my attention to responsive design principles. A key aspect of responsiveness is fluidity; I utilize flexible grid systems that allow my designs to adapt seamlessly to various screen sizes. I focus on using percentage-based widths rather than fixed pixel values, which ensures that elements resize proportionately. For instance, if I create a three-column layout for a website, I make sure that it shifts to a single-column format on mobile devices, allowing users to access the content without needing to zoom or scroll excessively. This adaptability is crucial for maintaining a positive user experience and ensuring that all viewers can engage with the material effectively.

As I create designs, I also pay attention to how content is organized. The hierarchy of information should be clear and logical, guiding users through the material effortlessly. I prioritize the most important elements—such as headlines, calls to action, and key images—ensuring they are prominent and easily identifiable. On mobile platforms, I often condense text and use larger, bolder fonts to enhance readability. This careful consideration of typography not only improves the visual appeal but also ensures that users can quickly scan and digest the content, even on smaller screens.

Visuals play a crucial role in engaging users, and I understand that different platforms may require distinct approaches to imagery and graphics. For example, high-resolution images are essential for web designs, where users may be viewing on larger screens. I often opt for high-quality visuals that enhance the overall aesthetic and provide a professional touch. However, when designing for mobile, I focus on optimizing image sizes to ensure fast loading times without compromising quality. Compressing images or using responsive formats like WebP allows me to strike a balance between visual impact and performance.

I also take into consideration the interaction patterns specific to each platform. Mobile users often engage with content through touch gestures, so I ensure that buttons and links are large enough for easy tapping. I aim for a minimum touch target size of 44 pixels, as this helps reduce frustration and improves the overall experience. In contrast, web users may interact with content through mouse clicks, allowing for different design choices regarding hover effects and other interactive elements. I use visual cues such as color changes or underlining to signal interactivity, ensuring users understand which elements they can engage with.

As I continue to develop my designs, I pay close attention to the context in which they will be used. For instance, if I'm creating a promotional banner for a website, I consider how it will be displayed on different pages. The banner should not only be visually striking but also relevant to the surrounding content, maintaining a cohesive look and feel. By aligning the design with the overall branding and messaging of the website, I can enhance the user's journey and reinforce brand recognition.

Moreover, I am acutely aware of the significance of accessibility in digital design. Users with disabilities should be able to navigate and engage with my content without barriers. I ensure that color contrast meets WCAG guidelines, making text readable against backgrounds. Additionally, I incorporate alt text for images, enabling screen readers to convey visual content to users with visual impairments. This commitment to accessibility is essential, as it broadens my audience and reflects an inclusive approach to design.

Incorporating analytics into my design process is another critical strategy. After deploying my designs across various platforms, I use analytical tools to track user engagement and performance metrics. This data provides insights into how users interact with the content, which elements are most effective, and where improvements can be made. For instance, if I find that a particular call to action has a high click-through rate on a mobile platform but underperforms on desktop, I can adjust the placement or design for the desktop version to enhance its effectiveness. This continuous feedback loop allows me to refine my designs iteratively, ensuring they remain relevant and impactful.

Collaboration with other team members also plays a significant role in the design process. I find that engaging with content creators, marketing teams, and developers can lead to a more holistic approach to design. By understanding the goals and needs of different stakeholders, I can create designs that align with broader marketing strategies and technical requirements. This collaborative effort not only enhances creativity but also ensures that the final product is cohesive and effective across all platforms.

Finally, I recognize that staying current with design trends and technological advancements is crucial for creating relevant and engaging content. The digital landscape is continually evolving, and users' expectations change over time. By attending workshops, participating in webinars, and following industry leaders, I can stay informed about emerging practices and tools. This commitment to ongoing education allows me to implement innovative techniques that elevate my designs, ensuring they meet the needs of a dynamic audience.

In summary, designing for different digital platforms requires a multifaceted approach that takes into account user experience, responsiveness, and accessibility. By prioritizing clear communication, effective organization, and data-driven decisions, I can create visually appealing designs that resonate with users, regardless of the device they choose to engage with. The ability to adapt my designs for various platforms not only enhances their effectiveness but also contributes to a cohesive brand experience that users can trust and connect with.

As I continue to explore the nuances of designing for different digital platforms, I recognize the importance of understanding user behavior across various devices. Each platform presents unique challenges that require a tailored approach, particularly regarding user interactions and expectations. Mobile users, for example, often engage with content differently than desktop users. They may be on the go, multitasking, or seeking quick information, which necessitates a design that prioritizes efficiency and accessibility.

In mobile design, I focus on simplifying navigation to accommodate these behaviors. Since screen space is limited, I streamline menus and often implement a vertical scrolling layout, which is intuitive for users accustomed to scrolling through content on their devices. I ensure that key information is front-loaded, meaning the most important elements are easily accessible without excessive scrolling. This approach aligns with mobile users' expectations, allowing them to find what they need swiftly.

The implementation of touch gestures is another critical consideration in mobile design. I incorporate swipe features and other touch interactions to enhance usability. For instance, allowing users to swipe between images in a gallery or scroll through testimonials creates a more interactive experience. I ensure that buttons are appropriately sized for touch, following guidelines that suggest touch targets should be at least 44 pixels in height and width. This attention to detail minimizes user frustration and enhances the overall experience.

In contrast, when designing for desktop platforms, I have the advantage of increased screen real estate. This allows me to present more information without overwhelming the user.

However, I must remain vigilant about the layout, ensuring that it remains organized and easy to navigate. I often employ a grid system to structure content, which helps maintain a visual hierarchy. For example, I can utilize sidebars to feature secondary information or calls to action, ensuring that the main content remains the focal point. This clear organization is crucial, as desktop users are typically more likely to explore content in depth.

One aspect that I find particularly valuable is the ability to incorporate multimedia elements into my desktop designs. While mobile devices may require more consideration when embedding videos or animations, desktops can handle these elements with greater ease. I strategically use multimedia to enhance storytelling, ensuring that any video or animation serves a purpose and contributes to the overall message. For example, a short promotional video on a product page can engage users more effectively than text alone, illustrating features and benefits in a dynamic manner.

Another essential factor in designing for different platforms is optimizing loading times. Users expect fast performance regardless of the device they are using, and slow-loading graphics can lead to frustration and abandonment. I take proactive steps to compress images and optimize file sizes without sacrificing quality. Tools like Canva allow me to export graphics in formats that balance visual fidelity and performance. For example, I might choose PNG for graphics with transparent backgrounds and JPEG for photographs, ensuring each image is optimized for the best loading speed.

User testing is a critical step in my design process, especially when creating responsive designs for different platforms. I conduct usability testing with real users to observe how they interact with my designs on various devices. This process helps me identify any friction points in navigation, readability issues, or areas where users may struggle. By gathering qualitative feedback during these sessions, I can make informed adjustments to enhance the user experience. For instance, if users struggle to locate a specific call to action on a mobile layout, I might adjust its size or reposition it to a more prominent location.

In addition to usability testing, I also pay close attention to analytics post-launch. Using tools like Google Analytics, I track user behavior, conversion rates, and engagement metrics across platforms. Analyzing this data provides valuable insights into which designs perform best and how users interact with my content. If I notice that a particular landing page has a high bounce rate on mobile but performs well on desktop, I investigate the mobile layout to identify potential issues. This ongoing analysis allows me to iterate and refine my designs continuously.

Responsive typography is another vital aspect that I prioritize in my designs. I recognize that font size and style can significantly impact readability across different devices. On mobile, I often use larger font sizes for headings and body text to ensure clarity. I typically select sans-serif fonts, which tend to be easier to read on screens. For desktop, I may use a combination of serif and sans-serif fonts to create a more sophisticated look, but I always ensure that legibility remains paramount. The goal is to create a harmonious balance between aesthetics and functionality, allowing users to engage with the content effortlessly.

As I design for various platforms, I also consider the context in which users will engage with my content. For instance, if I am creating graphics for a social media campaign, I focus on designs that are visually striking and shareable. These designs often include bold colors, eye-catching typography, and clear calls to action that encourage users to interact. Conversely, for email marketing materials, I prioritize a clean layout that presents information succinctly, making it easy for users to absorb key messages at a glance. Understanding the context informs my design choices, allowing me to create materials that resonate with users based on their expected interactions.

Finally, as I strive to create cohesive experiences across platforms, I remain committed to maintaining a consistent brand identity. I leverage tools like Canva's Brand Kit to ensure that logos, color schemes, and typography remain uniform across all designs. Consistency is key to building brand recognition and trust, and I take pride in ensuring that my visuals reflect the essence of the brand. By applying these elements consistently, I create a recognizable presence that reinforces my message and enhances user engagement.

In conclusion, designing for different platforms demands a thoughtful approach that considers user behavior, screen size, and context. By adopting responsive design principles, optimizing performance, and engaging in continuous testing and iteration, I can create effective marketing materials that resonate across both mobile and web platforms. The tools and resources available allow me to execute my vision, enabling me to produce designs that not only captivate audiences but also provide meaningful interactions. As I navigate this dynamic landscape, I remain eager to explore new techniques and strategies that will further enhance my ability to connect with users across various devices.

As I dive deeper into the nuances of designing for different platforms, I find that user feedback continues to play a crucial role in shaping the effectiveness of my designs. Once my materials are deployed, I prioritize gathering insights from users about their experiences interacting with the content. This can take various forms, including direct surveys, user testing sessions, and monitoring user behavior through analytics. Each feedback mechanism provides valuable data that informs future design iterations, ensuring that I am responsive to the needs and preferences of my audience.

In user testing, I typically recruit participants who mirror my target demographic. By observing their interactions with my designs across multiple devices, I gain insight into any usability issues they encounter. For instance, during a testing session for a mobile app, I might notice that users struggle to locate a specific feature due to poor placement or lack of visual hierarchy. This immediate feedback allows me to make real-time adjustments to enhance usability, ensuring that users can navigate the app effortlessly. I often find that small changes, such as repositioning buttons or adjusting text sizes, can significantly improve the overall user experience.

Analytics tools further complement my design evaluations. By analyzing metrics such as page views, click-through rates, and time spent on specific sections, I can identify patterns in user behavior. For example, if I notice a high drop-off rate on a particular mobile landing page, it prompts me to investigate potential design flaws, such as slow loading times or unclear calls to action. This data-driven approach allows me to pinpoint issues that may not be immediately apparent during user testing, helping me refine my designs with concrete evidence.

A focus on accessibility remains paramount in my design process. I strive to create content that is inclusive and usable for everyone, including individuals with disabilities. To achieve this, I adhere to established accessibility guidelines, ensuring that my designs meet the necessary standards. For instance, I carefully select color palettes that provide adequate contrast between text and backgrounds, making it easier for individuals with visual impairments to read the content. Additionally, I incorporate alt text for images and ensure that all interactive elements can be navigated using a keyboard, accommodating users with motor disabilities. This commitment to accessibility not only broadens my audience but also demonstrates a responsible approach to design.

The choice of typography is another critical aspect of effective design across different platforms. I carefully consider how font choices can influence readability and user engagement. For mobile designs, I often select sans-serif fonts, which tend to be clearer and more legible on small screens. I also pay attention to line spacing and paragraph length, ensuring that text is easy to scan and digest quickly. On the desktop, I can experiment with a wider variety of font styles and sizes, but I maintain a consistent hierarchy that guides the user's eye through the content. Consistency in typography reinforces brand identity while also improving the overall aesthetic appeal of my designs.

When creating visuals for various platforms, I understand the importance of incorporating brand elements effectively. Consistency in branding fosters recognition and trust among users. I leverage tools such as Canva's Brand Kit to ensure that my logos, color schemes, and typography remain uniform across all materials. By embedding these elements seamlessly into my designs, I create a cohesive experience that resonates with users regardless of the platform they are using. This cohesive branding not only strengthens the visual identity of my materials but also enhances user recall and connection with the brand.

In terms of imagery, I recognize that visuals play a significant role in capturing attention and conveying messages quickly. High-quality images are essential, but I must also consider how they perform on different platforms. On mobile, where loading speed is critical, I optimize images by compressing file sizes without sacrificing quality. Tools within Canva allow me to export images in the most suitable formats for web use, ensuring that visuals load quickly and maintain their visual integrity.

When designing for social media, I adapt my graphics to fit

the unique dimensions and requirements of each platform. Each social media platform has specific guidelines regarding image sizes and formats, and adhering to these guidelines is essential for ensuring that my content is displayed correctly. I often create multiple versions of a design, tailored to the specifications of each platform, while maintaining a consistent look and feel. This adaptability is crucial for maximizing engagement and ensuring that my brand message is communicated effectively.

The importance of storytelling in digital design cannot be overstated. I strive to craft narratives that resonate with users, drawing them into the content and fostering emotional connections. By using images, typography, and layouts strategically, I can guide users through a visual journey that highlights key messages and engages their senses. This storytelling approach transforms static designs into dynamic experiences, allowing users to relate to the content on a deeper level.

As I finalize my designs, I also consider the overall user journey from initial contact to conversion. Each interaction with my content should be smooth and intuitive, guiding users seamlessly toward their goals, whether that's making a purchase, signing up for a newsletter, or exploring additional resources. I ensure that calls to action are prominent and clear, encouraging users to take the next step. By focusing on the user journey, I can create designs that are not only visually appealing but also drive desired actions.

In summary, designing for different platforms requires a multifaceted approach that considers user behavior, accessibility, and visual coherence. By employing responsive design principles, optimizing visuals, and actively seeking user feedback, I can create engaging materials that effectively communicate my message across various devices. The insights gained from testing and analytics further inform my design choices, allowing me to make data-driven decisions that enhance usability. As I continue to navigate the complexities of digital design, I remain committed to creating impactful visuals that resonate with users and elevate their experience across all platforms.

CHAPTER 25: MASTERING CANVA'S ANIMATION TOOLS**

As I delve into the world of Canva's animation tools, I discover that adding movement to my designs is not merely an embellishment but a strategic way to engage my audience and convey messages more effectively. Animation can breathe life into static graphics, transforming them into dynamic presentations that capture attention and enhance storytelling. Understanding how to leverage these features allows me to create visually stimulating content that resonates with viewers across various platforms.

I begin by familiarizing myself with the various types of animations available within Canva. The platform offers a diverse range of animation styles, each serving different purposes and effects. For instance, text animations can draw attention to key messages, while image animations can add fluidity to presentations, making transitions smoother and more engaging. I explore options such as "Fade," "Rise," and "Pan," assessing which animations align best with the overall theme of my project. Each animation style carries its own emotional connotation; for example, a subtle "Fade" may evoke sophistication, while a more pronounced "Pop" can convey excitement.

The first step in using animation effectively is selecting the right elements to animate. I take a moment to consider the hierarchy of information within my design. Important messages should take precedence, and I often choose to animate headings and calls to action first. By applying animations to these elements, I can ensure that they catch the viewer's eye and encourage interaction. For instance, I might animate a call to action button with a "Bounce" effect to draw attention and invite clicks. This not only makes the button more noticeable but also encourages user engagement by suggesting a sense of urgency.

Once I have selected the elements to animate, I move on to the process of applying the animations. Canva's interface allows me to easily access animation options from the top toolbar after selecting an element. I can experiment with different animation styles and preview their effects in real time. This trial-and-error approach is vital, as it enables me to gauge how each animation contributes to the overall flow of the design. I find that it's often beneficial to keep animations subtle; excessive or rapid movements can overwhelm viewers and detract from the intended message. Striking a balance between dynamic movement and clarity is essential for maintaining audience engagement.

In addition to selecting the type of animation, I also consider the timing and duration of each effect. Canva allows me to adjust the duration, ensuring that animations do not move too quickly for the audience to absorb. I often opt for slower animations for key messages, giving viewers time to read and process the information before the next element enters the scene. Conversely, I may choose quicker animations for less critical elements or transitions, maintaining a sense of momentum without causing confusion. This careful consideration of timing is crucial for creating a cohesive viewing experience.

As I experiment with the animation features, I also explore the option to animate entire pages or slides in my presentations.

Canva's page animations allow me to create transitions between different slides that maintain a consistent visual language. For example, I might use a "Slide In" transition for new slides, creating a seamless flow that keeps the audience engaged throughout the presentation. This strategy not only adds a layer of professionalism to my work but also enhances the overall storytelling aspect, making it easier for the audience to follow along.

Moreover, I delve into the power of layering animations. By staggering the entry of different elements, I can create a more dynamic and layered effect. For instance, in a social media post, I might have the text appear first, followed by images or icons that slide in from the side. This layered approach guides the viewer's eye and maintains interest by introducing elements one at a time. It encourages viewers to stay engaged as they anticipate what comes next, fostering a sense of curiosity.

I also recognize the importance of context when it comes to using animations. Different platforms and audiences may respond to animations in varied ways. For instance, animations that work well for social media posts might differ from those suited for formal presentations. In social media, where attention spans are shorter, I may opt for more attention-grabbing effects that create a sense of excitement. In contrast, for professional presentations, I focus on subtle and sophisticated animations that enhance the message without distracting from the content.

As I finalize my designs, I consider the export options available for animated graphics. Canva allows me to export animations in several formats, including GIF and video, enabling me to share my work across different platforms easily. I often choose to export as a GIF for social media posts, as this format supports animation while keeping file sizes manageable. For presentations, I may opt for video formats that retain the quality of the animations while allowing for smooth playback on different devices. This versatility in exporting ensures that my animations maintain their impact regardless of where they are viewed.

Finally, I find that continuous learning and experimentation are key to mastering Canva's animation tools. As I create more animations, I actively seek inspiration from other designers and platforms. I analyze successful social media campaigns and presentations to understand how they utilize animation effectively. This exploration not only helps me refine my techniques but also opens my mind to innovative approaches that I can incorporate into my own work.

In summary, mastering Canva's animation tools involves a thoughtful and strategic approach. By selecting the right elements to animate, adjusting timing and duration, and considering the context in which the animations will be viewed, I can create engaging and dynamic designs that resonate with my audience. The ability to layer animations and use different export options enhances the versatility of my work, allowing for effective communication across platforms. As I continue to explore the possibilities within Canva, I am excited to push the boundaries of my creativity and create animations that captivate and inspire.

As I further explore the intricacies of Canva's animation tools, I recognize that the effectiveness of animations goes beyond mere aesthetics; it significantly impacts how messages are conveyed and received by audiences. One of the fundamental principles I embrace is the importance of coherence between the animated elements and the overall theme of the design. Each animation should not only serve a purpose but also align seamlessly with the content it enhances. For example, if I am working on a social media post aimed at promoting a product launch, I may choose energetic animations that convey excitement and urgency, reflecting the enthusiasm I wish to generate among potential customers.

In practice, I often start by identifying the core message I want to communicate. Once I have a clear understanding of the desired emotional response, I can strategically select animations that complement this message. For instance, if the goal is to evoke a sense of calm and tranquility, I might opt for gentle fades or slow zoom-ins that create a serene atmosphere. This thoughtful alignment between animation style and message not only enriches the viewer's experience but also reinforces the effectiveness of the communication.

When working with text animations, I find that timing plays a crucial role in enhancing viewer engagement. I experiment with staggering the entrance of text elements, allowing them to appear one after the other rather than simultaneously. This sequential display guides the audience's focus, helping them digest information gradually. For example, when presenting key statistics or data points, I might animate each point to fade in with a brief pause between them. This method prevents overwhelming viewers and gives them a moment to absorb each piece of information before moving on to the next, thus fostering better retention.

Additionally, I leverage Canva's ability to create animated infographics that blend visuals with dynamic text elements. For instance, when depicting a process or timeline, I can use animated arrows that lead the viewer's eye from one step to the next. Coupled with text that appears alongside these arrows, I can create a narrative flow that makes complex information more digestible. This approach not only maintains engagement but also aids in comprehension, as users can visually follow the progression of ideas.

Moreover, I delve into the mechanics of animating images and graphic elements. Canva allows me to apply animations such as "Slide," "Grow," or "Tumble" to images, making them more engaging. When incorporating product images in promotional material, I often choose a "Grow" animation, which enlarges the image as it enters the frame. This dynamic effect captures attention and draws the viewer's focus to the product, reinforcing its importance in the message. The animation must feel natural and not overly exaggerated, as this can detract from the professional quality of the design.

As I work with different media types, I also consider the impact of combining animations with audio elements. While Canva primarily focuses on visual designs, I explore opportunities to enhance my presentations by incorporating sound effects or background music that aligns with the animations. For example, a light, uplifting tune can enhance the emotional resonance of a presentation about community engagement, making the overall experience more immersive. This synergy between visuals and audio creates a multi-sensory experience that can captivate audiences and leave a lasting impression.

I also pay close attention to the pacing of animations. Effective pacing ensures that animations do not feel rushed or sluggish, allowing viewers to process information comfortably. I typically aim for a duration of around 0.5 to 1.5 seconds for most animations, adjusting as needed based on the context and content. For instance, transitions between slides in a presentation may require slightly longer durations to ensure that the audience has time to read and absorb the content before moving on to the next point. Conversely, for social media posts where users may only view the content briefly, quicker animations may be more appropriate to capture attention effectively.

Another essential aspect of mastering Canva's animation tools is consistency across all animated elements. I strive to maintain a unified animation style throughout a project to avoid distracting viewers. For instance, if I choose to use the

"Fade" animation for text elements, I consistently apply this style across similar elements in the design. This coherence not only enhances the visual appeal but also reinforces the overall narrative structure, allowing viewers to focus on the content rather than becoming sidetracked by varying animation styles.

As I finalize my animated designs, I take the time to preview them thoroughly. This allows me to assess the flow and ensure that all animations complement one another effectively. I look for any potential distractions, such as elements that may enter the frame too abruptly or animations that feel out of sync with the overall pacing. It is crucial to create a polished final product that seamlessly integrates all components, as this reflects professionalism and attention to detail.

The process of mastering Canva's animation tools is an ongoing journey, and I actively seek out new ideas and techniques to enhance my work. I regularly engage with design communities and explore resources that showcase innovative uses of animation. Learning from other designers' experiences allows me to adopt fresh perspectives and apply new techniques to my projects. This commitment to continuous improvement ensures that I remain adaptable in the fast-paced world of digital design.

In conclusion, mastering Canva's animation tools provides me with the opportunity to create engaging and dynamic designs that effectively communicate messages across various platforms. By thoughtfully selecting animations, considering timing and pacing, and ensuring coherence in style, I can enhance the viewer's experience and foster deeper engagement with the content. As I continue to experiment with these features, I look forward to pushing the boundaries of creativity and discovering new ways to captivate audiences through animated design.

As I continue to deepen my understanding of Canva's

animation tools, I recognize that the way I choose to animate elements can profoundly impact the narrative structure of my designs. Each animation has the potential to tell a story, drawing the viewer's attention and guiding them through the information I wish to convey. I begin by considering the specific objectives of my project. Whether it's a promotional video, a social media graphic, or a presentation, I align my animation choices with the overall goals and messaging.

One critical aspect I focus on is the use of entrance and exit animations. Entrance animations serve to introduce elements to the audience, while exit animations can help conclude the narrative of a design. For instance, if I'm designing an Instagram story to promote an event, I might use a "Slide In" animation for the event details to create a sense of anticipation. After the details have been shared, an "Out" animation, such as "Fade," can help gracefully remove the content, allowing the viewer to transition smoothly to the next piece of information. This thoughtful orchestration of entrance and exit animations adds a layer of professionalism to my work, ensuring that the audience's experience is cohesive and engaging.

Furthermore, I explore the concept of animated sequences. By coordinating multiple animations to occur in a specific order, I can craft a more complex narrative. For example, in a presentation slide showcasing a product launch, I may first animate the product image to appear with a "Zoom In" effect, capturing immediate attention. Next, I can follow this with a series of bullet points that slide in one at a time, each emphasizing a key feature of the product. This sequence not only keeps the audience engaged but also allows me to build anticipation as I reveal information incrementally, rather than overwhelming them with too much content at once.

Timing becomes increasingly important as I experiment with animated sequences. I often take care to stagger the timings of each animation, ensuring there is a natural flow. This not only enhances readability but also creates a rhythmic pace that maintains viewer interest. I find that a well-timed animation can effectively highlight key messages, while poorly timed animations may detract from the overall experience. As I tweak these timings, I aim to balance fluidity with clarity, enabling the audience to follow along without feeling rushed.

Another area I explore is the use of animated backgrounds. By incorporating subtle animations in the background of my designs, I can create a more dynamic visual environment without detracting from the primary content. For instance, a soft, moving gradient or a gentle parallax effect can add depth and intrigue to a presentation slide. I ensure that these animations are not overly distracting, instead serving as a complementary backdrop that enhances the overall aesthetic. This technique allows me to create immersive experiences that invite viewers to engage with the content on a deeper level.

In addition to visual elements, I recognize the power of incorporating audio elements into my animations. While Canva primarily focuses on visual design, I understand that sound can significantly enhance engagement. For instance, when creating a video presentation, I can pair my animations with a suitable background track that reflects the mood of the content. This audio-visual synergy elevates the overall experience, making it more memorable for the audience. I pay careful attention to the volume levels and pacing of the audio, ensuring it complements rather than overwhelms the visuals.

As I refine my use of Canva's animation tools, I also consider the platforms on which my designs will be shared. Different platforms may have varying requirements or limitations regarding animations. For example, while animated GIFs are ideal for social media, they may not be suitable for formal presentations where video formats might be preferred. I adapt my animations to fit the context of each platform, ensuring that they retain their intended impact regardless of where they are viewed. This adaptability showcases my ability to tailor my designs to meet the specific needs of different audiences.

Collaboration plays an essential role in my design process, especially when working with teams. I often share my animated designs with colleagues or stakeholders for feedback. This collaborative approach helps me gain diverse perspectives on the effectiveness of my animations. Constructive criticism enables me to refine my animations further, ensuring they align with the overall messaging and branding goals. I find that involving others in the review process enhances the final product, as multiple viewpoints contribute to a more polished outcome.

Continuous learning remains a vital component of mastering Canva's animation tools. I actively seek out tutorials, webinars, and design communities that focus on animation techniques. Engaging with the design community allows me to share insights and learn from others' experiences, enriching my own understanding of effective animation practices. I also keep abreast of industry trends, as emerging animation styles can provide fresh inspiration for my work. This commitment to ongoing education fosters a sense of creativity and adaptability, enabling me to push the boundaries of my designs.

As I conclude my exploration of Canva's animation features, I reflect on the profound impact animations can have on user engagement and storytelling. By thoughtfully incorporating animations into my designs, I can create dynamic experiences that resonate with audiences, encouraging them to connect with the content on a deeper level. The interplay of movement, timing, and sound transforms static visuals into compelling narratives that captivate viewers and invite interaction.

In mastering Canva's animation tools, I have learned that the key lies in thoughtful application and strategic execution. By balancing aesthetics with functionality, I can enhance the overall user experience and ensure that my designs stand out in an increasingly crowded digital landscape. As I continue to experiment and innovate, I look forward to creating animations that not only delight but also inspire action, fostering meaningful connections between my content and its audience. The journey of mastering animation is one of continuous growth, and I embrace the challenges and opportunities that lie ahead.

CHAPTER 26: CREATING AND USING DESIGN TEMPLATES**

In the pursuit of efficiency and consistency in design, the creation and utilization of design templates emerge as indispensable tools. As I delve into the art of crafting custom templates within Canva, I recognize that templates not only save time but also ensure a unified visual identity across a wide array of projects. This approach allows me to maintain brand integrity while streamlining the design process, enabling a more focused and cohesive output.

The journey begins with understanding the fundamental purpose of a template. A well-designed template serves as a framework that houses key elements such as color schemes, typography, and layout structures. By establishing these foundational components, I can create a reusable asset that aligns with my brand's identity. I start by identifying the core elements that represent my brand visually. This includes selecting a color palette that encapsulates the essence of the brand—whether that be vibrant and energetic or calm and sophisticated. I ensure that the colors are versatile enough to be adapted across various types of content, from social media graphics to printed marketing materials.

Next, I consider typography, recognizing that font choices convey personality and tone. I select a primary typeface for headings and a complementary font for body text. This harmonious combination not only enhances readability but also reinforces brand recognition. By defining these typographic rules within my template, I can ensure that all future designs adhere to a consistent style, creating a cohesive experience for the audience.

With these foundational elements established, I move on to the structural design of the template itself. I analyze the types of projects I frequently undertake—such as flyers, presentations, and social media posts—and create layouts that can be easily adapted for each format. I utilize Canva's grid and alignment tools to create a balanced layout that directs the viewer's eye through the content in a logical manner. For instance, in a social media post template, I may position key elements such as headlines, images, and calls to action in a way that maximizes visual interest while remaining functional.

Once I have developed the layout, I begin populating the template with placeholder text and images. These placeholders serve as visual cues for future designs, indicating where specific content should be placed. I make a point to include instructions or notes within the template to remind myself or other users of the intended use for each section. This clarity ensures that anyone accessing the template can easily navigate and modify it without confusion.

Another critical aspect of template creation is adaptability. I consider the various scenarios in which my templates may be used. For example, if I design a flyer template, I think about how it might be adapted for different events or promotions. I create versions of the template that allow for easy modifications, such as changing the headline or adjusting the color scheme to fit a specific theme. This flexibility not only enhances the usability of the templates but also encourages creativity, as users can experiment with different designs while remaining anchored to the original framework.

In addition to creating custom templates, I also explore the vast library of existing templates available in Canva. These pre-designed options can serve as an excellent starting point for projects, providing inspiration and structure. I sift through the extensive collection, seeking templates that resonate with my brand identity and can be customized to suit my needs. I evaluate each template for its layout, visual hierarchy, and overall aesthetic, ensuring that it aligns with the cohesive image I aim to project.

When I select an existing template, I focus on how to personalize it effectively. I modify the color scheme to match my brand palette, ensuring that the visual language remains consistent. I also adjust the typography, replacing the default fonts with my chosen typefaces. This attention to detail transforms a generic template into a tailored asset that reflects my brand identity. Additionally, I consider the imagery used within the template, opting to replace stock images with original graphics or photos that resonate more with my audience.

Using templates not only enhances efficiency in my design process but also streamlines collaboration with team members. When multiple people are involved in a project, having a set of templates ensures that everyone is working from the same visual framework. This minimizes the risk of inconsistent branding and allows for a more cohesive output. I establish clear guidelines regarding the use of templates, encouraging team members to adapt them as needed while maintaining adherence to brand standards.

I also implement a feedback loop for my templates, seeking input from colleagues and users to identify areas for improvement. By engaging with those who utilize the templates, I gain valuable insights into their effectiveness and usability. This feedback informs my ongoing refinement process, ensuring that my templates evolve in response to the needs of the users.

As I continue to master the art of creating and using design templates, I recognize that the process is not static. Design trends and audience preferences change over time, necessitating ongoing adjustments to my templates. I commit to periodically reviewing and refreshing my templates to keep them relevant and appealing. This proactive approach ensures that my designs remain current and engaging, aligning with the evolving expectations of my audience.

In conclusion, the creation and utilization of design templates are pivotal in achieving efficiency and consistency in my design work. By establishing clear guidelines for color, typography, and layout, I can craft reusable assets that reflect my brand identity. Whether creating custom templates or adapting existing ones, I remain focused on enhancing usability and maintaining visual coherence across all projects. As I continue to refine my template strategy, I look forward to leveraging these tools to elevate my design process and strengthen my brand presence in the digital landscape.

As I delve deeper into the process of creating and using design templates, I become acutely aware of the significant impact that thoughtful template design can have on both the efficiency of my workflow and the overall quality of my output. The ability to save time while ensuring consistency across various projects is invaluable, especially in environments where deadlines are tight and quality expectations are high. By developing a robust library of templates, I can streamline my design processes, allowing for greater focus on creativity and innovation.

Creating effective templates begins with a clear understanding of the intended audience and the specific goals of the materials I am producing. Each template I develop must not only be visually appealing but also serve a functional purpose. For example, when designing a template for a marketing brochure, I start by outlining the key messages and information that need to be conveyed. This ensures that the layout supports the flow of information logically, allowing the reader to navigate the content effortlessly. I consider how the design elements—such as headings, subheadings, and images—interact to guide the viewer's eye across the page.

One of the key benefits of using Canva for template creation is the ability to utilize grids and alignment tools. These features help maintain visual harmony and ensure that elements are spaced consistently. As I create the layout for my templates, I pay close attention to the alignment of text and images, ensuring that there is a clear visual hierarchy. For instance, larger headings draw attention and signal the start of new sections, while smaller body text provides supporting information. This hierarchy not only enhances readability but also reinforces the overall structure of the design.

I also prioritize the integration of brand assets within my templates. Having established a clear brand identity, I make it a point to incorporate logos, color palettes, and specific font choices directly into the templates. This not only saves time during the design process but also ensures that all materials created using these templates remain consistent with the brand's visual identity. For instance, if my brand uses a particular shade of blue in its logo, I ensure that this color is prominent in the template's design, creating a cohesive look that resonates with audiences across various platforms.

When developing templates, I also take into account the adaptability of the designs. Flexibility is crucial, as the same template may be used for a variety of purposes. For example, a presentation template may need to accommodate different types of content, such as text-heavy slides, image-focused slides, or data visualizations. I build in flexibility by including various layout options within the template itself, allowing users to choose the format that best fits their content. This adaptability encourages creativity while still adhering to the established brand guidelines.

As I create my templates, I find it helpful to incorporate guidance for users. Whether it's through placeholder text, instructional notes, or design tips embedded within the template, providing clear directions can significantly enhance the user experience. For example, I may add a note reminding users to replace placeholder text with their own copy or to adjust image sizes to fit specific layout dimensions. These simple prompts help maintain the integrity of the design and ensure that users feel confident in modifying the templates to meet their specific needs.

Once I have created a set of templates, I shift my focus to testing their usability. I often seek feedback from colleagues or team members who will be utilizing the templates. Their insights are invaluable in identifying any potential issues or areas for improvement. During testing sessions, I encourage them to work with the templates as they would in real scenarios, paying attention to how intuitive the process feels. Are there elements that seem unclear or cumbersome? Do the instructions provided facilitate ease of use? This iterative feedback process allows me to refine the templates further, enhancing their overall effectiveness.

In addition to creating custom templates, I also explore the wealth of existing templates within Canva. These pre-designed options can serve as excellent starting points, saving time and providing inspiration for my projects. When I select a template from the library, I evaluate it based on its alignment with my brand identity and the specific objectives of my project. If I find a template that resonates, I modify it to better fit my needs, adjusting colors, fonts, and layouts while retaining the core structure of the original design.

I recognize that effective use of templates requires ongoing education and adaptation. Design trends evolve, and audience preferences shift over time. Therefore, I commit to regularly reviewing and updating my templates to ensure they remain relevant and appealing. This may involve refreshing the visual elements, re-evaluating color palettes, or even redesigning layouts to align with current best practices in design. Staying attuned to industry trends not only enhances the quality of my templates but also demonstrates a commitment to excellence.

As I work with templates, I also consider the collaborative aspect of design. In a team environment, having a standardized set of templates promotes cohesion and unity in visual communication. It allows multiple team members to contribute to projects while maintaining a consistent brand identity. I establish clear guidelines for template usage, encouraging team members to utilize the templates as a foundation for their own designs. This collaborative spirit fosters a sense of ownership and creativity, as team members feel empowered to adapt templates to suit their unique projects.

In summary, the process of creating and using design templates is a multifaceted endeavor that combines strategic thinking with practical application. By focusing on the foundational elements of effective design, I can craft templates that not only enhance efficiency but also uphold a cohesive brand identity. Whether creating custom templates or modifying existing ones, I remain committed to ensuring that every design element serves a purpose and contributes to the overall narrative. As I continue to refine my approach to templates, I look forward to leveraging these powerful tools to elevate my design work and foster meaningful connections with my audience.

As I delve into the intricacies of creating and using design templates, I find that the true power of templates lies not only in their ability to save time but also in their capacity to foster creativity while maintaining brand consistency. By developing a comprehensive template library, I can ensure that my design process is both efficient and effective, allowing for a more streamlined approach to various projects, from marketing materials to social media graphics.

One of the most significant advantages of using templates is their capacity for customization. While the initial design may serve as a foundation, the real magic happens when I adapt these templates to suit specific campaigns or initiatives. For example, if I have a flyer template created for a general event, I can modify it to fit a specific theme by adjusting the colors, fonts, and images. This flexibility allows me to leverage the hard work invested in the original design while tailoring it to the unique context of each project. This adaptability also extends to the content; placeholder text can easily be replaced with event-specific details, ensuring that each iteration of the template remains relevant and engaging.

As I create templates, I also pay close attention to the concept of scalability. Different projects may require various levels of detail or information density. For instance, a social media post might require a concise message with bold visuals, while a brochure may need more extensive text and detailed explanations. To accommodate this, I design templates that can easily scale in complexity. By providing multiple layout options within a single template, I can cater to different content types while maintaining a consistent aesthetic. This thoughtful approach allows users to select the layout that best fits their needs without having to start from scratch each time.

In addition to scalability, I also emphasize user-friendly design in my templates. It's important to create templates that are not only visually appealing but also intuitive for anyone who might use them. To achieve this, I incorporate clear labels and visual cues within the template to guide users. For instance, I might include a color-coded system that indicates which sections are customizable and which elements should remain unchanged. This clarity is particularly beneficial in collaborative settings, where team members with varying levels of design experience may be using the templates. By making the process straightforward, I empower others to contribute effectively while ensuring that the brand's integrity is upheld.

Feedback plays a critical role in refining my templates. After sharing my initial designs with colleagues or clients, I actively solicit their input on usability and effectiveness. This collaborative feedback loop helps me identify any areas for improvement. Perhaps certain sections are unclear, or the layout may not effectively accommodate different types of content. By incorporating this feedback into my iterative design process, I can enhance the usability of my templates, making them more intuitive and effective for users.

As I explore the use of existing templates available in Canva, I realize that they provide a wealth of inspiration and serve as a valuable resource. While I appreciate the flexibility of creating custom designs, I also recognize that there is a vast library of professionally designed templates that can serve as a solid starting point. I sift through these options, selecting templates that resonate with my brand identity and project goals. Upon choosing a suitable template, I make necessary adjustments to align it with my brand's visual language, ensuring that the final product reflects our identity.

Another vital aspect of working with templates is ensuring consistency across different types of materials. As I design for various platforms—ranging from social media posts to printed brochures—I maintain a unified brand identity by adhering to a set of established design guidelines. This consistency reinforces brand recognition, making it easier for audiences to connect with our messaging. I pay careful attention to the use of logos, colors, and typography across all templates, ensuring that each piece of collateral complements the others.

In addition to maintaining visual consistency, I also focus on the emotional impact of my designs. Each template must resonate with the target audience, evoking the desired feelings and responses. When creating templates for promotional materials, for instance, I consider the emotions associated with the products or services being offered. Bright, vibrant colors might evoke excitement for a new product launch, while muted tones could convey sophistication for a luxury brand. By aligning the emotional undertones of my designs with the intended message, I can create a more compelling narrative that engages viewers.

As I refine my templates, I also consider the importance of accessibility in design. I strive to create templates that are inclusive, ensuring that they can be effectively utilized by individuals with diverse needs. This may involve selecting color combinations that are colorblind-friendly or ensuring that text is legible against various backgrounds. By prioritizing accessibility, I can expand the reach of my designs and ensure that they resonate with a broader audience.

Finally, I embrace the idea of ongoing evaluation and adaptation. As design trends evolve, I commit to revisiting my templates periodically to assess their relevance and effectiveness. I monitor industry changes, paying attention to emerging styles and preferences. This proactive approach allows me to refresh my templates as needed, ensuring they remain current and engaging.

In summary, the creation and use of design templates represent a critical aspect of my design process. By focusing on customization, scalability, usability, and consistency, I can craft templates that not only save time but also elevate the quality of my work. The combination of feedback, collaboration, and ongoing refinement ensures that my templates remain effective tools that resonate with audiences and maintain a cohesive brand identity. As I continue to master the art of template creation, I look forward to leveraging these resources to streamline my design efforts and inspire creativity in my projects.

CHAPTER 27: ENHANCING DESIGN WITH CANVA'S PHOTO EDITOR**

As I delve into the capabilities of Canva's photo editor, I am continually impressed by the toolset it provides for enhancing and manipulating images directly within the platform. The ability to edit photos without needing external software significantly streamlines my workflow, allowing me to focus on the creative aspects of my designs. Mastering these features not only improves the quality of my images but also elevates the overall impact of my projects.

The first step in my photo editing process is to upload the images I intend to work with. Canva supports various file formats, including JPEG and PNG, making it easy to import images from different sources. Once my images are uploaded, I can begin the editing process by selecting the image and navigating to the editing toolbar. The intuitive interface allows me to make adjustments seamlessly, fostering an efficient editing experience.

One of the foundational adjustments I frequently apply is brightness. Properly managing brightness can dramatically alter the mood of an image. For instance, a well-lit photo can evoke feelings of positivity and warmth, while a darker image might create a more dramatic or moody atmosphere. As I manipulate the brightness slider, I pay close attention to how the changes affect the image's overall appearance. I often find that slight adjustments yield the best results, preserving the integrity of the image while enhancing its visual appeal.

Closely related to brightness is the contrast adjustment. This feature allows me to control the difference between the darkest and lightest areas of an image. Increasing contrast can make an image pop, emphasizing details that might otherwise be overlooked. For example, when working with a portrait, enhancing contrast can bring out the facial features and create a more dynamic representation. However, I am cautious not to overdo it; excessive contrast can lead to loss of detail in shadows or highlights. My goal is to find a balance that maintains the natural look of the image while enhancing its vibrancy.

Saturation is another crucial adjustment I frequently use. This setting controls the intensity of the colors within the image. Increasing saturation can make colors appear more vivid and engaging, which is particularly effective for marketing materials or social media posts aimed at capturing attention. Conversely, reducing saturation can lend a more subdued, sophisticated quality to an image, which may be desirable in certain contexts, such as corporate branding or formal presentations. As I adjust saturation, I take care to maintain a natural appearance, avoiding overly bright colors that might detract from the image's message.

Retouching is a key component of enhancing images, and Canva offers various tools that allow me to refine my photos with precision. One of the features I often utilize is the "Blur" tool, which I apply to backgrounds to create a subtle depth of field effect. By blurring the background of a portrait, for instance, I can draw attention to the subject, enhancing the overall focus of the image. This technique is particularly useful in creating professional-looking photos that can elevate the quality of marketing materials and presentations.

In addition to blurring, I explore the "Crop" tool to refine my images further. Cropping allows me to remove unnecessary elements and focus on the subject matter. I often find that a well-cropped image can dramatically enhance composition, guiding the viewer's eye towards the most important aspects of the design. Canva's cropping feature includes various aspect ratio options, enabling me to adjust the dimensions based on the platform where the image will be displayed, whether it's for social media or print.

Filters are an exciting way to add a distinct style to my images, and Canva's library of filters allows for creative expression with just a click. I enjoy experimenting with different filters to see how they transform an image. A filter can enhance the mood of a photograph or lend a consistent aesthetic across multiple images in a project. For instance, using a vintage filter can create a nostalgic feel that aligns with certain brand narratives, while a modern filter may impart a fresh, clean look that appeals to a contemporary audience.

When applying filters, I remain mindful of the context in which the image will be used. While filters can create a striking effect, it's essential to ensure that they complement the overall design and message rather than overpower it. This nuanced approach allows me to enhance my images effectively while maintaining brand integrity.

Once I have completed my edits, I take the time to review my work, ensuring that the final images align with my project's objectives. This step includes examining the image in relation to other design elements, such as text and graphics, to ensure cohesiveness. I may also zoom in to check for any imperfections or areas that need further refinement. This meticulous attention to detail helps me produce high-quality images that contribute to the effectiveness of the overall design.

In conclusion, mastering Canva's photo editor allows me to enhance images in ways that elevate the quality of my designs significantly. Through thoughtful adjustments to brightness, contrast, saturation, and retouching, I can create professional-quality images that resonate with my audience. By understanding the interplay between different editing features and applying them strategically, I can ensure that my visuals effectively communicate the intended message while maintaining a cohesive brand identity. The seamless integration of these editing tools within Canva makes the entire design process more efficient, empowering me to focus on creativity and innovation in my projects.

In my exploration of Canva's photo editor, I find that the true potential of image enhancement lies not only in basic adjustments but also in the finer details that elevate an ordinary image to a professional standard. The robust toolset available allows me to manipulate various aspects of an image, and as I become more proficient with these tools, I am able to achieve stunning results that significantly enhance my overall designs.

One of the first aspects I delve into is retouching. This involves more than simply applying filters or adjusting brightness; it requires a careful examination of the image to identify imperfections that may detract from its visual appeal. For instance, if I'm working with a portrait, I often pay close attention to skin tones, blemishes, and distractions in the background. Canva provides a retouching tool that allows me to smooth skin textures and reduce blemishes without losing the subject's natural features. I find that subtle retouching can transform an image, providing a polished look while maintaining authenticity.

Additionally, I explore the cropping tool in greater depth.

Cropping is not merely about cutting away unwanted areas; it's about redefining the composition to create a more impactful visual. I analyze the rule of thirds and adjust the crop to place key elements along these lines. This technique helps to create balance and focus within the frame. For example, in a product photo, positioning the product off-center can add dynamism and interest, drawing the viewer's eye naturally across the image. After cropping, I also ensure that the aspect ratio suits the intended platform—whether for social media, print, or a presentation—thereby maintaining optimal visual integrity.

As I experiment with various editing features, I discover that applying adjustments like brightness and contrast in tandem can yield striking results. Increasing brightness can enhance clarity, but if not paired with a contrast adjustment, an image can appear flat and lifeless. I typically begin by adjusting the brightness to ensure that details are visible, followed by fine-tuning the contrast to give depth to the image. This careful balance allows the colors to pop while maintaining a realistic appearance. I make it a point to frequently toggle between the edited and original versions of the image to assess the effectiveness of my adjustments, ensuring I do not stray too far from the image's inherent qualities.

Saturation adjustments also play a significant role in my editing workflow. While vibrant colors can be eye-catching, over-saturation can lead to unrealistic images. I approach saturation with a nuanced understanding, often lowering it slightly if the image appears too bright or garish. For instance, in a scenic landscape photo, I might choose to increase saturation for the foliage to make it more vibrant while muting the sky to create a balanced color palette. The goal is to evoke the desired emotional response while ensuring the overall aesthetic remains harmonious.

When it comes to filters, I recognize their potential to change the tone and mood of an image dramatically. While Canva offers a variety of filters, I find it beneficial to apply them with restraint. My strategy involves layering a light filter over an image to enhance its qualities without overshadowing the original photo. For example, a soft vintage filter can add warmth and nostalgia, which may be perfect for a personal project like a family album. However, I remain vigilant about ensuring that the filter aligns with the purpose of the design. In marketing materials, I typically opt for clearer filters that maintain the product's authenticity and appeal.

Beyond simple editing, I also explore the artistic tools available in Canva. These tools allow me to manipulate photos creatively, incorporating elements such as overlays and textures. For instance, by layering a textured overlay, I can impart a sense of depth to an image, enhancing its visual interest. This technique can be particularly effective in social media graphics, where grabbing attention quickly is paramount. The combination of texture with a well-chosen color palette can create a stunning backdrop that elevates the primary content, whether it be text or a logo.

Furthermore, I consider the importance of maintaining image resolution throughout the editing process. High-resolution images are crucial for print materials, where clarity is paramount. As I work within Canva, I ensure that any adjustments made do not compromise the image quality. I regularly check the resolution settings and export options to ensure that the final product meets the required standards for both digital and print applications.

As I become more adept at using Canva's photo editor, I also embrace the opportunity to learn from other designers. Engaging with the design community, whether through forums or social media, provides valuable insights into different editing techniques and trends. I often seek inspiration from the work of others, analyzing how they achieve certain effects or enhance their images. This continuous learning journey not only enriches my own skills but also keeps my designs fresh and relevant.

In conclusion, the robust capabilities of Canva's photo editor empower me to enhance my images in ways that profoundly impact my design work. By mastering various editing techniques such as retouching, cropping, brightness and contrast adjustments, saturation management, and the use of filters, I can create polished, professional-quality images that resonate with my audience. The ability to manipulate images directly within Canva not only streamlines my workflow but also allows for greater creative expression. As I continue to refine my skills, I am excited to explore new possibilities for enhancing my designs and creating compelling visuals that leave a lasting impression.

As I continue to explore the vast capabilities of Canva's photo editor, I find that a deeper understanding of its advanced features allows me to push the boundaries of my creative projects. This section will delve into additional tools and techniques that enhance my images, offering layers of depth and sophistication that elevate the final product beyond standard editing practices.

One of the standout features in Canva's photo editing toolkit is the ability to manipulate specific areas of an image through selective adjustments. This allows me to enhance certain elements while leaving others untouched, creating a more dynamic and engaging composition. For instance, if I am working on a promotional image for a product, I might want to increase the brightness and saturation of the product itself while keeping the background muted. This technique draws the viewer's attention directly to the product, making it the focal point of the design. By selecting the specific area of the image I wish to edit, I can achieve a polished look that guides the viewer's eye precisely where I want it to go.

To employ selective adjustments effectively, I utilize Canva's masking tools, which enable me to create precise selections. This feature allows me to apply adjustments only to the areas I designate. For example, if the product is set against a busy background, I can isolate it and enhance its vibrancy without affecting the details in the background. This not only emphasizes the product but also maintains the integrity of the overall composition, ensuring that every element serves its purpose.

In addition to selective adjustments, I also make use of Canva's background remover tool, which has proven invaluable in creating clean and professional images. This tool allows me to eliminate distracting backgrounds or replace them entirely, giving me the freedom to create a more controlled environment for my subject. For example, if I have a product photo with a cluttered background, I can quickly remove that background, replacing it with a solid color or a textured backdrop that aligns with my brand identity. The background remover is intuitive and requires minimal effort, allowing me to maintain focus on my design goals rather than getting bogged down by complex editing processes.

As I enhance images, I often explore the application of overlays and textures. Adding a subtle overlay can imbue an image with a unique character, enhancing its depth and richness. I frequently experiment with different opacity levels to find the right balance; a semi-transparent overlay can soften an image without completely obscuring it. For example, applying a light grain texture can give a photograph a nostalgic feel, perfect for a vintage-themed design. These subtle touches add layers of complexity that draw the viewer in and create a more immersive visual experience.

While I appreciate the impact of overlays, I also recognize the importance of maintaining clarity in my images. Therefore, I pay close attention to the final output and ensure that any added effects do not detract from the primary subject.

This careful consideration allows me to enhance my images without compromising their integrity or the message I aim to convey. I consistently review my edits by toggling between the original and modified images, which helps me maintain a critical perspective on the changes I make.

Another crucial aspect of photo enhancement is the application of artistic filters. While I use filters to evoke certain moods, I am also deliberate about their application. Some filters can transform an ordinary image into something extraordinary, adding flair and creativity. For instance, a black-and-white filter can evoke a timeless quality in portraits, making them feel more evocative and emotionally resonant. However, I remain cautious to not over-rely on filters; their use should enhance the image rather than overshadow the subject. By employing filters judiciously, I can create a distinct style that aligns with my brand's visual identity while still allowing the original image to shine.

As I become more familiar with Canva's editing tools, I also engage in the practice of creating presets for frequently used adjustments. This feature allows me to save specific editing settings, enabling a quick application across multiple images. For instance, if I find a particular brightness and contrast setting that works well for my product photography, I can save this as a preset and apply it consistently. This not only saves time but also ensures that my images maintain a cohesive look throughout my design projects.

Furthermore, I delve into the world of image effects, such as shadows and reflections, which can add a three-dimensional quality to my designs. By subtly applying shadows to an image, I can create depth that makes elements appear as though they are lifted off the page. This technique can be particularly effective in presentations or social media graphics where visual engagement is key. Shadows can provide context, helping viewers understand the spatial relationships between different elements in a design.

Reflective effects can also enhance the perceived quality of an image. When used appropriately, reflections can impart a sense of sophistication, particularly in product displays. I often experiment with the reflection settings to find the right balance, ensuring it complements the overall aesthetic rather than detracting from it. This attention to detail is crucial in producing professional-quality designs that resonate with audiences.

As I wrap up my experience with Canva's photo editor, I take a moment to reflect on the journey through this robust toolset. The ability to enhance and manipulate images directly within Canva streamlines my workflow and significantly improves the quality of my designs. Through careful adjustments, thoughtful use of filters and overlays, and the incorporation of advanced features like selective adjustments and artistic effects, I can create visually captivating images that enhance my projects. This holistic approach to photo editing not only enriches my design toolkit but also empowers me to communicate my ideas more effectively through visuals, reinforcing my commitment to excellence in every piece I create.

CHAPTER 28: DESIGNING ENGAGING PRESENTATIONS**

Creating an engaging presentation involves more than simply arranging text and images on slides; it requires a thoughtful approach to design that captures and retains the audience's attention. My journey into crafting effective presentations using Canva begins with understanding the fundamental principles of slide design. These principles help ensure that my visuals not only communicate information clearly but also resonate with viewers on a deeper level.

The first step I take in designing a presentation is to outline the key messages I want to convey. This foundational stage allows me to identify the main themes and supporting points for each slide. Once I have a clear outline, I can begin selecting a suitable template from Canva's extensive library. These templates serve as a springboard for my design, offering a cohesive structure that can be customized to fit my content. I often choose templates that align with the tone of my presentation, whether it be formal, creative, or educational, as this initial choice sets the stage for the overall aesthetic.

As I delve deeper into the design process, I focus on the importance of visual hierarchy. This concept involves organizing elements on each slide in a way that guides the viewer's eye toward the most critical information first. I utilize varying font sizes, bold text, and strategic placement of images to create a clear hierarchy. For instance, I make the title of each slide prominent and immediately noticeable, using a larger font size and contrasting color to differentiate it from the body text. This not only draws attention but also allows the audience to quickly grasp the main topic of each slide.

To further enhance visual clarity, I limit the amount of text I include. Each slide should serve as a visual aid that complements my spoken words rather than a script for them. I strive for succinct bullet points or key phrases that encapsulate the essence of my message. This approach encourages audience engagement, as it prompts viewers to listen actively instead of passively reading lengthy paragraphs. I often employ visuals such as icons or images to reinforce my points, as they can convey complex ideas more effectively than words alone.

When incorporating images, I ensure they are high-quality and relevant to the content being discussed. Canva provides an extensive library of stock photos, illustrations, and icons that I frequently utilize. I choose images that resonate with my message and evoke the desired emotions in my audience. For example, if I'm presenting a case study about environmental sustainability, I might select images depicting nature or community engagement in eco-friendly practices. This connection between visuals and content enhances retention and reinforces the overall narrative I'm aiming to convey.

As I design each slide, I also pay close attention to color schemes. The colors I select must not only align with my brand identity but also work harmoniously together to create a cohesive look. Canva's color palettes make it easy to choose complementary colors that evoke specific feelings or associations. For instance, a presentation focused on wellness might utilize soothing greens and blues to promote a sense of calm and trust. In contrast, a marketing pitch might employ vibrant reds and yellows to energize and excite the audience. Consistency in color not only enhances aesthetic appeal but also aids in creating a professional and polished presentation.

Transition effects also play a role in maintaining engagement throughout the presentation. While I avoid overly flashy transitions that can distract from the content, I appreciate the subtle animations that Canva offers. For instance, fading in elements can create a sense of progression and anticipation as I move through my slides. I apply these transitions judiciously, ensuring they enhance the flow of my presentation rather than disrupt it.

In addition to visual elements, I consider the use of storytelling techniques to enhance audience engagement. A compelling presentation often weaves together data, anecdotes, and examples that resonate with the audience's experiences. By framing my content within a narrative structure, I can make complex information more relatable and memorable. For instance, when discussing statistical data, I might share a personal story or case study that illustrates the real-world implications of the data. This blend of storytelling with design helps create a more immersive experience for the audience.

As I progress through my design process, I remain cognizant of the need for accessibility. This involves ensuring that my presentation is viewable and understandable for all audience members, including those with visual impairments. I pay attention to text readability, avoiding overly decorative fonts and ensuring sufficient contrast between text and background colors. Additionally, I consider alternative text for images and ensure that color choices do not convey information solely through color alone. By prioritizing accessibility, I strive to make my presentations inclusive, allowing everyone to engage with the material.

After finalizing my slides, I conduct a thorough review of the entire presentation. I look for any inconsistencies in formatting, typos, or areas where the flow might be improved. This step is critical, as even minor mistakes can detract from my credibility as a presenter. I also practice my delivery, using the slides as cues rather than crutches. Familiarity with the content allows me to engage with my audience more effectively, maintaining eye contact and responding to their reactions as I present.

As I prepare to present, I leverage Canva's sharing options to ensure that my presentation can be easily accessed by the audience. I consider exporting the presentation in various formats, such as PDF or PowerPoint, depending on the needs of the audience and the context of the presentation. Additionally, I explore options for online sharing, enabling remote participation if necessary. This flexibility allows me to adapt to different environments, whether presenting in person, via video conference, or sharing the content asynchronously.

In crafting engaging presentations through Canva, I draw on a combination of effective design principles, storytelling techniques, and a focus on audience engagement. By strategically leveraging these elements, I create visually compelling presentations that not only communicate information clearly but also resonate with and captivate my audience. Through continuous practice and refinement of my skills, I aim to make each presentation a memorable experience that informs, inspires, and engages those who view it.

In crafting effective presentations, I find that the nuances of slide design play a pivotal role in conveying my ideas and keeping my audience engaged. As I delve into this process, I pay careful attention to various elements that can significantly enhance the visual impact of my presentations, ensuring that each slide not only looks appealing but also communicates my message effectively.

One essential aspect of slide design is the use of white space, which refers to the empty areas around design elements. By strategically incorporating white space, I can create a sense of balance and clarity, allowing my audience to focus on the key points without feeling overwhelmed. I aim to avoid clutter by ensuring that each slide features only the most pertinent information and visuals. This not only helps in maintaining a clean aesthetic but also allows viewers to absorb the content more readily. For example, when presenting data, I opt for clean graphs or charts accompanied by minimal text. This combination facilitates understanding, allowing my audience to grasp complex information at a glance.

As I explore Canva's presentation templates, I notice the variety of layouts available, each designed to cater to different types of content. For instance, some templates are structured to emphasize text, while others prioritize visuals. I choose templates based on the type of content I am presenting. When discussing a narrative or concept, I might select a layout that features ample text space, whereas for data-heavy presentations, I lean towards layouts that emphasize charts and visuals. This tailored approach ensures that my presentation aligns with my goals and effectively communicates the intended message.

When integrating visuals, I am particularly attentive to the types of images I use. High-quality, relevant images can significantly enhance engagement. I often select images that resonate with the content of the slide, serving to illustrate the points I am making. For instance, if I am discussing a marketing strategy, I might include images of successful campaigns or products that exemplify my arguments. This visual storytelling approach creates a stronger connection with the audience, making the information more relatable and memorable. Canva's extensive library of stock images allows me to find suitable visuals that align with my branding and the overall theme of the presentation.

In addition to images, I find that the use of icons can greatly enhance my slides. Icons serve as visual shorthand, helping to break down complex concepts into easily digestible pieces. I often incorporate icons next to bullet points or key phrases to visually represent the ideas being discussed. This not only adds a layer of visual interest but also aids in reinforcing the information for the audience. For example, using an icon of a lightbulb when discussing innovative ideas can create a quick visual cue that enhances comprehension.

Another important design element I consider is typography. The choice of fonts can dramatically impact the readability and overall aesthetic of my slides. I typically select two to three complementary fonts for my presentation—one for headings, one for body text, and occasionally a third for accent purposes. This approach ensures visual hierarchy and consistency throughout the slides. I prioritize clarity, opting for sans-serif fonts for their legibility, especially when viewed from a distance. By maintaining a consistent font size and style across my slides, I create a cohesive look that aligns with my brand identity.

In designing presentations, color also plays a critical role in influencing mood and attention. I select a color palette that aligns with the theme of my presentation and resonates with my audience. Using contrasting colors for text and backgrounds enhances readability, while a harmonious color scheme contributes to a professional appearance. For example, if I am delivering a presentation focused on environmental sustainability, I may opt for greens and earth tones that evoke nature. Canva provides pre-made color palettes that help streamline this process, allowing me to easily apply a consistent color scheme throughout my slides.

As I build my presentation, I also consider the pacing and flow of the content. Each slide should transition smoothly into the next, maintaining audience engagement and narrative coherence. I often employ transitions and animations available within Canva to enhance the movement between slides and elements. For instance, a subtle fade-in effect can draw attention to key points without distracting from the overall message. However, I am careful not to overuse animations, as excessive movement can detract from the seriousness of the content and diminish its impact. Instead, I aim for a balanced approach that enhances, rather than overwhelms, the presentation.

When preparing to present, I rehearse my delivery multiple times, using my slides as visual prompts rather than scripts. Familiarity with my content allows me to engage more authentically with my audience, encouraging interaction and discussion. I often ask rhetorical questions or incorporate anecdotes that relate to the visual elements on my slides. This strategy creates a more dynamic presentation, inviting the audience to connect with the material on a personal level.

After completing my design, I utilize Canva's sharing options to ensure that my presentation can be accessed easily. I consider exporting it in various formats, such as PDF or PPTX, depending on the needs of my audience and the context in which I will present. Additionally, I explore options for online sharing or collaborative editing, which can be particularly useful in group settings where multiple participants may need to provide input or feedback.

The process of designing engaging presentations in Canva requires a blend of creativity, strategy, and technical know-how. By focusing on visual clarity, effective use of templates, thoughtful integration of images and icons, careful font selection, and a harmonious color palette, I can create presentations that not only convey information clearly but also captivate my audience. With each presentation, I continue to refine my skills, adapting my approach to meet the specific needs of my audience and the objectives of my message. As I enhance my presentations through these methods, I remain committed to creating impactful visual experiences that inform, inspire, and engage.

As I delve further into the intricacies of designing engaging presentations, I recognize that the delivery of content is just as important as the visual design itself. A well-designed slide can only do so much if it is not accompanied by a confident and clear presentation style. Therefore, I prioritize understanding the nuances of effective communication as I prepare my presentations. This involves not only what I say but also how I say it, including my tone, body language, and the pacing of my delivery.

One critical aspect I consider is the structure of my presentation. I typically start with a strong opening that captures the audience's attention. This might involve an intriguing question, a compelling story, or a surprising statistic that immediately engages the listeners. By establishing a hook early on, I create an emotional connection that makes the audience more invested in what I have to share. Following this, I outline the main points I will cover, providing a roadmap for my audience. This sets clear expectations and helps them follow along as I transition from one point to another.

As I move through my presentation, I pay close attention to pacing. Maintaining an appropriate speed ensures that my audience can absorb the information I am presenting without feeling rushed or overwhelmed. I often practice my timing, aiming for a rhythm that allows me to emphasize key points while leaving room for audience reflection. Pausing after significant statements can also enhance understanding, allowing the audience to process the information before moving forward.

In conjunction with pacing, I incorporate rhetorical techniques to keep the audience engaged. I often pose open-ended questions throughout my presentation to stimulate thought and encourage participation. For instance, when discussing a new marketing strategy, I might ask, "What challenges do you think we will face in implementing this?" This not only invites engagement but also allows me to gauge audience reactions and adapt my delivery accordingly. I find that fostering an interactive environment makes my presentations more memorable and impactful.

Visual aids play a crucial role in my presentations, and I ensure that they complement my spoken words without overwhelming them. Each slide serves as a visual representation of the points I am discussing, reinforcing my message rather than distracting from it. I make a conscious effort to limit the amount of text on each slide, opting for succinct bullet points and impactful visuals. This allows me to maintain the audience's attention on what I am saying, rather than having them read extensive paragraphs. The visuals I choose are carefully selected to enhance understanding; for example, I might include a graph to illustrate a trend I am discussing, allowing the audience to visualize the data in a clear and concise manner.

Moreover, I leverage Canva's animation features to create dynamic presentations that capture attention. Subtle animations can enhance the flow of my presentation, guiding the audience through the information step by step. For instance, when introducing a new concept, I might animate text to appear in sequence, emphasizing each point as I speak. This technique helps to create anticipation and keeps the audience engaged, as they are visually prompted to focus on each new element being introduced.

As I prepare for the delivery of my presentation, I also consider the use of technology and tools available in Canva. The platform allows me to present directly from the application, which simplifies the logistics of managing my slides during the presentation. I often take advantage of this feature to ensure smooth transitions between slides. Additionally, Canva offers presenter notes, which serve as a useful tool for reminders and prompts during my delivery. These notes provide me with key points to address without cluttering my slides with excessive text, allowing me to maintain a clean and professional appearance.

Feedback is another integral part of refining my presentation skills. After each presentation, I seek constructive criticism from peers or mentors, allowing me to identify areas for improvement. I am particularly interested in understanding which aspects of my delivery resonated with the audience and which elements could be enhanced for future presentations. This iterative process of seeking feedback and implementing changes enables me to continuously evolve my presentation style and ensure that I remain an effective communicator.

Finally, I recognize the importance of preparation and practice in mastering the art of presentation. Familiarizing myself with the content and flow of my slides enables me to present with confidence and authority. I often rehearse my presentation multiple times, both alone and in front of others, to ensure I am comfortable with the material and can deliver it smoothly. This practice helps reduce anxiety and allows me to focus on connecting with my audience during the actual presentation.

In conclusion, designing engaging presentations in Canva requires a multifaceted approach that goes beyond visual design. By focusing on effective communication strategies, employing visual aids, and maintaining a dynamic delivery style, I can create presentations that resonate with my audience. Each presentation becomes an opportunity to connect, inform, and inspire, ultimately making a lasting impact through the combination of thoughtful design and compelling storytelling. As I continue to refine my skills and experiment with new techniques, I am excited to explore the potential of presentations to influence and engage diverse audiences.

CHAPTER 29: DESIGNING FOR MARKETING AND ADVERTISING**

In the realm of marketing and advertising, the ability to design materials that not only attract attention but also effectively communicate a message is paramount. As I embark on this journey of creating compelling marketing collateral, I draw upon foundational design principles while also adapting them to suit the specific needs of marketing. Whether it's a flyer, a poster, or a digital advertisement, the core objective remains the same: to engage the audience quickly and persuasively.

The first step in crafting effective marketing materials is to understand the target audience. This insight shapes every design decision I make, from color choices to typography. I begin by defining who I am trying to reach: What are their demographics? What are their interests and pain points? By identifying these factors, I can tailor my design to resonate deeply with the intended audience. For instance, if I am creating a flyer aimed at young professionals, I might opt for modern typography and vibrant colors that convey energy and innovation. Conversely, for a more corporate audience, I would choose a more subdued color palette and classic fonts that exude professionalism.

Once I have a clear understanding of my audience, I turn my attention to the layout of the marketing material. Effective layout is crucial in ensuring that information is presented clearly and that the viewer's eye is drawn to the most important elements. I often employ a grid system to organize content, which allows me to create a balanced composition. This structure not only enhances readability but also guides the viewer's journey through the material. I typically start with the most critical information at the top—such as a striking headline or an eye-catching image—followed by supporting details. The use of white space is also an essential consideration, as it helps to prevent clutter and allows each element to breathe. By providing enough space around text and images, I ensure that my message remains clear and digestible.

In the realm of marketing, the call-to-action (CTA) is perhaps the most vital component of any design. A persuasive CTA prompts the audience to take a specific action, whether it's visiting a website, making a purchase, or signing up for a newsletter. When designing a CTA, I focus on both its placement and its wording. I often position the CTA prominently within the layout, ensuring it stands out through the use of contrasting colors or bold typography. The wording is equally important; it must be direct and compelling. Instead of a generic "Click Here," I might use phrases like "Get Your Free Sample Today" or "Join the Revolution Now," which evoke a sense of urgency and encourage immediate action. This strategic approach to CTAs helps to maximize engagement and drive desired outcomes.

As I explore design elements specific to marketing, I also pay careful attention to imagery. Visuals play a crucial role in capturing attention and conveying messages quickly. High-quality images that align with the brand and message are essential. I utilize Canva's extensive library of stock photos, ensuring that the images I select are not only relevant but also resonate emotionally with the audience. For instance, if I am designing a flyer for a health food product, I would choose vibrant images of fresh fruits and vegetables that evoke feelings of vitality and wellness. Additionally, I often consider the use of icons and graphics to simplify complex ideas and make the material more visually appealing. Simple icons can break up text and make the information more digestible, guiding the viewer through the content seamlessly.

Color theory also plays a significant role in marketing design. The colors I select must reflect the brand identity while also eliciting the desired emotional response from the audience. Different colors can evoke various feelings; for example, blue often conveys trust and reliability, while red can evoke excitement and urgency. I am careful to maintain consistency with the brand's established color palette, as this reinforces brand recognition and creates a cohesive look across all materials. Canva provides me with the tools to easily apply these colors across my designs, ensuring that my marketing collateral feels unified and professional.

When it comes to typography, the choice of fonts can dramatically impact the effectiveness of my designs. I typically choose two to three fonts that complement each other; one for headings, another for body text, and possibly an accent font for emphasis. This not only aids in creating visual hierarchy but also helps maintain brand consistency. For marketing materials, I prioritize legibility, especially for headlines and CTAs. I often experiment with font sizes and weights, ensuring that the most critical information is easily readable even from a distance. This is particularly important for posters and banners, where viewers may only have a few seconds to absorb the content.

As I finalize my designs, I remember that feedback and revision are integral to the process. I often share my drafts with colleagues or friends, inviting their input on both the aesthetic and the message. Their fresh perspectives can uncover areas for improvement that I might overlook. I am especially attentive to their reactions regarding the clarity of the message and the effectiveness of the design elements. If the feedback indicates confusion or lack of engagement, I am prepared to make adjustments, whether it's rephrasing a CTA, altering the color scheme, or rethinking the layout. This iterative process of refining my designs ensures that the final product is not only visually appealing but also maximally effective in achieving its marketing goals.

In summary, designing engaging marketing materials is a multifaceted process that demands an understanding of the target audience, effective use of layout, strategic placement of CTAs, and the thoughtful integration of imagery and typography. By leveraging these principles and techniques in Canva, I can create marketing collateral that not only captures attention but also drives action, ultimately enhancing the effectiveness of the marketing efforts. Each design becomes an opportunity to connect with the audience, communicate messages clearly, and inspire engagement.

In designing marketing and advertising materials, one of the core principles I embrace is the importance of a strong visual hierarchy. This concept is fundamental in guiding the viewer's eye toward the most important elements of the design. I achieve this by strategically organizing the layout to emphasize critical information, such as the main message, offers, and calls-to-action. I begin by identifying the primary objective of the material—whether it's to promote a product, announce an event, or encourage sign-ups—and then craft the design to reflect that goal.

One effective way to establish visual hierarchy is through the use of size and scale. Larger elements naturally draw more attention, so I make sure to highlight key messages or headlines using larger fonts. This is particularly effective for promotional flyers where the goal is to quickly grab attention. For instance, in a flyer advertising a limited-time sale, I would prominently display the discount percentage or special offer in large, bold letters, making it the first thing that catches the eye. Following this, I would arrange supporting information—such as details about the sale or the products involved—in smaller text beneath the headline, ensuring that the reader can easily digest the content in order of importance.

Color contrast is another vital tool in creating a compelling design. Utilizing contrasting colors not only enhances readability but also helps to differentiate various sections of the marketing material. For example, if I'm designing a poster for a summer event, I might choose a bright yellow background, with contrasting dark blue text for the main details. This combination not only draws attention but also evokes a sense of excitement and energy, reinforcing the event's theme. I find it essential to maintain consistency with the brand's color palette, as this not only reinforces brand identity but also contributes to a cohesive look across different marketing materials.

When developing persuasive calls-to-action, I apply specific wording and design strategies to encourage the audience to take immediate action. Effective CTAs are clear, direct, and create a sense of urgency. Phrases such as "Limited Time Offer," "Join Now," or "Get Yours Today" can motivate the audience to respond quickly. I often emphasize these calls-to-action by enclosing them in buttons or contrasting shapes, making them visually distinct from other elements on the page. The placement of the CTA is also crucial; I position it in a prominent location, often at the bottom or center of the material, where the viewer's eye naturally lands after absorbing the key information.

In addition to visual hierarchy and color contrast, I pay

attention to the overall balance of the design. A well-balanced layout enhances visual appeal and ensures that the material does not feel overcrowded. I aim for a harmonious distribution of text and images, where each component has room to breathe. I often employ a grid layout to maintain consistency and alignment, ensuring that elements are evenly spaced and organized. This structured approach not only improves aesthetics but also aids in guiding the viewer through the information logically.

Imagery plays a critical role in the effectiveness of marketing materials. I prioritize using high-quality images that align with the message I am trying to convey. For instance, if I am promoting a new restaurant, I would select mouth-watering images of the dishes being offered, as these visuals create an immediate emotional response and entice potential customers. I ensure that the images I choose resonate with the target audience; using images of people enjoying the food can evoke feelings of community and enjoyment, which are effective in attracting new patrons.

Moreover, I understand that typography is more than just selecting a font; it's about setting the tone of the message and enhancing readability. I typically choose fonts that reflect the brand's personality—modern and clean fonts for tech-related products, or playful and rounded fonts for a children's brand, for example. In marketing materials, I often limit myself to two or three font styles to maintain consistency and avoid visual clutter. The primary font is usually used for headlines and calls-to-action, while a secondary font can be utilized for body text. This approach not only maintains readability but also ensures that the materials appear professional.

Another consideration in marketing design is the format in which the material will be displayed or distributed. For instance, a flyer that will be handed out in person may require different design considerations compared to a digital advertisement displayed on social media. In the case of digital designs, I often create materials that are optimized for various screen sizes, ensuring that all text and visuals remain legible and impactful on devices ranging from smartphones to desktop computers. By understanding the medium, I can adjust the design accordingly, making the necessary alterations to dimensions, resolutions, and formats.

As I develop these marketing materials, I continually remind myself of the importance of feedback and iteration. After completing a design, I seek input from peers or potential audience members to gauge their reactions. This feedback can provide valuable insights into how well the design communicates its intended message and whether it resonates with the target audience. I am often open to making adjustments based on this feedback, whether it involves refining the wording of a call-to-action or tweaking the layout for better balance.

Ultimately, my aim in designing marketing and advertising materials is to create visually compelling pieces that not only capture attention but also drive action. By employing effective design principles such as visual hierarchy, color contrast, strategic placement of CTAs, and thoughtful use of imagery and typography, I can craft materials that effectively communicate the intended message while resonating with the audience. Each marketing piece becomes an opportunity to connect with potential customers, invite engagement, and inspire action, ultimately contributing to the success of the overall marketing strategy.

In the pursuit of crafting effective marketing materials, I find that one of the most impactful strategies involves the meticulous selection of design elements that not only enhance aesthetics but also reinforce the core message of the advertisement. This requires a thoughtful integration of images, icons, and colors that align with the brand identity while also appealing to the emotions and expectations of the target audience. As I embark on this process, I consider how these elements work together to create a cohesive and engaging experience for the viewer.

When incorporating imagery, I always strive to choose high-quality, relevant visuals that resonate with the audience's interests and desires. For example, if I am designing a poster for a travel agency promoting exotic destinations, I select vibrant images that evoke a sense of wanderlust. These visuals serve not only to attract attention but also to create an emotional connection with potential customers, making them envision themselves at those breathtaking locations. The power of imagery in marketing cannot be overstated; it often conveys messages more effectively than words alone.

In addition to striking images, I also utilize icons and graphics to simplify complex ideas and reinforce the messaging. Icons can act as visual cues that guide the audience's understanding, breaking down information into digestible segments. For instance, if I am creating a flyer that outlines the benefits of a new health product, I might use icons to represent each benefit —such as a heart for improved health or a clock for time-saving convenience. This not only enhances comprehension but also adds an engaging visual layer that draws the viewer in.

Color choices are equally crucial in the design of marketing materials. Each color can evoke specific emotions and associations, and I am deliberate in my selections to ensure they align with the message I wish to convey. For instance, using green often signifies health and wellness, while blue can evoke trust and reliability. I carefully analyze the brand's existing color palette to maintain consistency and ensure that the materials are instantly recognizable to the audience. The interplay of colors in the design can dramatically impact the viewer's perception; a well-coordinated color scheme can create a sense of harmony and professionalism.

Typography also plays a pivotal role in the effectiveness of marketing materials. The fonts I select must not only be legible but also convey the tone of the message. For example, a modern sans-serif font may be appropriate for a tech company aiming to convey innovation, while a classic serif font might be better suited for a law firm seeking to project authority and tradition. I often experiment with different font sizes and weights to create a visual hierarchy within the text, ensuring that the most critical information stands out. This hierarchy helps the audience quickly identify key messages, such as promotional offers or essential details, leading to increased engagement.

As I continue developing my marketing materials, I remain mindful of the concept of balance in my designs. A well-balanced layout ensures that no single element overwhelms the others, creating a harmonious visual experience. I often use a grid system to achieve this balance, allowing me to arrange text and images in a way that feels structured yet visually appealing. The placement of elements should guide the viewer's eye naturally from one section to another, leading them through the narrative of the advertisement without causing confusion or distraction.

Another aspect of effective marketing design is the inclusion of persuasive language. The words I choose for headlines, body text, and calls-to-action must be carefully crafted to elicit a response. I often use active voice and action-oriented language to create urgency, encouraging the audience to take immediate action. Phrases such as "Limited Time Offer" or "Join Us Today" can spur quick responses and enhance the likelihood of engagement. I also consider the use of testimonials or social proof within the materials; incorporating quotes from satisfied customers can significantly boost credibility and persuade potential clients to consider the offering.

Testing different versions of marketing materials through A/B testing is a technique I find valuable for refining my designs. By creating two variations of an ad—such as different headlines or image choices—I can gather data on which version resonates more with the audience. This empirical approach allows me to make informed decisions based on real feedback, ultimately enhancing the effectiveness of my marketing efforts.

Lastly, I recognize the significance of tailoring designs for specific platforms and formats. Different advertising mediums have unique requirements; for instance, social media graphics must be optimized for quick viewing and engagement, while printed flyers may allow for more detailed information. I ensure that my designs are adaptable, adjusting dimensions, layouts, and elements according to the specific platform where they will be displayed. This adaptability ensures that the marketing message remains consistent and impactful, regardless of where the audience encounters it.

Through a comprehensive understanding of these design principles—visual hierarchy, effective use of imagery and color, strategic typography, balance, persuasive language, and adaptability—I can create marketing and advertising materials that not only capture attention but also convey messages clearly and compel the audience to take action. Each design serves as a powerful tool to connect with the target audience, drive engagement, and ultimately contribute to the success of marketing initiatives. By continually refining my approach and incorporating feedback, I enhance my ability to create compelling marketing collateral that resonates with viewers and achieves desired outcomes.

CHAPTER 30: LEVERAGING CANVA'S BRAND KIT**

Establishing and maintaining a cohesive brand identity is crucial for any organization, and Canva's Brand Kit feature offers an effective solution to achieve this goal. As I delve into the nuances of setting up and utilizing the Brand Kit, I recognize the importance of consistency in reinforcing brand recognition and ensuring that all visual materials convey a unified message. The Brand Kit serves as a centralized resource for all essential brand elements, making it easier for me to create designs that align with the established identity of the brand.

To begin setting up the Brand Kit, I first gather all the necessary components that define the brand. This typically includes the brand's color palette, which plays a vital role in establishing the visual identity. Color choices evoke specific emotions and associations, so it is essential to select a palette that reflects the brand's values and resonates with its target audience. I ensure that I have a primary color, which often becomes the dominant hue in most designs, accompanied by secondary and accent colors that provide flexibility and variety while maintaining harmony. By entering these colors into the Brand Kit, I ensure that they are readily accessible for all future designs, streamlining the process and minimizing the risk of inconsistency.

Next, I focus on the typography that embodies the brand's voice. Selecting the right fonts is not merely about aesthetics; it's about ensuring readability and creating a tone that aligns with the brand's messaging. I typically choose a primary font for headings that captures attention and conveys personality, along with a complementary font for body text that enhances legibility. It is essential to include any special fonts or variations, such as bold or italic styles, that may be used frequently. By storing these fonts in the Brand Kit, I can easily apply them across various designs, reinforcing a consistent visual style that helps the brand stand out.

Incorporating the brand's logos into the Brand Kit is equally important. A logo is often the first element that consumers associate with a brand, serving as a visual anchor in all marketing materials. I ensure that I upload various versions of the logo, including full-color, monochrome, and any alternative variations, so that I can select the most appropriate one for each design context. Having these logos readily available within the Brand Kit simplifies the design process, allowing me to maintain consistency without having to search through multiple folders for the correct logo file.

Once the foundational elements of the Brand Kit are established, I can begin to apply these components across various designs. As I create marketing materials, social media graphics, or presentations, I consistently refer back to the Brand Kit to ensure that I am using the correct colors, fonts, and logos. This not only helps to maintain a cohesive look but also fosters recognition among the audience. When viewers encounter a design that uses the brand's established elements, they are more likely to associate it with the brand itself, enhancing brand loyalty and trust.

One of the advantages of using Canva's Brand Kit is the ability to quickly create templates that incorporate the brand elements. By designing templates that reflect the brand identity, I can streamline future projects and ensure that any new materials adhere to the established visual standards. For instance, if I create a social media post template that features the brand colors and fonts, it becomes a reusable asset for future campaigns. This efficiency not only saves time but also reinforces consistency, as each new post will align with the brand's overall identity.

As I design, I remain vigilant about adhering to the guidelines established in the Brand Kit. This involves regularly reviewing completed materials to ensure they align with the defined brand standards. If I find that certain elements have deviated —perhaps a different shade of a brand color was used, or an unapproved font was selected—I make the necessary adjustments to realign the design with the brand identity. This proactive approach is essential for maintaining brand integrity across all platforms and materials.

In addition to visual elements, I also recognize the significance of messaging in building a strong brand identity. The language and tone used in marketing materials should reflect the brand's personality and values. Whether I am writing promotional copy or crafting a social media post, I ensure that the messaging aligns with the brand identity. By integrating the Brand Kit not only as a visual resource but also as a guide for tone and style, I can create a holistic representation of the brand that resonates with the audience.

Furthermore, I explore the collaborative features of Canva when working with teams. When multiple individuals are involved in the design process, it is crucial that everyone has access to the Brand Kit to ensure adherence to the brand standards. By sharing the Brand Kit with team members, I can facilitate a smoother design workflow and minimize discrepancies that may arise from different interpretations of the brand elements. This collaborative approach enhances the overall quality of the designs produced while ensuring that they remain true to the brand identity.

As I wrap up the process of leveraging Canva's Brand Kit, I reflect on how this tool has significantly streamlined my design efforts. The ease of access to essential brand elements and the ability to create templates fosters an efficient and consistent design workflow. Whether I am developing new marketing materials or updating existing ones, the Brand Kit serves as a cornerstone for maintaining a cohesive brand identity that resonates with the audience. This consistency not only enhances brand recognition but also reinforces the trust and loyalty that are vital for long-term success in today's competitive market. By fully utilizing the Brand Kit, I empower myself to create designs that effectively communicate the brand's essence and engage the audience in meaningful ways.

To effectively leverage Canva's Brand Kit, it is essential to first understand the significance of each element contained within it. As I work with the Brand Kit, I focus on three primary components: colors, fonts, and logos. Each of these elements plays a crucial role in establishing and maintaining a brand identity that is not only visually appealing but also consistent across various platforms and materials.

Starting with colors, I recognize that the palette I choose can greatly influence the perception of the brand. Colors evoke emotions and can significantly impact how a brand is perceived. For example, a vibrant color scheme might convey energy and excitement, making it suitable for a brand targeting a younger audience, while softer hues may suggest calmness and reliability, appealing to a more mature demographic. To create an effective color palette, I typically select a primary color that will dominate the design, supplemented by secondary and accent colors that provide contrast and variety. By entering these colors into the Brand Kit, I ensure that I can consistently apply them across all marketing materials, enhancing brand recognition.

Once the colors are established, I turn my attention to typography. The fonts selected for a brand communicate not just information but also the brand's personality. A modern sans-serif font might suggest innovation and forward-thinking, while a classic serif font might convey tradition and trustworthiness. When setting up the Brand Kit, I choose a primary font for headings that captures attention and aligns with the brand's voice. I complement this with a secondary font for body text that ensures readability and consistency. This careful selection of typography allows me to create designs that not only look cohesive but also resonate with the target audience on a deeper level.

As I incorporate logos into the Brand Kit, I am reminded of their pivotal role in branding. A logo serves as the visual cornerstone of a brand, representing its values and mission at a glance. When uploading logos into the Brand Kit, I ensure to include various versions—such as color, black and white, and simplified icons. This variety is essential for adapting the logo to different contexts and backgrounds while maintaining brand integrity. Having all these variations readily accessible allows me to streamline my design process, ensuring that I can quickly apply the correct logo in any situation.

With the foundational elements of the Brand Kit established, I now focus on practical application across different design projects. Whenever I embark on creating new marketing materials—be it flyers, social media graphics, or presentations —I always refer back to the Brand Kit to ensure that I am utilizing the correct colors, fonts, and logos. This adherence to established brand elements is crucial for maintaining a consistent visual identity that audiences can easily recognize. For instance, if I am designing an Instagram post for a product launch, I will ensure that the colors and fonts used match those stored in the Brand Kit, enhancing recognition and trust among followers.

Utilizing the Brand Kit extends beyond merely applying colors and fonts; it also involves creating templates that embody the brand's identity. By developing customizable templates for different types of content, I not only save time in the design process but also ensure that every piece of content adheres to the brand guidelines. For instance, I might create a standard template for promotional flyers that incorporates the brand's color palette and typography, allowing for quick adaptations for various campaigns while retaining a unified look. This approach fosters efficiency and consistency, making it easier to manage large volumes of marketing materials.

As I continue to apply the Brand Kit, I remain vigilant about periodically reviewing and updating the elements within it. As brands evolve, so too can their visual identities. Whether due to rebranding efforts, changes in target audiences, or shifts in market trends, I understand the importance of ensuring that the Brand Kit reflects the current identity and values of the brand. This might involve adjusting color shades, updating logos, or even exploring new font styles that align with the brand's direction. By maintaining an adaptable Brand Kit, I can keep the brand relevant and resonant with its audience.

Collaboration is another significant aspect of leveraging Canva's Brand Kit. When working with teams, sharing the Brand Kit becomes essential to ensure that everyone is aligned with the brand's visual standards. By allowing team members access to the Brand Kit, I can facilitate a collaborative environment where design elements are uniformly applied across various projects. This reduces the chances of inconsistencies and enhances the overall quality of the materials produced. Team members can easily pull from the Brand Kit when creating their own designs, promoting a sense of unity and purpose in our branding efforts.

Additionally, I take advantage of Canva's collaborative features to gather feedback on designs. Once I create a marketing piece using the elements from the Brand Kit, I often seek input from colleagues or stakeholders. This collaborative feedback process can reveal insights that I might not have considered, such as how well the design resonates with the intended audience or whether any elements appear misaligned with the brand identity. By incorporating this feedback, I can refine the designs further, ensuring they effectively communicate the brand message.

In summary, leveraging Canva's Brand Kit is instrumental in establishing a cohesive brand identity across all design projects. By meticulously selecting and applying brand colors, fonts, and logos, I can create materials that are not only visually consistent but also reflective of the brand's values and personality. Through the development of templates and the integration of collaborative features, I enhance the efficiency of the design process while ensuring alignment with the established brand guidelines. This strategic approach ultimately strengthens the brand's presence in the market, fostering recognition, trust, and loyalty among the audience.

The functionality of Canva's Brand Kit extends beyond mere storage of visual elements; it serves as an integral tool in maintaining brand integrity throughout all forms of communication and marketing. As I utilize the Brand Kit, I find that the process of applying brand elements to various designs reinforces not only aesthetic consistency but also the overall message of the brand. This alignment is crucial in a world where consumers are bombarded with visual stimuli, making the need for a recognizable and cohesive identity more important than ever.

When I begin a new project, the first step involves a thorough review of the brand elements stored in the Brand Kit. This includes assessing how well the selected colors translate across different mediums. For instance, while a color may look vibrant on screen, it may appear muted when printed. I often run tests with different materials to see how these colors hold up in physical formats, adjusting the color codes in the Brand Kit as necessary to ensure fidelity across platforms. This meticulous attention to detail guarantees that the brand's visual identity remains consistent, regardless of how and where it is presented.

In addition to color considerations, I place significant emphasis on typography. The fonts chosen not only define the visual appeal of any design but also influence how the audience perceives the message. For example, a playful font might work well for a children's brand, while a more sophisticated typeface may suit a luxury product. By having these fonts readily available in the Brand Kit, I can swiftly implement them into any new designs, ensuring that all written content aligns with the overall tone of the brand.

As I explore the application of logos within the Brand Kit, I recognize their role as a visual anchor for the brand. Each version of the logo uploaded into the Brand Kit—be it full-color, monochrome, or simplified—serves a distinct purpose depending on the context of the design. For example, when creating a social media graphic that will appear on a busy background, a simplified logo may be more effective in maintaining visibility and impact. By accessing these variations effortlessly, I can select the most appropriate logo for each design without hesitation, ensuring that brand representation remains consistent and professional.

While the foundational elements of the Brand Kit are essential, it's also important to recognize the influence of messaging in brand identity. The visual aspects of a brand, while vital, are often intertwined with the language and tone used in marketing materials. As I develop content, I consistently refer back to the Brand Kit not just for visual elements, but also as a guide for the brand's voice. Whether crafting promotional copy for an email campaign or writing social media posts, I ensure that the messaging reflects the brand's personality. By aligning visual and textual elements, I create a comprehensive representation of the brand that resonates deeply with the audience.

An essential aspect of leveraging the Brand Kit is the integration of collaborative features in Canva. When working with teams, having access to a shared Brand Kit fosters a more cohesive approach to design. Team members can easily pull from the established brand elements, reducing the likelihood of discrepancies that may arise from miscommunication or differing interpretations of brand guidelines. I often conduct design reviews with my team, allowing us to assess how well the current designs align with the brand identity as outlined in the Brand Kit. This collaborative feedback not only enhances the quality of the materials produced but also promotes a sense of ownership and pride among team members.

As I develop templates within Canva using the Brand Kit, I find that this practice significantly streamlines the design process. Templates act as a foundation, allowing for quick adjustments while ensuring adherence to brand standards. For example, when creating a flyer for an upcoming event, I can start with a pre-designed template that includes the brand's colors, fonts, and logos. This not only saves time but also ensures that every detail aligns with the established brand identity.

The importance of regular updates to the Brand Kit cannot be overstated. Brands evolve over time, and it is vital that the Brand Kit reflects these changes. As new products are introduced or as audience preferences shift, I revisit the elements within the Brand Kit to ensure they remain relevant. This may involve incorporating new color trends, refreshing the typography, or even redesigning the logo to better align with current market dynamics. By keeping the Brand Kit dynamic, I ensure that the brand continues to resonate with its audience and stands out in a competitive landscape.

Furthermore, as the digital landscape evolves, the need for adaptability becomes paramount. Platforms such as social media frequently update their design guidelines and dimensions, and it's essential to have a Brand Kit that can accommodate these changes. I regularly assess the effectiveness of our designs on various platforms, making adjustments as necessary to ensure optimal performance. This agility allows the brand to maintain its relevance and appeal, ultimately driving engagement and loyalty.

In conclusion, leveraging Canva's Brand Kit is an integral part of creating a cohesive and recognizable brand identity. By carefully managing colors, fonts, and logos, I can produce designs that not only adhere to established standards but also resonate with the target audience. This meticulous attention to detail ensures that every design element contributes to a unified brand message, enhancing the overall perception of the brand. By embracing collaboration, adaptability, and ongoing refinement, I empower myself and my team to create designs that truly capture the essence of the brand, ultimately fostering lasting connections with our audience.

CHAPTER 31: INTEGRATING CANVA WITH OTHER TOOLS**

Integrating Canva with other tools and platforms is essential for optimizing my design workflow and maximizing productivity. By connecting Canva with applications like Google Drive, Dropbox, and various social media platforms, I can streamline the entire process of design, storage, and distribution. This interconnectedness not only saves time but also enhances collaboration and access to resources, allowing me to focus on creativity rather than logistics.

To begin with, linking Canva to Google Drive provides a seamless way to store and access my design files. With this integration, I can easily save my completed designs directly to my Google Drive, ensuring they are securely stored and accessible from any device. This is particularly useful when I am working on multiple projects across different locations or devices. Whenever I need to retrieve a file, I simply navigate to my Google Drive, eliminating the need to search through multiple folders or worry about losing files. This ease of access enhances my workflow significantly, allowing me to shift focus back to design without interruption.

Furthermore, the ability to import images and assets from

Google Drive into Canva simplifies the design process. Instead of having to download files and then upload them again, I can directly pull in the necessary images or documents from Google Drive while I'm working in Canva. This not only saves time but also reduces the chances of version mismatches, as I always have the latest files available at my fingertips. Additionally, collaborating with team members becomes more straightforward; they can access shared files from Google Drive, and I can incorporate their input directly into my designs without any back-and-forth email exchanges.

Another valuable integration is with Dropbox, which offers similar benefits to Google Drive but with some unique features. Dropbox allows me to organize my files in a way that makes sense for my workflow. I often create specific folders for different clients or projects, which helps me maintain clarity and order in my design assets. By connecting Canva to Dropbox, I can access these organized files and easily drag and drop them into my designs. This efficient file management system streamlines my creative process, enabling me to concentrate on the design itself rather than on locating assets.

Moreover, utilizing Dropbox's collaborative features is particularly advantageous when working with clients or team members. By sharing folders with collaborators, I can invite them to contribute images, files, or feedback directly. This collaborative space fosters communication and helps ensure that everyone is on the same page throughout the design process. The ability to incorporate real-time feedback directly into my Canva designs means I can make adjustments quickly and efficiently, leading to faster turnaround times on projects.

Integrating Canva with social media platforms takes my design process to another level. Canva allows for direct sharing of designs to platforms such as Facebook, Instagram, and Twitter. This integration eliminates the need for intermediate steps like downloading and then uploading files to social media. Instead, I can publish my designs with just a few clicks, ensuring that my content goes live promptly and accurately reflects my brand's visual identity.

When creating content specifically for social media, I pay close attention to the recommended dimensions and specifications for each platform. Canva's templates for social media posts are designed with these requirements in mind, making it easier for me to create visually appealing graphics that fit perfectly within the platform's constraints. By linking my Canva account to social media, I can directly share these posts, ensuring that they maintain their intended quality and format. This integration reduces the likelihood of errors that could arise from manual uploads, such as incorrect sizing or formatting issues.

Additionally, integrating Canva with scheduling tools like Buffer or Hootsuite allows me to plan and automate my social media content more effectively. Once my designs are complete, I can schedule them to be posted at optimal times, reaching my audience when they are most active. This not only enhances engagement but also frees up my time for other tasks. By automating the posting process, I can focus on creating fresh content and engaging with my audience, knowing that my scheduled posts are being handled efficiently.

Collaboration extends beyond file sharing and scheduling; it also involves communication. Using tools like Slack or Microsoft Teams in conjunction with Canva facilitates real-time discussions about design projects. I can easily share design links within these platforms, allowing team members to view and provide feedback directly. This level of integration ensures that everyone involved in the project can contribute their insights without the need for lengthy email chains or meetings, which can often detract from the creative process.

As I dive deeper into the various integrations available,

I also explore how Canva can work with analytics tools. Understanding how my designs perform on social media is crucial for refining my strategies. By connecting Canva to analytics platforms, I can track engagement metrics, such as likes, shares, and comments, directly related to my designs. This data is invaluable in understanding what resonates with my audience and what might need adjustment. Using insights from these analytics, I can create more targeted and effective designs in the future, continually improving the impact of my marketing efforts.

In conclusion, integrating Canva with other tools and platforms not only enhances my design workflow but also amplifies the overall effectiveness of my marketing strategies. By linking Canva with storage solutions like Google Drive and Dropbox, I streamline file access and improve collaboration. Sharing directly to social media platforms accelerates the distribution of my content while maintaining brand integrity. Furthermore, leveraging scheduling and communication tools ensures that my team remains connected and engaged throughout the design process. Ultimately, these integrations empower me to focus on creativity and deliver high-quality designs that resonate with my audience.

Integrating Canva with various tools and platforms profoundly enhances my workflow, providing an efficiency that allows me to focus on the creative aspects of design rather than getting bogged down by logistics. When I begin working on a project, the first tool I often connect to Canva is Google Drive. This integration facilitates seamless access to my files, enabling me to import images, documents, and other assets directly into my designs without the hassle of downloading and uploading each file manually. The ease with which I can pull in resources helps maintain the flow of creativity, allowing me to experiment with different elements on the fly.

When I save a design in Canva, it can be instantly uploaded to my Google Drive. This is particularly beneficial when working on collaborative projects where multiple team members may need access to the same materials. By storing all designs in a shared Google Drive folder, I ensure that everyone involved has access to the most up-to-date versions of our work. This real-time collaboration significantly reduces the likelihood of miscommunication or duplication of efforts, as team members can contribute their own ideas directly within Canva, making adjustments that align with our collective vision.

Using Google Drive also allows for easy organization of my design files. I can create folders for different clients, projects, or campaigns, providing a clear structure that helps me locate files quickly. This level of organization is crucial, particularly when juggling multiple projects simultaneously. When I need to find a specific asset, such as a logo or a previous design template, I can quickly search within Google Drive and access it directly in Canva, streamlining the design process further.

Another valuable integration is with Dropbox, which provides similar advantages. Dropbox offers robust file organization and sharing capabilities, and its integration with Canva allows for direct access to my stored images and documents. I appreciate how I can organize my assets within Dropbox into folders by project or asset type, making it intuitive to locate the files I need. The ability to drag and drop files from Dropbox directly into my Canva workspace is a feature that I utilize frequently, as it cuts down on the time spent switching between applications.

Moreover, Dropbox facilitates real-time collaboration on design projects. By sharing folders with clients or team members, I can invite them to upload their own images, provide feedback, or even comment directly on the designs we are working on. This collaborative approach fosters a dynamic environment where ideas can be exchanged freely, ensuring that the final product reflects a collective effort. As a result, the designs I produce are often richer and more diverse, benefiting from the input and perspectives of various stakeholders.

Integrating Canva with social media platforms significantly enhances my ability to share designs promptly and effectively. With just a few clicks, I can publish graphics directly to platforms like Facebook, Instagram, and Twitter. This integration is invaluable, especially when timing is critical for marketing campaigns or event promotions. I can ensure that my content reaches the intended audience at peak engagement times, maximizing visibility and impact. The convenience of sharing directly from Canva eliminates unnecessary steps and streamlines the process of getting my work out into the world.

When designing content for social media, it is imperative to consider the unique specifications and dimensions required by each platform. Canva's templates are designed to accommodate these specifications, and this integration allows me to focus on creativity rather than the technical details of sizing. I can create tailored graphics for each platform while maintaining a cohesive brand identity, as the templates ensure that all designs are consistent in terms of color, typography, and overall aesthetic.

Another critical aspect of this integration is the ability to analyze performance metrics through various analytics tools. By connecting Canva with platforms that provide insights into engagement, I can track how well my designs resonate with the audience. Understanding metrics such as likes, shares, and comments helps me refine my design strategies for future projects. This data-driven approach informs my creative process, allowing me to make adjustments based on what works and what doesn't.

Additionally, integrating Canva with scheduling tools, such as Buffer or Hootsuite, allows me to plan and automate my social media content. After designing a series of posts, I can schedule them for optimal release times, ensuring that my audience receives consistent and timely updates. This automation not only enhances my productivity but also frees up time to focus on other aspects of my work, such as strategizing new campaigns or exploring fresh design ideas.

I also find that integrating communication platforms, such as Slack or Microsoft Teams, with Canva improves collaboration across my team. Sharing design links and assets within these platforms allows for swift feedback and discussions, creating an environment of constant engagement. When I present a new design or concept, my team can provide input and suggestions in real time, enabling us to iterate quickly and ensure that everyone is aligned with the project goals.

The integration of Canva with tools like Trello or Asana can further enhance project management. By incorporating design tasks within these project management tools, I can track the progress of each project, assign responsibilities, and set deadlines. This visibility not only keeps everyone informed but also helps me manage my time more effectively, ensuring that I stay on track and deliver high-quality designs within established timelines.

In essence, integrating Canva with a variety of tools and platforms creates a synergistic workflow that empowers my design process. The combination of easy access to files, real-time collaboration, and efficient sharing capabilities means that I can concentrate on what truly matters: producing exceptional designs that capture my audience's attention. As I continue to explore and leverage these integrations, I am constantly reminded of the potential for creativity that lies within a well-connected ecosystem of tools, enabling me to bring my vision to life more effectively than ever before.

Integrating Canva with a variety of tools and platforms not only enhances my workflow but also fosters a more dynamic and efficient design environment. One of the most beneficial aspects of this integration is the seamless connection it provides between Canva and various cloud storage solutions, such as Google Drive and Dropbox. By linking these services, I am able to streamline my asset management, ensuring that my images, videos, and other resources are readily accessible without interrupting my creative flow.

When I connect Canva to Google Drive, I gain instant access to my files directly within the Canva interface. This means I can easily import images or documents I've stored in Google Drive without needing to switch applications or manage multiple downloads. The convenience of this integration becomes particularly evident when working on large projects where I need to access numerous assets quickly. For instance, while designing a marketing brochure, I can pull in product images and related content without the hassle of navigating through various folders on my computer.

In addition, saving designs directly to Google Drive after completion is a game-changer. It ensures that my work is always backed up and easily accessible from any device. If I need to present a design to a client or colleague, I can quickly share a link to the Google Drive folder containing all relevant materials, providing a centralized location for feedback and collaboration. This collaborative aspect is further enhanced when multiple team members are involved in a project; everyone can access the same set of files, reducing the risk of version confusion and ensuring that all changes are logged and accounted for.

Similarly, integrating Canva with Dropbox offers its own advantages, particularly in terms of file organization and sharing. I often utilize Dropbox's folder structure to categorize my design assets by project or client, which allows for a clear and systematic way to locate files. When I import images or graphics from Dropbox into Canva, I can easily navigate through these organized folders, ensuring that I'm always using the most relevant and up-to-date materials. Additionally, Dropbox's sharing features enable me to invite team members or clients to collaborate on specific folders. They can upload files directly or provide feedback on the designs, fostering an environment of shared creativity and productivity.

Social media integration is another critical component that enhances my workflow within Canva. By connecting my Canva account to various social media platforms, I can share my designs directly from the platform to places like Facebook, Instagram, Twitter, and LinkedIn. This integration eliminates the need for additional steps in the process, such as downloading and then uploading content, which can often lead to errors in formatting or sizing. Instead, I can publish my posts directly, ensuring they maintain their intended appearance and reach my audience promptly.

When creating social media content, the specifications for each platform can vary significantly. Canva's templates are designed to meet these specific requirements, and with the social media integration, I can ensure that my graphics are optimized for the intended platform. For example, an Instagram post will have different dimensions and aspect ratios compared to a Facebook banner. With direct integration, I can create multiple versions of a design tailored to various platforms, maintaining consistency in branding while also adhering to each platform's unique visual standards.

In addition to sharing, this integration also allows me to analyze the performance of my designs once they are live. By utilizing analytics tools connected to my social media accounts, I can track engagement metrics like likes, shares, and comments. This data provides valuable insights into what resonates with my audience and informs future design decisions. Understanding which types of posts generate the most interaction helps me refine my content strategy and focus on creating designs that effectively engage my audience.

Integrating Canva with project management tools such as Trello or Asana enhances my organizational capabilities. By incorporating design tasks into these platforms, I can manage deadlines, assign responsibilities, and track progress all in one place. This integration ensures that I stay on schedule, particularly when juggling multiple projects with varying timelines. I can set reminders for upcoming tasks and follow up with team members, keeping everyone accountable and aligned with our project goals.

Moreover, communication tools like Slack or Microsoft Teams play a vital role in fostering collaboration. By sharing design links directly within these platforms, I can facilitate discussions around specific projects or designs. This integration allows for quick feedback and adjustments, making it easy for team members to comment on designs and suggest modifications in real time. The back-and-forth conversations that typically occur via email can be condensed into a single thread, streamlining communication and enhancing productivity.

As I continue to explore the various integrations available with Canva, I also consider the benefits of connecting to analytics and reporting tools. By incorporating these resources, I can evaluate how well my designs perform in the context of my overall marketing strategy. Understanding key performance indicators and metrics gives me the ability to adjust my design approaches based on data-driven insights, leading to more effective and targeted campaigns.

The flexibility and adaptability offered by these integrations significantly enhance my creative process, allowing me to focus on producing high-quality designs that resonate with my audience. By leveraging the capabilities of Canva in conjunction with other tools and platforms, I can create a comprehensive and cohesive workflow that not only boosts my efficiency but also enriches the quality of my work. In a fast-paced digital landscape, these integrations empower me to stay organized, collaborative, and ultimately successful in my design endeavors.

CHAPTER 32: EXPLORING CANVA'S ADVANCED FEATURES**

Canva is not just a platform for creating basic designs; it also provides a suite of advanced features that empower power users to take their projects to new heights. One of the standout functionalities within Canva is the ability to set custom dimensions for your designs. While Canva offers a wide array of pre-set dimensions for various formats—be it for social media posts, presentations, or print materials—the option to create custom dimensions allows for unparalleled flexibility. This feature is particularly beneficial when working on specific projects that require unique sizing not covered by the standard templates.

When I begin a new design project, I often start by defining my canvas dimensions based on the intended use of the graphic. For instance, if I am designing a promotional banner for a website, I will consider the website's layout and how the banner will fit within that space. By setting custom dimensions, I can ensure that my design is perfectly tailored to the needs of the platform it will occupy. This precision not only enhances the visual impact of the design but also ensures that all elements fit cohesively without compromising on aesthetics or clarity.

In addition to custom dimensions, Canva's advanced filter options allow me to manipulate images and graphics in sophisticated ways. The filters provide a range of stylistic choices that can dramatically alter the mood and tone of an image. For example, when creating promotional materials, I often apply filters that align with the branding of the product or service. If the brand has a vintage aesthetic, I might choose a filter that softens the image and adds a warm tone. Conversely, for modern and sleek brands, I may select a filter that emphasizes clarity and vibrancy. This ability to customize the visual attributes of my images helps in creating a more cohesive design that reflects the brand's identity.

Beyond just basic filters, Canva also offers advanced editing tools that enhance my creative control over every aspect of an image. I can adjust brightness, contrast, saturation, and sharpness to fine-tune how an image appears within the overall design. This level of detail is crucial when aiming for a polished, professional look. For instance, if I'm working with a product image, I might increase the saturation to make the colors pop, thereby attracting the viewer's attention more effectively. Additionally, the ability to crop and rotate images ensures that I can focus on the most impactful parts of an image, directing the audience's gaze precisely where I want it.

Another powerful feature that enhances the design process is Canva's collaborative tools. In a world where teamwork often spans different geographical locations, the ability to work on a project simultaneously with others is invaluable. Canva facilitates real-time collaboration, allowing team members to edit and comment on designs as they evolve. This immediate feedback loop ensures that all voices are heard and that the design aligns with the team's vision before finalizing it.

I frequently utilize this collaborative feature when working on group projects. For example, when developing a marketing campaign, I create a shared design project in Canva that allows team members to contribute their ideas and suggestions. As we brainstorm, each member can add their designs or modify existing ones, which fosters a sense of collective ownership. The comments section enables constructive discussions around specific elements of the design, such as color choices or layout preferences. This not only enhances the design itself but also strengthens team dynamics as we work together towards a common goal.

Moreover, Canva's version history feature is a lifesaver when it comes to collaborative projects. As changes are made, Canva automatically saves different versions of the design, enabling me to revert to previous iterations if necessary. This capability is particularly useful when experimenting with different design approaches, as it allows for exploration without the fear of losing valuable work. If a particular direction doesn't resonate with the team, we can simply revert to an earlier version and continue refining our ideas without starting from scratch.

Exploring Canva's advanced features also leads me to discover how templates can be enhanced through collaboration. While I often begin with pre-existing templates, the ability to customize them collaboratively means that we can adapt them to better fit our unique needs. For instance, if a team member suggests a new layout or specific branding elements, we can seamlessly incorporate those adjustments into the existing template. This flexibility ensures that our designs not only remain on-brand but also resonate more effectively with our target audience.

The integration of Canva with other tools further amplifies its advanced functionalities. For instance, connecting Canva to Google Drive allows me to access and save files directly within my projects. This integration means that I can pull in documents, images, and assets stored in the cloud without having to switch between different platforms. It streamlines my workflow, allowing me to focus on the creative aspects of design rather than getting bogged down in file management.

As I delve deeper into Canva's advanced features, I begin to realize that it is not just about creating visually appealing designs; it's about leveraging these tools to enhance communication, collaboration, and overall productivity. The combination of custom dimensions, advanced filters, and robust collaborative tools empowers me to produce high-quality designs that effectively communicate messages and connect with audiences. Each feature plays a crucial role in elevating my design process, ensuring that my final outputs are not only aesthetically pleasing but also strategically sound.

As I dive deeper into the advanced features of Canva, I discover that the platform's capabilities extend far beyond the basics, allowing for a more nuanced and sophisticated approach to design. One particularly valuable feature is the ability to create and utilize custom dimensions for any design project. This functionality is critical when working on specialized projects that do not conform to standard sizes. By defining specific dimensions, I can ensure that my designs fit perfectly within the constraints of their intended application, whether it be for print materials, social media graphics, or web elements.

When I initiate a project, I often consider the end goal: Where will this design be used? For example, if I'm designing a promotional flyer that needs to be printed at a specific size, I set the dimensions accordingly right from the start. This proactive approach eliminates the frustration of adjusting the design later, ensuring that every element is proportioned correctly from the outset. The ability to create a custom canvas allows me to tailor my designs specifically to the medium, maximizing their visual impact and functionality.

Moving beyond dimensions, the advanced filtering options available in Canva provide a powerful means to enhance my images and graphics. The filters allow for real-time adjustments that can dramatically transform the appearance of an image. When I work with photographs, for instance, I often utilize filters to establish a certain mood or aesthetic that aligns with the overall theme of my design. If I want to convey a sense of warmth and nostalgia, I might opt for a vintage filter that softens the image and imbues it with a sense of history. Conversely, for a modern and clean look, I would select a filter that enhances brightness and clarity.

Additionally, the ability to adjust brightness, contrast, and saturation within Canva's photo editing tools enables me to refine my images further. When creating marketing materials, it's crucial that the visuals are not only appealing but also effective in communicating the desired message. For instance, if I am designing a social media post for a summer sale, I might increase the saturation of vibrant colors to make the image pop and catch the eye of potential customers scrolling through their feeds. This level of control over the aesthetic quality of my images empowers me to make strategic choices that enhance the effectiveness of my designs.

As I experiment with these advanced features, I also recognize the importance of collaborative tools in facilitating a more efficient design process. Working with a team often involves multiple perspectives and ideas, and Canva's collaborative functionality allows for seamless integration of these contributions. When embarking on a group project, I create a shared design workspace where team members can access and edit the project in real-time. This fosters an environment of creativity and innovation, where ideas can be exchanged and refined as the design evolves.

The comments feature in Canva proves invaluable during collaborative efforts. Team members can leave feedback directly on the design, allowing for focused discussions on specific elements. This method eliminates the need for lengthy email threads or separate communication channels, streamlining the feedback process. When someone suggests a change to a particular graphic or layout, I can immediately see their comment in context, making it easier to understand their perspective and implement the necessary adjustments.

Another aspect of collaboration that I find particularly beneficial is the version history feature. As a project progresses, it's common for designs to undergo several iterations. Canva automatically saves each version of the design, allowing me to track changes and revert to previous iterations if needed. This functionality provides peace of mind, especially when experimenting with different design directions. If a new approach doesn't resonate with the team, we can easily return to a prior version, preserving the integrity of our creative process.

Furthermore, Canva's integrations with other platforms, such as Google Drive and Dropbox, enhance my workflow by enabling easy access to external assets. When I work on a project, I often pull in images, documents, or graphics stored in my cloud storage. This ability to access and incorporate materials from various sources directly within Canva saves time and keeps my focus on the creative aspects of design. For example, if I need to include a logo or branding asset stored in Google Drive, I can quickly import it without having to navigate away from the design interface.

As I delve into the advanced features of Canva, I discover that the potential for creativity and efficiency is greatly enhanced. Custom dimensions allow me to tailor designs to specific needs, while advanced filters and photo editing tools provide the ability to manipulate visuals with precision. Collaboration tools facilitate teamwork and feedback, and integrations streamline the design process by connecting various platforms.

By mastering these features, I am equipped to push the boundaries of my design capabilities, creating professional-quality materials that resonate with audiences and effectively communicate messages. Whether working independently or collaboratively, the advanced functionalities of Canva elevate my design projects, ensuring that I can deliver exceptional results that meet the needs of my clients and stakeholders.

As I continue exploring Canva's advanced features, I find myself increasingly engaged with the platform's custom dimensions functionality. This aspect not only allows for the creation of designs tailored to specific requirements but also provides an opportunity to experiment with unconventional layouts. By setting custom dimensions, I can craft unique formats for everything from social media graphics to business cards, ensuring that my designs stand out and meet the precise needs of various applications.

The process of defining custom dimensions is straightforward yet powerful. I can choose the exact width and height in pixels, inches, or millimeters, which enables me to align my designs with industry standards or personal specifications. For instance, when designing a banner for an event, I might specify dimensions that adhere to the venue's requirements, ensuring that my graphic will fit seamlessly within the allotted space. This level of customization enhances my efficiency and creativity, allowing me to visualize and execute concepts that might otherwise be constrained by predefined templates.

In conjunction with custom dimensions, Canva's advanced filtering tools offer a wealth of options for enhancing the aesthetic quality of my designs. These filters enable me to apply a wide array of visual styles that can dramatically alter the mood of an image. When working on a project, I often experiment with different filters to discover how they impact the overall feel of my design. For instance, a subtle sepia filter can lend an air of nostalgia to a photo, perfect for vintage-themed marketing materials. Conversely, a high-contrast filter can create a more dynamic and modern aesthetic, suitable for contemporary branding efforts.

Moreover, the ability to adjust individual parameters such as brightness, contrast, and saturation further empowers me to fine-tune images to my liking. I recall a particular instance where I needed to highlight the vibrancy of a product in a promotional graphic. By increasing the saturation and adjusting the brightness, I was able to make the product pop against a neutral background, capturing the attention of potential customers. This level of detail is crucial in marketing, where the visual representation of a product can significantly influence consumer perception.

As I delve deeper into the collaborative tools available within Canva, I am reminded of the importance of effective teamwork in the design process. Collaboration is enhanced through features such as real-time editing, where multiple users can work on a design simultaneously. This capability transforms the workflow, allowing for immediate feedback and iterative design improvements. When collaborating with colleagues, I find it invaluable to see changes reflected in real-time, facilitating dynamic discussions that lead to more refined outcomes.

The comments feature plays a significant role in this collaborative process, enabling team members to leave feedback directly on specific elements within the design. This targeted approach to communication eliminates confusion and ensures that all voices are heard in the design process. For example, if a team member suggests altering the font on a particular slide, their comment appears adjacent to that element, making it easy for me to understand the context of their feedback. This direct line of communication not only speeds up the design process but also fosters a collaborative atmosphere where creativity can flourish.

Additionally, Canva's version history feature provides an essential safety net during collaborative projects. As I make changes to a design, I can track the evolution of my work and revert to previous versions if needed. This capability is particularly beneficial when experimenting with different design approaches. If a new direction does not resonate with the team, I can easily restore a prior iteration without losing valuable time or progress.

The integration capabilities of Canva also enhance its functionality, allowing me to connect with other applications and streamline my design workflow. By linking Canva to tools such as Google Drive, Dropbox, and social media platforms, I can effortlessly access and share assets without disrupting my creative flow. For instance, if I need to incorporate a logo stored in my Google Drive, I can import it directly into my design within Canva. This seamless integration reduces the friction associated with switching between platforms and enhances my productivity.

The power of Canva's advanced features truly lies in their ability to elevate the design process, transforming it into a more efficient and enjoyable experience. By leveraging custom dimensions, advanced filters, collaborative tools, and integrations with other applications, I am equipped to create professional-quality designs that effectively communicate ideas and resonate with audiences.

As I explore these advanced functionalities, I find myself continually inspired to push the boundaries of my creativity. Whether I am working independently or collaborating with a team, Canva's robust toolset provides the support I need to bring my vision to life. This exploration of advanced features is not just about mastering the tools but also about understanding how to utilize them strategically to achieve impactful results. The journey of design is a dynamic one, and with Canva at my fingertips, I feel empowered to navigate it with confidence and flair.

CHAPTER 33: TROUBLESHOOTING AND DESIGN BEST PRACTICES**

Design challenges are an inevitable part of the creative process, and while Canva provides a powerful platform for design, encountering issues is commonplace. Understanding how to troubleshoot these challenges not only saves time but also enhances the overall quality of the work produced. In my experience, the most effective way to address design issues is through a structured approach that allows for clear identification and resolution of problems.

One of the most frequent challenges I face is ensuring that my designs maintain clarity and visual appeal across various platforms and devices. This often involves scrutinizing elements such as text size, color contrast, and image resolution. For instance, while a design might look stunning on a desktop screen, it may lose impact on a mobile device if the text is too small or colors do not stand out. To troubleshoot this, I recommend consistently previewing designs in different formats. Canva allows for instant previews, which can help identify potential issues before finalizing the design. By toggling between views, I can adjust the size of text and the layout accordingly, ensuring that my design is visually engaging no matter the medium.

Another common issue arises with image quality. When importing images, it is crucial to use high-resolution graphics to avoid pixelation, especially in print materials. If I notice that an image appears blurry or unclear, I first check its original resolution. If it is too low, I seek higher-quality alternatives. Canva's built-in photo editor can also enhance certain aspects of an image, but it is always best to start with a sharp, clear image. Additionally, I have learned to pay close attention to the file formats I'm using. For instance, PNG files are typically better for images with transparency, while JPEGs work well for photographs. Understanding these nuances helps to maintain the integrity of the visuals in my designs.

Color issues are also paramount in the design process. Ensuring that the chosen colors not only represent the brand accurately but also provide adequate contrast is essential for readability and overall appeal. I often utilize Canva's color palette generator to explore complementary colors that maintain harmony in the design. If I encounter a situation where colors seem off, I revisit the color settings and experiment with variations until I find a palette that resonates. This might involve adjusting hues or saturation levels to better fit the overall aesthetic and purpose of the design.

When creating marketing materials, an area of focus must be the call-to-action (CTA). Often, I find that a design may look visually appealing but lacks an effective CTA. This can lead to missed opportunities for engagement. If my initial designs do not lead to the desired responses, I evaluate the placement, size, and wording of the CTA. It is vital that it stands out, prompting the viewer to take the intended action. Utilizing contrasting colors for the CTA and ensuring it is prominently placed in the design helps to improve visibility and response rates. Furthermore, I analyze the phrasing to ensure it is direct and compelling, guiding the audience toward the next step clearly.

Collaboration within teams can also present unique challenges. When multiple people are working on a design, conflicting styles or changes can lead to confusion. To manage this, I encourage establishing clear guidelines on design elements such as fonts, colors, and layout prior to starting a project. When I notice inconsistencies in a collaborative design, I initiate discussions to realign on our objectives. Canva's comments feature has proven invaluable in this regard, allowing team members to provide feedback directly on the design, facilitating better communication about necessary adjustments.

In terms of best practices, maintaining a systematic approach to design is essential. I prioritize organization within my Canva workspace by categorizing designs into folders based on projects or themes. This not only helps streamline my workflow but also makes it easier to locate specific designs for revision or reference. Consistently naming files in a descriptive manner ensures I can quickly identify the content without having to open each file individually.

Moreover, I find it beneficial to establish a template for recurring design projects. By creating and saving templates, I can maintain consistency across different materials while significantly reducing the time required for future designs. This practice is particularly advantageous for branding purposes, as it ensures that every design adheres to established visual guidelines, reinforcing the brand's identity in the marketplace.

In my experience, continual learning is crucial to overcoming design challenges. I frequently explore new features that Canva introduces, as well as resources and tutorials available within the platform. Engaging with the broader design community through forums and social media can provide fresh perspectives and solutions to common problems. Staying informed about design trends and software updates ensures that I am equipped to adapt and innovate as challenges arise.

Ultimately, troubleshooting in design requires a combination of analytical skills, creativity, and proactive measures. By adopting a systematic approach, focusing on clarity and quality, and leveraging the resources at hand, I can navigate common design challenges effectively. Each hurdle I encounter provides an opportunity for growth, enhancing my skills and improving the quality of my designs. As I continue to master these processes, I not only become a more proficient designer but also contribute to the overall success of the projects I undertake.

As I continue to navigate the intricacies of design in Canva, it becomes clear that even the most experienced designers encounter challenges that require thoughtful solutions. One area that often presents difficulties is the alignment and spacing of elements within a design. It is essential to maintain visual harmony, ensuring that text, images, and other components are well-balanced. If I notice that elements appear cluttered or unevenly spaced, I take a step back and assess the layout. Canva offers helpful alignment guides and grids that can significantly simplify this process.

Utilizing the alignment tools effectively allows me to ensure that all elements are correctly positioned in relation to each other. For instance, aligning text boxes to the left or right can create a more cohesive look. I often find that using even spacing between elements enhances readability and visual appeal. If I'm designing a flyer, I make sure to maintain consistent margins, creating a border around the text and images to frame the content attractively. This not only improves aesthetics but also draws the viewer's eye to the essential information.

Another common issue I face is ensuring that my designs

are accessible to all audiences. This includes considering color choices that accommodate individuals with color vision deficiencies. I utilize tools within Canva to check the contrast ratios between text and background colors. By adhering to accessibility guidelines, I ensure that my designs are inclusive and convey messages effectively to a broader audience. This not only demonstrates professionalism but also reflects a commitment to inclusivity in design.

When it comes to typography, I often wrestle with the challenge of selecting fonts that resonate with the intended message while also being legible. Choosing the right typeface can drastically affect how a design is perceived. In moments where the text feels crowded or difficult to read, I reevaluate the font size and line spacing. A common best practice is to limit the number of fonts used in a single design, ideally to two or three that complement each other. I have found that this approach not only enhances readability but also reinforces the overall aesthetic cohesion of the design.

In addition to typography, I also pay close attention to the imagery I select. High-quality images are fundamental to creating engaging designs, yet it can be tempting to overlook this aspect. If I notice that an image appears grainy or pixelated, I promptly replace it with a higher resolution option. Canva provides a wealth of stock images, and I often explore these resources to find visuals that align with my design goals. When integrating images, I make sure they complement the text and overall layout, reinforcing the intended message rather than detracting from it.

Feedback is another crucial aspect of the design process. While working independently can be rewarding, I have learned that seeking input from peers or colleagues can significantly enhance the quality of my designs. When I share my work, I invite constructive criticism and focus on specific aspects, such as color usage, layout, and overall impact. This collaborative approach often reveals blind spots I may have overlooked, allowing me to refine my work further.

As I refine my designs, I also keep in mind the importance of consistency in branding. Each piece of marketing collateral, whether a flyer or a social media post, should reflect the brand's identity. This includes using the same color palette, typography, and logo placement across various materials. If I find that a design diverges from established brand guidelines, I make the necessary adjustments. Canva's Brand Kit feature simplifies this process, allowing me to apply consistent colors and fonts effortlessly.

Another challenge I often encounter is time management. The creative process can be unpredictable, and I may find myself spending more time on a design than initially planned. To combat this, I set clear goals for each design session, outlining what I hope to accomplish. Breaking projects into smaller tasks not only makes the process more manageable but also helps maintain focus. When I feel stuck or overwhelmed, I take short breaks to recharge my creativity, which often leads to renewed inspiration.

Additionally, staying organized within Canva is paramount to maintaining efficiency. I categorize designs into specific folders based on projects or themes, making it easier to locate files quickly. I label each design clearly, incorporating descriptive titles that convey the content at a glance. This organizational system saves me valuable time, especially when deadlines loom.

Lastly, it is essential to embrace a mindset of continuous improvement. The design landscape is ever-evolving, and staying updated on trends, tools, and techniques is vital. I regularly explore new features within Canva and participate in online design communities to share insights and learn from others. Engaging in this way not only enhances my skill set but also cultivates a sense of community among fellow designers.

Through these practices and insights, I have developed a more robust approach to troubleshooting design challenges in Canva. Each obstacle serves as an opportunity for growth, pushing me to refine my skills and elevate the quality of my work. By maintaining a focus on best practices, fostering collaboration, and committing to ongoing learning, I can navigate the complexities of design with confidence and creativity.

When diving into the intricacies of design in Canva, one common challenge that surfaces is the need for images and graphics to be seamlessly integrated into the overall design. It is essential to ensure that every visual element aligns not only with the branding but also with the message being conveyed. If I find that an image feels out of place or detracts from the intended message, I reassess its relevance. Selecting high-quality, relevant images is crucial. I often browse through Canva's extensive library of stock photos, illustrations, and icons, filtering options to suit the context of my design. If a chosen image appears overly busy or clashes with other elements, I don't hesitate to explore alternatives or apply Canva's editing tools to crop or adjust the image to better fit the layout.

Another issue that frequently arises is the balance of colors within a design. When experimenting with different color combinations, I pay close attention to how colors interact with one another. If I perceive that certain colors clash or make the text difficult to read, I revisit my color palette. I utilize Canva's color wheel to identify complementary and analogous colors, ensuring that the overall composition remains harmonious. Additionally, I incorporate white space intentionally; this breathing room around elements can make a design feel less cluttered and more sophisticated, drawing attention to the most critical aspects of the content.

As I refine my designs, the use of text must also be carefully considered. The legibility of text is paramount, especially when conveying important messages. If I notice that a particular font style complicates readability, particularly at smaller sizes, I explore alternative typefaces that maintain the intended aesthetic while ensuring clarity. I also experiment with text hierarchy—using varying font sizes, weights, and colors to guide the viewer's eye through the design effectively. This practice not only enhances readability but also strategically emphasizes key points within the design, ensuring that the audience grasps the essential information quickly.

One challenge that often leads to frustration is the need to meet specific dimensions for various platforms or materials. Each platform has unique requirements for graphic sizes, which can be daunting when designing multiple assets. To navigate this, I leverage Canva's ability to create custom dimensions for each design. Understanding the dimensions necessary for social media posts, web banners, and print materials allows me to streamline my workflow significantly. By setting the correct dimensions from the outset, I can focus on the creative aspects of the design without worrying about resizing elements later, which could lead to a distorted or imbalanced final product.

In cases where I encounter design elements that do not align as intended, I utilize Canva's alignment tools and guidelines to ensure everything is perfectly positioned. This attention to detail is crucial in maintaining a professional look. If alignment issues persist, I sometimes take a moment to step away from the project and return with fresh eyes; this can often help in spotting inconsistencies or areas needing adjustment that I might have overlooked initially.

The use of layers is another advanced technique that can

alleviate some design challenges. As I work, I strategically layer elements, using transparency settings to create depth and interest. If an image or shape is obscuring important text or graphics, I adjust the layering order, ensuring that critical components are visible and prominent. This ability to manipulate layers enhances the visual complexity of the design without overwhelming the viewer.

As I finalize my designs, the export settings are crucial to consider. Depending on the intended use of the design—be it digital or print—different file formats and resolutions are required. If my design is meant for digital sharing, I typically opt for PNG or JPEG formats, ensuring the quality remains high while keeping file sizes manageable. For print materials, I focus on exporting in PDF format, often selecting the option for high-quality print. Paying attention to these details ensures that my designs look as vibrant and polished in their final forms as they do within the Canva interface.

Throughout this process, I remain cognizant of the importance of gathering feedback on my designs. Whether through informal discussions with colleagues or structured critiques, external perspectives can highlight areas for improvement that I may not have noticed. Constructive feedback helps refine my work, ensuring that the final design resonates with the intended audience.

Moreover, I continuously seek to expand my knowledge of design best practices by exploring online resources, engaging in workshops, and following industry leaders in the design space. Staying updated on trends and new tools available within Canva allows me to push the boundaries of my creativity and adapt to evolving design standards.

Ultimately, troubleshooting design challenges in Canva is not merely about fixing problems; it is an opportunity to grow and enhance my skills. By embracing a systematic approach to identifying issues, utilizing the plethora of tools and features available, and remaining open to feedback, I can produce high-quality designs that not only meet but exceed my goals. Each design project becomes a chance to learn, experiment, and elevate my craft, reinforcing the notion that even challenges can lead to unexpected and rewarding outcomes in the world of design.

CHAPTER 34: FUTURE TRENDS AND EVOLVING WITH CANVA**

As the design landscape continues to evolve, staying abreast of emerging trends is essential for any designer, particularly those using tools like Canva. In the ever-changing digital environment, it becomes increasingly important to recognize the shifts in consumer preferences and technological advancements that influence how we create and present our work. Canva, being a leading design platform, has not only embraced these trends but has also anticipated them, making it a vital tool for designers looking to maintain relevance and effectiveness in their projects.

One significant trend shaping the future of design is the emphasis on personalization. Users now expect tailored experiences that resonate with their individual preferences. This trend is evident in how Canva has expanded its features to allow for greater customization in designs. From personalized templates to the ability to upload and save custom fonts and color palettes, Canva empowers users to create materials that reflect their unique identities. By leveraging these personalization options, I can enhance engagement with my audience, ensuring that my designs speak directly to their tastes and preferences.

Moreover, as the demand for visual content continues to rise, the need for high-quality imagery and graphics cannot be overstated. Canva has responded to this need by continually updating its library of stock images, illustrations, and icons. The introduction of advanced search features, including the ability to filter by style, color, and orientation, allows me to find the perfect visuals quickly and efficiently. As I navigate through these resources, I also appreciate the importance of selecting images that align not only with my message but also with current aesthetic trends, such as minimalism and authenticity. Incorporating authentic visuals helps create a deeper connection with the audience, as they often prefer relatable content over overly polished stock imagery.

Another noteworthy trend is the integration of motion and animation within design. In an era where attention spans are diminishing, adding dynamic elements can significantly enhance the viewer's experience. Canva's animation features enable me to incorporate movement into text, images, and other design elements. As I experiment with different animation styles—such as fade-ins, slide-ins, and bounces—I find that they can effectively draw attention to key messages, making presentations and social media posts more engaging. The ability to create short, animated graphics or videos within Canva further emphasizes the importance of versatility in modern design. By embracing this trend, I can ensure that my designs stand out in a crowded digital space.

As I continue to explore the potential of Canva, I also recognize the increasing importance of collaboration in the design process. With more teams working remotely, tools that facilitate effective collaboration are becoming essential. Canva's collaborative features, such as real-time editing, commenting, and sharing, have made it easier for teams to work together seamlessly, regardless of their physical locations. This capability not only fosters creativity through diverse input but also streamlines workflows, allowing projects to progress more efficiently. I make it a point to leverage these collaborative tools, inviting colleagues and clients to provide feedback directly within the design, ensuring that we remain aligned throughout the creative process.

Additionally, the rise of mobile-first design is another trend that has significantly impacted how I approach my projects. With an increasing number of users accessing content through their smartphones and tablets, it is essential to create designs that are not only visually appealing but also optimized for smaller screens. Canva's mobile-responsive templates serve as an excellent foundation for this, allowing me to easily adjust layouts and elements to ensure clarity and impact on any device. I consistently test my designs on various screen sizes, ensuring that text remains readable and important information is easily accessible, regardless of the medium.

In light of these trends, continuous learning and adaptation are crucial. Canva has positioned itself as a leader in providing educational resources, from design courses to tutorials that explore new features and design principles. I actively participate in these learning opportunities, which help me stay informed about the latest design trends and tools available within the platform. This commitment to ongoing education not only enhances my skills but also enables me to implement fresh ideas and techniques into my work, thereby elevating the quality of my designs.

As the design industry continues to shift, it is clear that tools like Canva will play an integral role in shaping the future of creative work. By embracing personalization, high-quality imagery, animation, collaboration, mobile-first design, and continuous learning, I can effectively adapt to these evolving trends. The ability to leverage Canva's features in alignment with these trends will not only enhance my design capabilities but will also ensure that my work remains relevant and impactful in a fast-paced digital landscape.

Ultimately, navigating the future of design requires a proactive approach, embracing change while maintaining a focus on quality and effectiveness. As I move forward, I remain committed to harnessing the full potential of Canva, ensuring that my designs not only meet current standards but also anticipate future needs and expectations. This journey of continuous growth and adaptation is essential for any designer striving to excel in the modern creative environment, and I look forward to exploring the possibilities that lie ahead.

As I delve deeper into the future trends shaping the design landscape, it becomes increasingly clear that the integration of artificial intelligence (AI) is revolutionizing how we approach design tasks. Canva has embraced this shift by incorporating AI-driven features that enhance efficiency and creativity. One such feature is the AI-powered design suggestions that offer personalized recommendations based on the user's previous work and design preferences. This capability not only streamlines the creative process but also allows for greater experimentation without the fear of missteps. I find that utilizing these intelligent suggestions can lead to unexpected design breakthroughs, as they often introduce elements I might not have considered on my own.

Moreover, the rise of augmented reality (AR) and virtual reality (VR) is redefining how we visualize designs. As these technologies become more accessible, the potential for immersive design experiences expands significantly. Canva is already exploring ways to integrate AR elements into its platform, allowing users to create content that can be viewed in augmented environments. This advancement presents exciting opportunities for marketers and designers alike, enabling them to engage audiences in more interactive and impactful ways. As I keep an eye on these developments, I can envision using AR to showcase products in realistic settings, creating a compelling narrative that enhances customer connection.

In addition to these technological advancements, the trend toward sustainability in design is becoming increasingly prominent. As awareness of environmental issues grows, consumers are seeking brands that prioritize sustainability not only in their products but also in their marketing materials. Canva's initiatives to offer eco-friendly templates and options for digital-first designs align perfectly with this shift. By utilizing Canva's resources, I can ensure that my designs reflect a commitment to sustainability, reducing waste associated with traditional print materials. This alignment with consumer values not only enhances brand perception but also contributes to a more sustainable future for the industry.

Another critical aspect of the evolving design landscape is the growing emphasis on inclusivity and accessibility. Designing with diverse audiences in mind is no longer an option but a necessity. Canva has made strides in promoting inclusivity by providing tools that allow for accessible design practices. For instance, features such as contrast checkers and text readability suggestions help ensure that my designs are accessible to individuals with visual impairments. As I create materials, I make it a point to incorporate diverse imagery and culturally relevant content, recognizing the importance of representation in visual communication. By prioritizing inclusivity, I can foster a deeper connection with my audience and contribute to a more equitable design environment.

Moreover, the trend toward micro-interactions in design is gaining traction. These subtle animations or design elements that respond to user actions can enhance the overall user experience, making designs feel more dynamic and engaging. Canva's animation features allow me to easily incorporate micro-interactions into my projects, creating a sense of playfulness and responsiveness. I find that adding these small details can significantly improve user engagement, encouraging viewers to interact with the content in a meaningful way. This emphasis on user experience aligns with the broader trend of prioritizing the end-user in the design process.

As I reflect on these trends, I also recognize the importance of continuous learning and adaptability. The design landscape is fluid, with new tools, techniques, and methodologies emerging regularly. To stay ahead of the curve, I actively seek out educational resources, webinars, and tutorials offered by Canva and other design experts. This commitment to lifelong learning ensures that I am equipped to leverage new features and trends effectively. By embracing a growth mindset, I can continuously refine my design skills and remain relevant in a competitive field.

In conclusion, the future of design is characterized by the integration of advanced technologies, a commitment to sustainability, a focus on inclusivity, and an emphasis on user experience. As I navigate this evolving landscape, Canva serves as a powerful ally, providing me with the tools and resources necessary to adapt and thrive. By embracing these trends, I can create designs that not only meet the demands of the modern audience but also push the boundaries of creativity and innovation. The journey of exploration and growth in design is ongoing, and I am excited to see how I can contribute to this dynamic field in the years to come.

As I explore the future trends in design, it becomes increasingly evident that the role of data visualization is paramount. With the ever-growing volume of information that organizations generate and utilize, the need for clear, effective ways to present this data is more critical than ever. Canva's capabilities for creating infographics and charts are invaluable in this context. The platform allows me to take complex datasets and transform them into visually appealing and easily digestible graphics. By utilizing the various templates and design tools available, I can highlight key insights and trends that would otherwise be lost in a sea of numbers. This approach not only enhances comprehension but also engages my audience, allowing them to absorb information more readily.

The integration of interactive elements into presentations and digital content is another trend that is gaining traction. Audiences today expect more than static visuals; they crave engagement and interactivity. Canva is evolving to meet this demand by introducing features that allow for the creation of clickable presentations and interactive infographics. These tools enable me to design experiences where viewers can explore data at their own pace, diving deeper into areas of interest. This dynamic interaction not only keeps the audience engaged but also fosters a more profound understanding of the material being presented. As I incorporate these interactive elements, I am finding that they significantly enhance the storytelling aspect of my designs.

Moreover, the concept of personalization in design is on the rise, driven by the expectation that content should be tailored to individual preferences. Canva supports this trend through its ability to create customizable templates that can be adapted for different audiences. By leveraging data insights and user feedback, I can create targeted marketing materials that speak directly to the interests and needs of specific groups. This level of personalization helps in building stronger connections with the audience, as it demonstrates an understanding of their unique perspectives. In a landscape where consumers are inundated with generic content, crafting personalized designs can set my work apart and foster brand loyalty.

As I delve into the emerging technologies that are shaping

the design landscape, artificial intelligence continues to be a significant player. Canva's implementation of AI-driven features, such as automatic background removal and smart resizing, has transformed the efficiency of my design process. These tools save time and reduce the complexity of tasks that would otherwise require considerable manual effort. The introduction of AI also suggests a future where design software will become increasingly intuitive, enabling users to achieve professional results with minimal technical expertise. This democratization of design empowers individuals from diverse backgrounds to express their creativity without the traditional barriers imposed by technical skill requirements.

Additionally, the shift toward remote work and digital collaboration has underscored the importance of tools that facilitate teamwork across geographical boundaries. Canva's collaborative features allow multiple users to work on a single design in real time, making it easier to gather input and iterate quickly. This is particularly beneficial for marketing teams or project groups where diverse perspectives can enhance the overall quality of the design. By using comments and feedback directly within the platform, I can streamline communication and ensure that all team members are aligned with the project's vision. This collaborative approach fosters a sense of community and collective ownership over the design process.

In parallel to these trends, there is a growing recognition of the importance of mental well-being in the design field. As the demand for high-quality content increases, so does the pressure on designers to produce quickly and efficiently. This has led to a focus on creating supportive environments where creativity can thrive without burnout. Canva's user-friendly interface and extensive resources contribute to this supportive atmosphere, making design accessible and enjoyable. By simplifying complex processes and providing a wealth of templates and elements, Canva helps alleviate some of the stress associated with design tasks. As I embrace this more holistic view of design, I find that my creativity flourishes in an environment that prioritizes well-being.

Ultimately, the future of design is characterized by adaptability, innovation, and inclusivity. As I integrate these emerging trends into my work, I am not only enhancing the quality of my designs but also aligning with the evolving needs of audiences and industries. By leveraging Canva's tools and staying informed about the latest advancements in design, I can ensure that my skills remain relevant and that my work continues to resonate with viewers. The journey of growth and exploration in the realm of design is ongoing, and I am excited to embrace the challenges and opportunities that lie ahead. As I look to the future, I remain committed to pushing the boundaries of my creative capabilities while fostering a design ethos that values collaboration, accessibility, and engagement.

www.ingramcontent.com/pod-product-compliance
Lightning Source LLC
Chambersburg PA
CBHW052139220526
45471CB00004B/1438